TB

First Edition (LONDON)

MW01155703

SAS: WITH THE MAQUIS

Acknowledgements

The author wishes to acknowledge the support and encouragement received from the SAS Regimental Association, the Very Reverend Dr Fraser McLuskey, MC, Dr Alex Muirhead, Tony Trower, Eric Adamson and many other old friends, which emboldened him to submit for publication these recollections of a raw young officer on his first campaign.

In particular, he wishes to acknowledge the contribution of his daughter, Gail Gardiner, who compiled the index, and of his brother, Raife, who so painstakingly prepared the sketch maps, which illustrate the range and scope of SAS operations in the Morvan.

SAS WITH THE MAQUIS

In Action with the French Resistance
June – September 1944

IAN WELLSTED

PREFACE BY THE VERY REVEREND
DR J. FRASER MCLUSKEY, MC

Greenhill Books, London
Stackpole Books, Pennsylvania

Greenhill Books

SAS: With the Maquis
First published 1994 by Greenhill Books, Lionel Leventhal Limited,
Park House, 1 Russell Gardens, London NW11 9NN
and
Stackpole Books, 5067 Ritter Road, Mechanicsburg, PA 17055, USA

© Ian Wellsted
The moral right of the author has been asserted

All rights reserved. No part of this publication may be reproduced,
stored in a retrieval system or transmitted in any form or by any means,
electrical, mechanical or otherwise without first seeking the written
permission of the Publisher.

British Library Cataloguing in Publication Data
Wellsted, Ian
SAS: With the Maquis – In Action with the
French Resistance, June–September 1944
I. Title
940.5344
ISBN 1–85367–186–X

Library of Congress Cataloging-in-Publication Data available

Typeset by DP Photosetting, Aylesbury, Bucks
Printed and bound in Great Britain by Butler & Tanner, Frome and London

Contents

Illustrations

Glossary

Arctic tent	Small, easily portable tent
Compo rations	Tinned rations providing balanced meals
Cordtex	Detonating cord for linking explosive charges
Denison smock	Thigh-length camouflaged water-resistant smock
DZ	Dropping Zone – where men or supplies are dropped by parachute
Eureka beacon	Man-pack radar beacon for use on DZs
FANY	First Aid Nursing Yeomanry – women's auxiliary, providing drivers for Army ambulances and other vehicles
FFI	Force Française d'Interieur – military organisation directing the Resistance movement within France
FM	Fusil-mitrailleur – French light machine gun
Gammon bomb	Plastic bomb for use against tanks
Gasogene	Gas produced through imperfect combustion in a metal cylinder, used as fuel in some maquis vehicles
Jock column	Small mobile raiding parties, including artillery, used by the British in North Africa
Lewis bomb	Small charge of plastic explosive mixed with thermite for destroying parked aircraft
Milice	French fascist para-military police
Parachutage	Arrival of men or supplies by parachute
PC	Poste de Commandement – Military Command Post
Pressel switch	Means of initiating a detonation by pressure
Shleuh	Maquis slang for Germans
SOE	Special Operations Executive – British agency involved in locating, encouraging and supplying guerrilla organisations
S-phone	Man-pack wireless for short-range ground-to-air communication
Time pencil	Pencil-shaped fuse initiating a detonation at a predetermined time after the breaking of a seal
Todt worker	Member of a German civilian labour organisation
War Box	Army slang for the War Office

Maps

Conventional Signs

Départements Boundaries (Overview Maps only)	- - - - - - - - - -
Départements Names (Overview Maps only)	**NIÈVRE**
Roads	——————
Major Journeys	▬▬▬▬▬
Towns and Villages	Lucy-sur-Yonne
Actions with date	✕ La Verrerie 24 June
Parachute Drops with date	DZ A 7/6
SAS Camps with initial of Commander and date	CF 2 21-27/6
Maquis Camps with date	M Serge to Sept

Sketch Maps drawn by Raife Wellsted

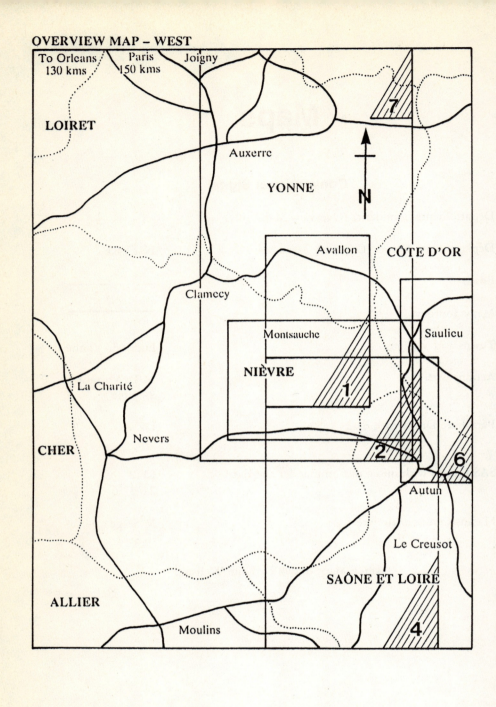

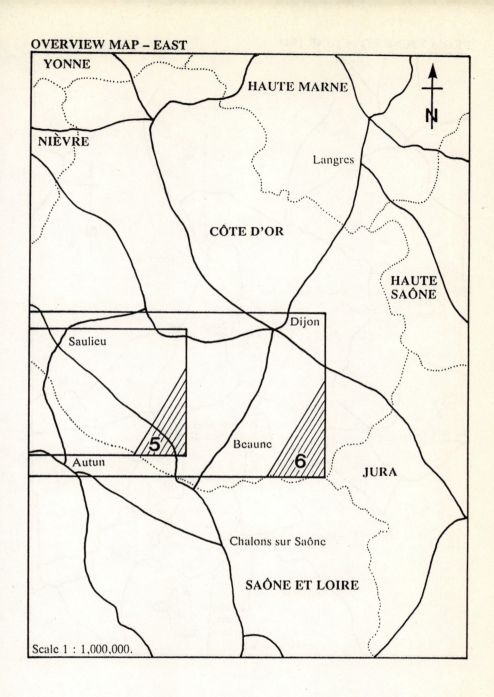

YONNE

HAUTE MARNE

NIÈVRE

Langres

CÔTE D'OR

HAUTE SAÔNE

Dijon

Saulieu

5

Beaune

6

Autun

JURA

Chalons sur Saône

SAÔNE ET LOIRE

Scale 1 : 1,000,000.

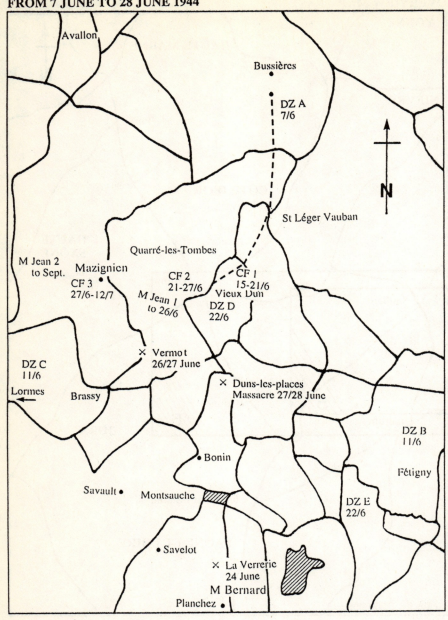

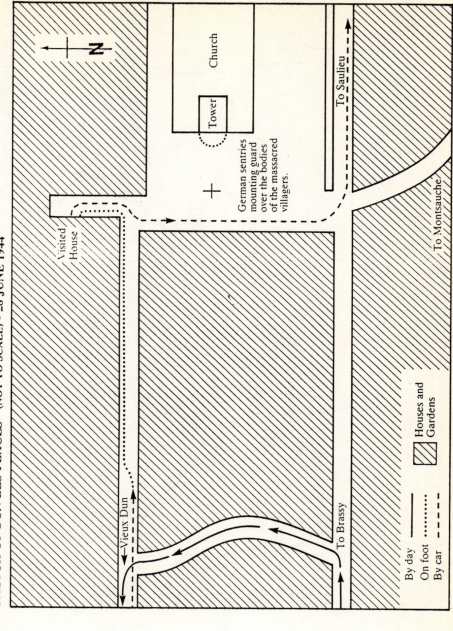

SKETCH OF DUN LES PLACES - (NOT TO SCALE) - 28 JUNE 1944

N

Church

Tower

To Saulieu

Visited House

German sentries mounting guard over the bodies of the massacred villagers.

To Montsauche

←Vieux Dun

To Brassy

Houses and Gardens

By day
On foot
By car

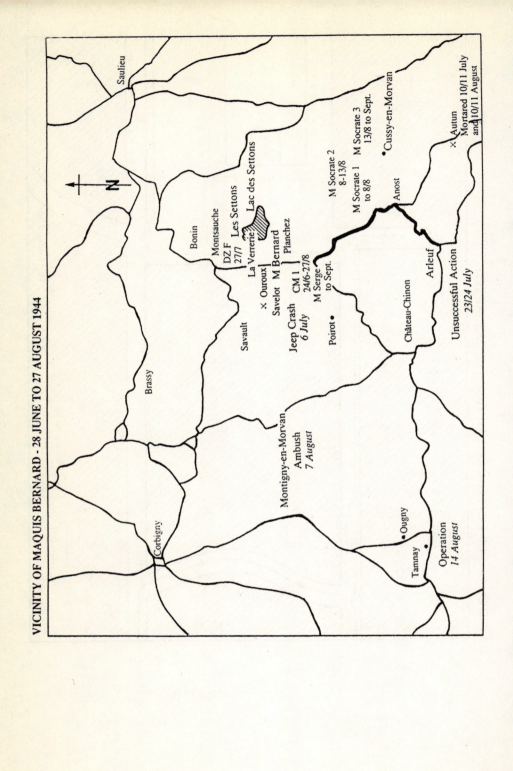

VICINITY OF MAQUIS BERNARD - 28 JUNE TO 27 AUGUST 1944

ACTIONS FURTHER NORTH - 28 JUNE TO 6 AUGUST 1944

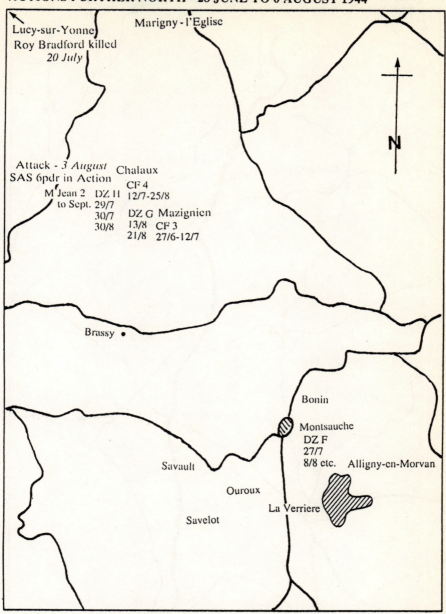

Lucy-sur-Yonne
Roy Bradford killed
20 July

Marigny - l'Eglise

N

Attack - *3 August*
SAS 6pdr in Action
Mt Jean 2   DZ H
to Sept.   29/7
30/7
30/8

Chalaux
CF 4
12/7-25/8

DZ G Mazignien
13/8   CF 3
21/8   27/6-12/7

Brassy •

Bonin

Montsauche
DZ F
27/7
8/8 etc.   Alligny-en-Morvan

Savault

Ouroux

La Verriere

Savelot

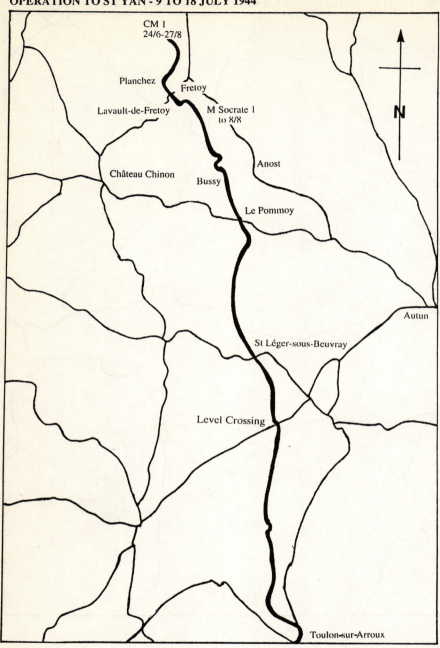

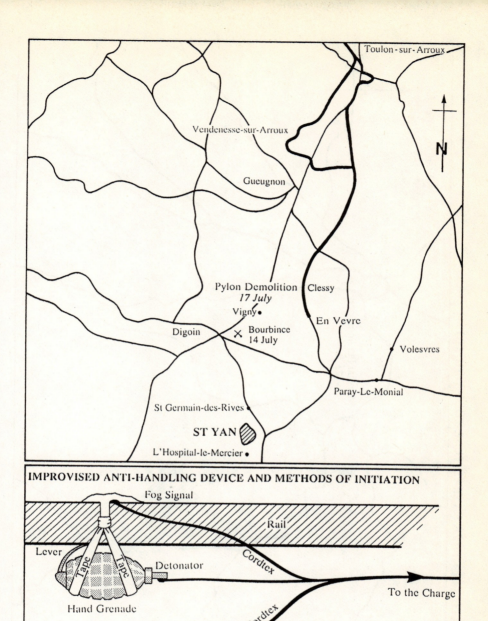

Toulon-sur-Arroux

N

Vendenesse-sur-Arroux

Gueugnon

Pylon Demolition
17 July
Vigny •

Clessy

En Vevre

Digoin

× Bourbince
14 July

Volesvres

Paray-Le-Monial

St Germain-des-Rives •

ST YAN

L'Hospital-le-Mercier •

IMPROVISED ANTI-HANDLING DEVICE AND METHODS OF INITIATION

Fog Signal

Rail

Cordtex

Lever

Tape   Tape

Detonator

To the Charge

Hand Grenade

Cordtex

Time Pencil

Detonator

(See page 124-5)

SORTIES FURTHER EAST - 29 JUNE TO 29 AUGUST 1944

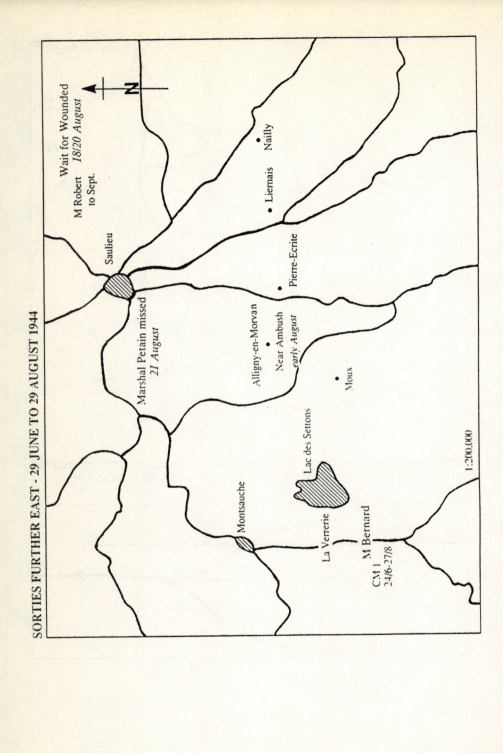

N

Wait for Wounded
M Robert *18/20 August*
to Sept.

Saulieu

Nailly

Liernais

Pierre-Ecrite

Marshal Petain missed
21 August

Alligny-en-Morvan

Near Ambush
early August

Moux

Lac des Settons

Montsauche

La Verrerie

CM 1 M Bernard
24/6-27/8

1:200,000

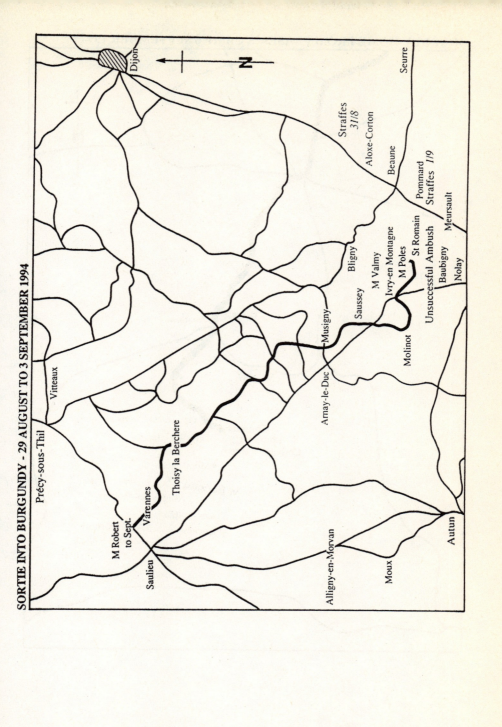

SORTIE INTO BURGUNDY - 29 AUGUST TO 3 SEPTEMBER 1994

N

Dijon

Seurre

Straffes
31/8
Aloxe-Corton
Beaune
Pommard
Straffes 1/9
Meursault
St Romain
M Poles
Unsuccessful Ambush
Baubigny
Nolay
Ivry-en Montagne
M Valmy
Molinot
Saussey
Bligny
Musigny
Arnay-le-Duc
Vitteaux
Précy-sous-Thil
Thoisy la Berchere
Varennes
Saulieu
M Robert
to Sept.
Alligny-en-Morvan
Moux
Autun

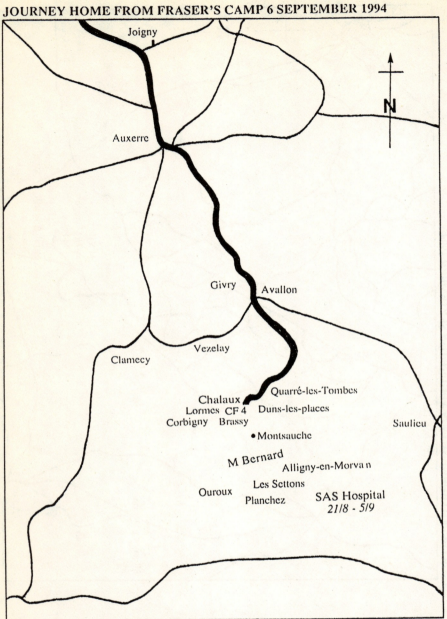

Preface

When the Allied armies launched their invasion in the summer of 1944, the Special Air Service Regiment engaged in one of its own. By courtesy of the RAF and the exercise of its parachuting skills, members of the Regiment took up residence in German-occupied France wherever they were most likely to inconvenience the enemy and hasten his departure. Their contribution on both counts was to receive the highest praise from the Commander-in-Chief. As Padre of First SAS I accompanied our 'A' Squadron to the scene of its operations in the Nièvre. After the Squadron had dispersed I began my parish visitation of the scattered encampments. I have the most vivid and pleasant recollections of my sojourn with Two Troop. Having spent my first night in my sleeping-bag under a friendly tree, I was wakened the following morning by a gentle tap. A familiar voice then announced that breakfast in bed was being served. Our author had placed a mug of tea and a plate of tinned bacon at my side. No minister of religion could have received a kinder or more acceptable welcome from his parishioner.

I knew Ian Wellsted well. We had both joined the Regiment at the same time and had shared the weeks in Darvel preparing for our role in France. Before 'A' Squadron could take off, the necessary reconnaissance had to be done. Ian was charged with this duty along with another subaltern, Ian Stewart. On the night of 6 June they emplaned with their three specialist companions. When some two weeks later the main body of the Squadron arrived, complete with medical officer and padre, Ian was there to receive us.

How much we owed to our advance reconnaissance team. They had found our required dropping zone. They had established good relations with the neighbouring Maquis. They had explored possible campsites. Not least they had gathered valuable information as to the locations and habits of the occupying forces. It was a considerable achievement involving incessant and arduous travel in unfamiliar territory that appeared to hold the world record for drenching downpours. Equipment was minimal and food meagre. When, as frequently happened, communication with the home base broke down, the nightmare must have been complete. However, in the best traditions of the Regiment, they soldiered on, giving the Squadron its eventual chance to embark on the campaign.

Just what that involved becomes clear as we read this vivid and fascinating account. Originally written soon after the events described, the narrative has all the authority and strength of an eyewitness. We are given memorable pictures of the Morvan. We meet various groups of Maquis, that motley assembly of French patriots differing so greatly in organisation and equipment and, sometimes at least, in political orientation.

In the early stages of the mission the SAS leant heavily on Maquis aid which was later repaid with equipment for those mostly likely to use it to good effect. From time to time SAS and Maquis engaged in combined operations but as a rule it was essential for the SAS to operate independently if the appointed tasks were to be performed. In the main these involved relaying useful information to the Home Command, sabotage of selected targets and strafing enemy forces when opportunity offered.

It may well be questioned how British troops hundreds of miles from the main forces could operate with such comparative freedom and success in strongly held enemy territory. As the story proceeds we are given clear and conclusive answers. The Morvan provided excellent cover. The French were on our side and, despite the risks involved, constantly supplied vital information. Supply drops brought jeeps to supplement locally commandeered vehicles. Petrol, weapons, ammunition, food, new recruits, all fell from the night sky. Maquis co-operation was of inestimable value throughout. One must add that the expertise of the desert raiders plus the enthusiasm of the comparative new boys constituted a striking force of formidable power.

Ian Wellsted is to be congratulated on recording the events in which he participated with a nut-and-bolt accuracy and with a down-to-earth assessment both of success and failure. If genius is to be defined, as it has been, as 'an infinite capacity for taking pains', then he has a good claim to the title. As an officer come lately to the Regiment, he succeeded in winning the trust and respect of officers and men alike. He has written the kind of book I would have expected, as revealing of the author as of the life we shared together behind the German lines.

Dr J. Fraser McLuskey, MC
1994

Introduction

Even though I walk through the valley of the shadow of death,
I will fear no evil.

When I started to write this tale in December 1944, I intended it to be a publishable autobiography entitled *By Guess, by God, and by Gremlin!* I had very little time and progress was slow. Then I was sent to Germany for the battle of the Rhine. This stalled me completely.

It was November 1945, after the war had ended, before I began again. But because of the current spate of war stories, I abandoned the idea of trying to get the work published. Accordingly, I just wrote down everything as it had happened, leaving the whole as a personal memoir for my old age, or for the present amusement of my friends and relatives.

My original plans were based in part on my personal diary up to the moment that I went into the concentration area, and on my log of the recce party and the work of the Squadron up to 8 July 1944.

With these sources to form the skeleton of my tale, I moulded on to them the flesh and form of the incidents as I remembered them. Many scenes flashed back most vividly, conjured up by a single line of dry official report, and other events were branded with startling clarity upon the image of my mind, and have remained so for close on fifty years.

I am surprised and grateful that Greenhill Books have thought fit to publish my book at this late stage of my life. Rereading it after this long interval, I have no reason to make any but the smallest amendments and corrections.

Every personal reminiscence is true as far as I remember it. The stories of other people are their stories as they recounted them to me. Where I am not sure of the veracity of an anecdote, I say so. Dates are as nearly correct as is possible and certainly never more than a day or two out. Apart from the above, the history is as true as I can make it. If any friend or colleague from those days feels slandered, maligned or neglected, I offer my apologies in advance and beg the opportunity to amend my version in the light of any further facts he can disclose.

Ian Wellsted
Owhango
King Country
New Zealand
1994

Song of the Regiment

There was a song we always used to hear,
Out in the desert, romantic, soft and clear
Over the ether, came the strain,
That soft refrain, each night again,
To you Lili Marlene, to you Lili Marlene.

Check you're in position, see your guns are right,
Wait until the convoy comes creeping through the night,
Now you can press the trigger, son,
And blow the Hun to kingdom come,
And Lili Marlene's boy friend will never see Marlene.

Twenty thousand rounds of tracer and of ball,
Forty thousand rounds of the stuff that makes 'em fall,
Finish your strafing, drive away,
And live to fight another day,
But Lili Marlene's boy friend will never see Marlene.

Creeping into Fuka, forty planes ahead,
Belching ammunition, and filling them with lead,
A 'flamer' for you, a grave for Fritz,
He's like his planes, all shot to bits,
And Lili Marlene's boy friend will never see Marlene.

Afrika Korps has sunk into the dust,
Gone are its Stukas, its Panzers lie in rust,
No more we'll hear that haunting strain.
That soft refrain, each night again,
For Lili Marlene's boy friend will never see Marlene.

Lyric by Paddy Mayne, to the tune of *Lili Marlene*

CHAPTER I

The SAS:
Preparations for Action

At the beginning of the war, I was commissioned into the Royal Tank Regiment and by August 1943 was a captain in the 49th Battalion but still stationed in England. Longing to see action, I volunteered for parachute training in the hope of joining the Parachute Regiment in Italy, but unfortunately broke my leg on my second jump.

During my convalescence in London, while dining at a restaurant with my wife, Margot, I noticed strange wings on the breast of a fellow diner – a tall lieutenant colonel with DSO and bar wearing the uniform of the Royal Ulster Rifles. When I learned what the wings stood for, I longed for an opportunity to join the SAS, but did not know how to go about it nor how soon I was destined to become a part of it . That chance encounter was my first meeting with the legendary Paddy Mayne.

Lieutenant Paddy Mayne had won his first DSO on 14 December 1941, when the Special Raiding Squadron of the SAS attacked Tamet airfield in Tripolitania. After destroying twenty-four enemy planes on the field, a detachment led by him systematically wiped out the officers' mess with Tommy-guns. Having run out of ammunition, Paddy Mayne then leapt out of his Jeep, ran over to the one surviving plane and pulled out the control panel with his bare hands.

Such initiative and courage was typical of the man who had a few months previously volunteered for Desert Warfare service with Colonel David Stirling's newly formed Squadron.

Lieutenant Colonel Paddy Mayne, as he became, took over command of the regiment on its entry into Tunisia after the capture of David Stirling. The SAS played a leading role in the invasion of Sicily and the subsequent landings in mainland Italy. Meanwhile, in early 1944, an SAS Brigade, made up of two British regiments, two French parachute regiments and one Belgian parachute company, was set up to operate behind enemy lines as part of the impending invasion of Europe.

To bring the British element of this brigade up to strength, Paddy went on a recruiting tour. Thus it was that one day during my second parachute course at Ringway, we were paraded in the gymnasium for a talk by Paddy. He spoke of the work of the SAS, called for volunteers and interviewed applicants afterwards. I was one of the first in the queue. I heard nothing for several weeks, but, at last, on 10 February, while posted to the Airborne Forces Holding Unit at Chesterfield, the eagerly awaited news came through. Six of us, including Les Cairns, a Scottish gunner officer, and 'Puddle' Poole, an instructor at the Airborne Depot Battle School, were to report to the 1st SAS Regiment in Kilmarnock the following day.

*　　*　　*

Our introduction to the SAS was informal in the extreme. The adjutant was out. The doctor, Phil Gunn, was sitting on his table. 'I'll show you round,' he said and pulling the woolly lining of an aged trench-coat over the shoulders of his leather-patched service dress, he donned a battered peaked cap and led us across to the 'Turf' Hotel, Darvel, home from home for the officers of the SAS, where a splendid tea was spread before us.

One or two other officers of the original 1st wandered in and we were introduced. One major in particular made a deep impression. He was a Scotsman, dark and of medium height, but his humorous mouth and eyes gave his whole face a puckish, irresistibly jolly expression. This was Bill Fraser, the Officer Commanding A Squadron. When he disappeared into the depths of the hotel, returning on the stroke of 5.30 with a brimming tankard of beer, I determined that he was the commander for me.

The next day, fortunately enough, gave us the opportunity to choose our Squadron, and 'Puddle', Les and I were happy to be sent to A.

For the next few months our training continued apace. Our fellow-officers included Johnny Wiseman, commanding One Troop, short and stout, with broad grin and touchy temper; Alex Muirhead, commanding Two Troop, familiarly known as Bertie Wooster, tall and slim, always cool; and fair-haired Roy Bradford, then a new bloke like ourselves, but later to command Three Troop. And there were the other subalterns, Dickie Grayson, Ian Stewart, Tony Trower, Johnny Cooper and many more.

Our WO and NCOs were Squadron Sergeant Major Reg Seekings, with DCM and MM: Sergeant Jack Terry, who got his DCM in the attack on Rommel's HQ; and Sergeant 'Chalky' White DCM, MM, with his peculiar jinx on the officers who operated with him. On exercises and in pubs, at dances and on parade, we got to know and like our men and their fellows.

In the months of waiting and training, we had two of those age-old SAS institutions, the Squadron party. Men and selected guests, from the major down to the last non-operational sanitary man, would get uproariously drunk on a dreadful concoction of red wine and rum, known as 'Suki'. Throughout the evening this was backed up by barrels of beer. It was on these occasions that we almost raised the roof as we sang the Regimental Song to the tune of *Lili Marlene*.

These parties were a regular custom and remarkably useful. The men were too good and understood too well their value to abuse them. It was an admirable opportunity to compose quarrels, learn the truth about one's juniors, one's seniors and oneself, and really to get to know one's men.

Apart from drinking, we took a lot of exercise and practised hard at moving across country in small parties by night, prepared for minor sabotage. We learned about explosives. We tried, with conspicuous lack of success, to learn French and German and we marched and marched and marched.

On one exercise we made experiments with pigeons, to be released after successful landings. We carried them in the aeroplanes in little cardboard containers strapped to our chests. Unfortunately, it was a very rough day and the birds proved complete failures. Many pigeons escaped during unskilful attempts to get them out of their basket and into the container. Some of the containers were strapped on upside down, so that after a long flight the bird, when released, could only stagger round drunkenly and sit down. Then, horror of horrors, a number of men were thoroughly airsick all over their pigeons which, quite understandably, proved unable to fly.

Day after day, training continued. Winter wore into spring and spring gave way to early summer. The smell of operations was in the air. Towards the end of May, we knew that the Great Day was coming. We were moved down into a barbed-wire concentration camp in the south of England and we knew that thence there was to be no exit, except by aircraft bound for France.

*   *   *

On 1 June, 'Puddle', Ian Stewart and I were warned that we would be the first officers of the Squadron to go in. 'Puddle' was on a special mission that bore the code name of 'Titanic'. Ian and I were to be an advance recce party to the Squadron as a whole in an operation to be known as 'Houndsworth'.

From then on, our days were spent in studying maps and aerial photographs, in learning the ways to avoid being tracked by trained police dogs and other methods of eluding the enemy.

We had a final overhaul and packing of our kit, wrote our final farewell letters and cut and folded with care the maps we were going to take with us.

On 3 June, a 15-cwt truck bore Ian and me, John Tonkin and Richard Crisp of B Squadron, and Mike Sadler, our intelligence officer, away from the organised inactivity of the concentration camp to the hurly-burly of London. We were off to be briefed.

That journey was quite unforgettable. We knew pretty well where we were going and a great deal of imagination was not required to guess how soon. The great dumps of ammunition along the roadsides were grim reminders of our approaching fate and even the people in the streets, sensing how soon our day would come, waved to us as we passed and drivers gave us the thumbs-up sign as we overtook them.

Our destination was a little two-storey house nestling in an out-of-the-way London mews, where the full secrets of our respective reconnaissances were to be revealed to us. There we were welcomed by our understanding and efficient briefing officers and met the Special Operations Executive (SOE) officers who were to accompany us.

After quick introductions and a short time to dump our kit, we went out to lunch. As the munificent Foreign Office and not the niggling War Box was responsible for our entertainment, we were allowed to choose our own eating place and the government footed the bill. We lunched at Martinez, just off Regent Street and dined at Bagatelle where we saw a pleasant and diverting cabaret. The next day we lunched at the Hungaria: we did not stint ourselves. What a motley selection we must have looked to the casual observer. There was 'Cal', our American briefing officer, resplendent in US Service dress; there were the three SOE officers, one an Englishman with the *nom-de-guerre* of Denby, and two Frenchmen, Gapeau and Centime. There were Mike Sadler, Ian and myself to complete the party, with our '1st SAS' flashes on our shoulders and rather incongruous corduroys draping our nether extremities.

Our briefing was admirably meticulous, with nothing left to chance. Everything in that small house was conducted in separate rooms and every-thing was so secret that people virtually looked over their shoulders and behind doors before they said anything. Such was the atmosphere that one felt it would occasion no surprise if a Jap spy wearing a red nose and blue whiskers had been hauled suddenly out of the linen cupboard. It was the last word in security.

It was here that I actually adopted the *nom-de-guerre* by which I came to be known in France. Both Ian and I had the same Christian names, so to avoid confusion I had to find a new one. Les Cairns always used to call me the 'Gremlin', so, for the purposes of this operation, the Gremlin I became.

On the afternoon of the second day another 15-cwt truck took us from our secluded mews to a 'Hush-hush House' in the country where, to greet us on the steps, was our good friend 'Puddle'. Here, fenced in with barbed wire and guarded by police dogs, we found ourselves in the company of people whose existence I had believed was confined to the realm of fiction – the beautiful spies.

Since D-Day was at the last minute postponed for one day, we spent the whole of 5 June playing at jigsaw puzzles with the spies and waiting for the night.

One of the spies was a particularly attractive, dark-haired young woman. It was hard to tell her nationality as she deliberately confused the issue by talking, quite indiscriminately, with a French, Cockney and educated English accent.

She was paired off with a young American wireless operator and I am pretty sure, though not certain, that she was Violette Szabo.

Paddy came to see us that day and wished us luck. Our departure was, however, delayed a further day since it was hoped that a reception committee could be arranged to lay out guiding lights for us as was being done for B Squadron. In the evening, we saw 'Puddle' with his men, and John Tonkin with the B Squadron party, set off on their respective missions. We shook them firmly by the hand and wondered when we would see them again. One of the RAF dispatchers went with 'Puddle' to help with their drop. He returned with the dawn and told us how, in the hurried scramble for the exit, 'Puddle' had tripped over his kitbag, being probably the only man ever to do a head-first exit through the small floor-hole in the fuselage of a Halifax bomber with a kitbag tied to his feet. The next day his pigeon returned and that was the last that I heard of 'Puddle' Poole.

The vivacious young spy and her operator went over that night, but they were unable to find their reception committee and had to return.

Thus throughout the fateful 6 June, we went on doing jigsaws and listening to the news. As evening approached, we did a final pack and check of our kit. After an early supper we stepped aboard fast saloon cars driven by members of the First Aid Nursing Yeomanry, familiarly known as Fannies, who took us to the 'drome.

To Gapeau I said, 'Off to your homeland at last.' But with a shrug he replied, 'When I see the red light (Action Stations) I will say "Peut-être"; when I see the green light (Go) I will say "Probablement"; I have been disappointed many times.'

We fitted our chutes, talked to the pretty Fannies, listened to the radio and heard the king's speech. How we blessed those girls whose pleasant chatter kept our minds off what was in store.

Violette Szabo, if indeed it was she, donned her parachute that night for the last time. Within ten days she was ambushed by the Gestapo and sent to Ravensbruck, where she was shot. She earned a posthumous George Cross for her gallantry, but I remember her best fitting pieces into a big jigsaw puzzle with a slim steady hand, looking bright and beautiful in our sombre waiting room.

At last, as darkness was falling and the full glowing pink of the western horizon was beginning to fade, we made our way across to the waiting plane. It was a Lockheed Hudson fitted with a special slide, rather like those that kids slither down on a playground, but now adapted for the more warlike purpose of slipping out poor parachutists.

My rucksack, which was to be strapped to my leg and used to carry my food, ammunition and personal gear like a normal parachutist's kitbag, was enormous and weighed about 100 pounds. I feared that it would be too large for the hole at the end of the slide and said so. The wiseacres scoffed at my fears. I tried the damned thing for fit and proved myself right. I asked for a minute to repack my kit and was told that since we were to take off in one minute, I must do my adjusting in the plane.

A few seconds later the engines opened up with a roar and soon we were taxiing out across the airfield. Next, we were all huddled well forward for the take-off. The plane was racing up the runway. We were airborne. The great adventure had begun.

Meanwhile, in the tail of the plane, a forlorn figure was busily engaged in repacking his rucksack. And as I finished I looked out to see the waves of the English Channel dancing and swaying thousands of feet below.

CHAPTER II

Advanced Reconnaissance

The plan, briefly, was this. We, as an advanced reconnaissance party, were to be landed to find out whether there were any Germans in the neighbourhood, to gather what information we could about local conditions and to prepare a reception committee for the main reconnaissance party which would be dropped two or three nights later. The latter, including Bill Fraser himself, would decide on the suitability of the area for SAS operations, the force required, and the nature of any special equipment, if any, to be sent. They would also find lying-up areas for the main body, arriving two or three days later, and lay on reception committees for them.

The advance reconnaissance party was equipped with two transmitting and three receiving wireless sets; and since the French Resistance movement in the area was an unknown quantity, a Foreign Office agent was supposed to be in a position to contact us near our Dropping Zone (DZ) every morning between 3.00 and 5.00 am for five days after our drop. We hoped, too, that if nothing was heard from us, a plane would fly over our DZ two nights later and give us the opportunity of signalling by lamp.

The area in which we were to operate was the mountainous Morvan country in the centre of France, enclosed by the Loire to the west, the Bourgogne Canal to the north and the River Saône to the east. This is the whole *département* of the Nièvre and a bit more besides. Our DZ was to be a stretch of open country to the south-east of the little village of Vieux Dun, right in the centre of our area.

The reception committee which had caused the postponement of our departure was found after all to be impracticable and our drop was to be blind.

As we raced at full speed across the Channel, the Hudson's nose well down and her tail well up, we had our first moment of excitement, as the machine-gun in the upper turret suddenly broke into a chattering bark; but it was only the gunner warming up and we settled down once more. Swooping over the French coast, we saw a few enemy searchlights weaving patterns in the sky but they were not after us and we roared on through the darkness, relieved momentarily by the glow of a city over to the right burning under the fire of aerial attack.

The journey was over far quicker than any of us had expected and we were 300 miles deep into France and busily engaged in strapping our rucksacks on and making last-minute adjustments by 1.30. Luck was against us that night, however, for mist shrouded our DZ, and the mountains made it difficult and dangerous for the pilot to go in really low and have a look. As we took up our positions on the slide ready for the long-awaited jump into action, the pilot was circling the area hoping for a gap in the clouds, or a thinning of the mist.

Ian and I had tossed up beforehand as to which of us should have the doubtful honour of being the first to touch down in the mountains of the Morvan. He had won, and as we circled he was seated on the bottom of the slide, barely holding himself into the aircraft, while I, as number 2, kept inadvertently kicking him a little further down every few minutes. For nearly three-quarters of an hour we were thus suspended over the hole waiting anxiously for the great moment. At last the co-pilot came back to us. 'We can't find your DZ,' he said, 'but at present we are between Rouvray and St Léger-Vauban. The pilot would like to know whether this will do, or whether you'd like to try again tomorrow night.'

There was no doubt as to which was the better course. After two days of jigsaw puzzles and forty minutes over the aperture, we would happily have jumped on to Hitler's lair at Berchtesgaden. 'Drop us,' said Denby, the senior member of the party, and as the plane ran in again the red light flicked on and off, the green light came on with a steady glow, and Ian had disappeared into the night.

There followed a slight mishap. The metal supports of my rucksack had for the last forty minutes been wedging themselves even more tightly into the slide, and when the black bulk of Ian's silhouette suddenly whipped away, exposing the yawning void, it behoved me to follow him as quickly as possible, but could I move? Like hell. My rucksack was completely stuck. For a very brief instant I struggled, then two strong hands grasped me firmly by the shoulders and I was heaved, with compelling force, through the hole.

As I tipped off the bottom of the slide, the slipstream seized me, and as the chute jerked open I felt the rucksack rip away from its frame. Luckily I was holding it, and it did not whistle straight down, as Ian's had done, like some unshapely bomb. In fact, as I was a good thirteen stone, while Ian was tall and slim, I have always maintained that with my 100-lb pack I probably beat him down and landed first in France. Be that as it may, I made one of my usual misjudged landings, stretched out my feet, and slightly twisted my ankle.

I can remember that moment most vividly. It was lightly misty and the watery moon shone down upon us. I could see the other three swinging down behind me and there was dew on the grass. The crickets were chirping all around. I was very glad to be down and I felt that I ought to do something symbolic, so I kissed the ground of France and have never since dared to admit this lapse into sentimentality.

I rolled up my parachute and inspected my rucksack. I fastened the broken canvas to the frame with a piece of rigging line. I opened my rucksack and checked my bottle of whisky, which mercifully had survived the impact. I repacked my rucksack and took out my rum flask. This, I felt, called for a celebration, and I was still celebrating when Ian found me.

Together we made our way up toward the end of our field. The plane, having circled again to drop our wireless and other kit, had flown away. Except for the interminable chirp of the crickets, the world seemed very quiet. There was movement in the hedge in front, a muttered password to which we replied. It was Denby. We held a hasty conference. I stood guard over the kit which we collected close to a cart track. Ian returned to the scene of his drop to try to retrieve his smashed rucksack, while Denby went off to find the others and the dropped wireless sets.

I waited for what seemed an age. The pips that I had worn on a sort of sleeve on my shoulders had got torn off and I tried to find them. I attempted to get my bearings, without much success, and I listened.

All of a sudden I heard footsteps coming heavily down the road. I did not want to use the Colt that I carried for fear of the noise. I drew my knife. I have never liked the idea of knifing a man. It has always struck me as rather messy, but it looked as though there wasn't much option this time. I gripped the hilt hard and waited. Then softly I heard a voice. 'Gremlin, are you there?' Denby had returned with Gapeau but Centime could not be found.

A few minutes later Ian rejoined us. He had not been able to find his rucksack either and none of the wireless sets or other kit had yet been located. It was obvious that we could do no more until daylight. So we gathered up our parachutes and the stuff that we still had with us and made our way into the nearby woods where we made a rendezvous. By this time dawn was beginning to break and a light drizzle was falling.

Once more I remained to watch the kit, while Ian searched for his rucksack, and the two SOE officers went out after Centime and their missing packages.

The lonely vigil in the woods seemed to last an eternity but at last Ian Stewart got back with some of his stuff. The rucksack was a shapeless pulp. Most of Ian's kit was damaged and his wireless receiver was totally destroyed. At 8 o'clock the others returned with Centime and a couple of retrieved rucksacks. They had also found one of the wirelesses but its parachute had failed to open and it, too, was a jumbled mass of twisted wires and broken valves.

It was now raining pretty hard and after brewing up some tea we wrapped ourselves in our parachutes and tried to sleep, without conspicuous success. About midday, the SOE went out again to find our position and look for the last remaining wireless. Ian and I took it in turn to stand guard and to dig the pit in which we were going to inter our parachutes. We heard a few woodsmen and saw a farmer's dog, but were not discovered. When Denby and his party got back they told us that they had established our position as about half a mile to the west of the town of Rouvray and rather closer to the German garrison town of Avallon than to our proper DZ, some twelve miles as the crow flies, over the hilly country to the south-west. The wireless still could not be found.

Later in the afternoon, Ian, Gapeau and I went down to a nearby lake to fetch water and conduct a further search. We, too, were unsuccessful. As we returned we heard voices in our wood. We dropped flat on our faces in the long grass. Gapeau crept forward to investigate and returned to tell us that it was only woodsmen. Nevertheless he crawled back stealthily and re-entered the wood from a different direction.

After a brief interval, the rain came on again harder than ever and we rigged up one of the parachutes as a shelter and huddled under it cold, wet and weary. We felt no hunger, but brewed some tea. We ate none of our unappetising emergency rations. As evening drew on, we buried all our surplus kit and our parachutes and set off for the distant DZ.

It was a truly nightmarish march. Partly we went across country, partly we followed cart-tracks and woodland paths. Our maps proved most inaccurate and the French SOE officer who was acting as guide was soon hopelessly lost. My extraordinarily heavy rucksack, made uncomfortable by the damage sustained in its drop, was chafing my back and bending my knees with its weight. At every farmhouse the dogs barked their resentment. In every village we advanced with the utmost care, Colts loaded and loose in their holsters, grenades ready with pins half-drawn.

At one village, shortly after midnight, we met a party of men going in the opposite direction. We slunk into the shadows but they passed so close that they could not avoid seeing us. They were in French civilian clothes. They attended to their business without molesting us and we continued to go about our own. At about 1.30 I was so dead tired that I felt I could not walk another step. I took one of the Benzedrine tablets which had been provided against just such an eventuality and felt a bit better, but the weight on my back and the raw flesh on my side, where the frame still chafed, made progress most uncomfortable. Worse still, my twisted ankle was beginning to bother me once more.

An hour later, Gapeau admitted that he was completely lost and we had a short conference. It was decided that he should go back alone to the last farm that we had passed and enquire our position. When he returned, we dumped our kit, and leaving Ian, Centime and Gapeau to rest and guard it, Denby and I set out on the five-mile trek still before us.

The need was too urgent for us to continue to keep to the woods and little tracks. It was essential for us to reach our rendezvous before 5 o'clock, or once more we would miss the agent and another valuable day would be wasted. We had to contact the agent as soon as possible so that he could get the message relayed to the Regiment that the DZ was clear of the Germans and that we were safe, sound and ready to receive the main recce party. The loss of our wireless had been a grave blow for us.

Now the Benzedrine stood me in good stead and as Denby began to flag, I was able to take his carbine and help him along a little. All the time we strode along good second-class roads. Several times we had to stop and read the maps. Once we got lost but found ourselves again without undue loss of time. At last we reached the bridge that was our rendezvous. There was no agent near it. No one was anywhere about.

We walked back and forward over the bridge. We waited the last few minutes that still remained before 5 o'clock and we spoke the passwords aloud to the bubbling stream, but nobody replied. Our walk had been in vain. The agent was not there.

Denby, utterly exhausted, lay down by the stream to rest and taking his carbine I walked on through the strengthening light of dawn to have a look at the village of Vieux Dun and the DZ beyond. The village still was swathed in a cloak of silence, but I did not venture near. The DZ was open rolling fields of grass, interspersed with a few trees and one or two large hedges. It looked all right to me. Now all that remained was to find some way of letting the Regiment know, but how?

I returned to the bridge to find Denby dead to the world. I shook him roughly to wake him and we started the long trek back. It was now broad daylight. We were both utterly worn out after two sleepless nights, a long hard march on an empty stomach and hearts filled with a bitter disappointment. The effects of my Benzedrine had now worn off and if anything I was more weary than Denby. Both of us swayed and staggered as we walked. God knows how far we had walked during the night, but it was upwards of twenty miles and our loads had been very heavy.

Suddenly Denby pulled me down into the ditch. 'Look at that man,' he said urgently.

'Where?' I whispered back.

'Over by the little tree,' he replied. 'There, didn't you see him move?'

I strained my eyes. I could see the tree all right but not the man. A small bush swayed in the breeze.

'There,' cried Denby. 'He moved again.'

'It's a bush,' quoth I, rising to my feet, and as we got to it so it proved to be. We laughed heartily, but not for long.

'Christ,' I said, pulling Denby into the cover of an overhanging rock. 'Look out for that lorry.' At the top of the slope up which we were steadily plodding I could dimly see the shape of a large truck with the distinctive brown and black camouflage colouring of the German army.

For some minutes we crouched in our meagre cover, watching the events on the road above us. Two grey-clad figures seemed to be discussing the lie of the land. Behind them I could see posts driven deep into the ground and the heavy cross beams of a permanent road-block. Denby suddenly discovered a steam-shovel mistily outlined against the drab hillside, while I made out a squad of men stripped to the waist as they bent their backs to the labour.

We were dead-beat. For a moment we wildly discussed the possibility of creeping up and stealing the lorry, or trying to brazen our way up the road pretending to be foreign workers in Todt organisation uniforms. But even in our numbed mental state we realised that these plans bordered on the suicidal and reluctantly we began to make our laborious way up the mountainside, doing our best to keep under cover and circumventing the danger point.

Suddenly, as we drew abreast of the road-block, Denby from his vantage point overlooking the road said, 'I don't believe that they are men at all!'

I crept closer and focused my binoculars to my tired eyes. He was right. The lorry dissolved into a pile of wood. The men were bushes, the steam-shovel a gaunt decaying tree. Only the road-block itself was no figment of our wearied imaginations and on closer inspection it proved to be an erection for loading lumber on to trailers. Not a Hun, not a man, not a living thing was to be seen. We were drugged with lack of sleep.

The rest of the journey was truly a nightmare. The sun rose higher, warming our backs and raising our thirsts. The risk of discovery increased with every minute that passed. Again and again we saw visions that existed only in our minds. Tanks and guns and lakes we passed, until we came to believe in nothing that our eyes told us, but only in the interminable dusty road which dragged beneath our feet. Every half-hour we would sink down to rest and slumber as we fell, but first one and then the other of us would wake, shake up his fellow, and keep just pushing on and on and on.

At last we reached a more important road which, though we had followed it by night, we dared not stick to by day, particularly as we could hear the voices of children on their way to school and the gruff shouts of the men as they drove out their cattle. Quietly we crept to the edge of the road, quickly we plunged across unseen. Now we were in an unfamiliar wood, we were very tired and our hunger was agonising.

I don't know what came over me then. I suddenly seemed to feel an urge; a sort of homing instinct; a minor revelation. 'I know the way,' I exclaimed, and we dived deeper into the wood, with Denby following me and muttering that he hoped I was right. Incredible as it may seem, I was, and after a ten-minute struggle across the wooded spur of a small hill we burst into a clearing and saw our temporary camp, with Gapeau and Centime washing in a small stream, while Ian prepared a condensed but palatable breakfast. It was a joyful reunion, though the tale of failure that we brought was by no means pleasant tidings.

After we had wolfed our morning meal we fell asleep in our fleabags, dead to the world and careless of the dangers that might so easily lurk around the corner.

It was early afternoon when we were awoken by cows which came inquisitively through the low bushes to examine us. Several French peasants passed close by, but none questioned us, though they appeared friendly. Centime went off to try to get some eggs but was unsuccessful. We washed and carried out repairs to our torn clothing and battered bodies. We prepared an evening meal and I collected the young leaves of nettles to form a vegetable, which tasted rather like spinach and took off the worst of the taste of our concentrated meat ration.

About 9 o'clock we set out, moving through the woods until it was dark and following back the course that we had taken that morning. Once, in trying to avoid a farm, we got a bit lost but at last, towards midnight, we reached a woodsman's hut on the edge of the river close to our rendezvous. Here we dumped the kit, rested a while, and then moved out on to the DZ to wait for the plane that we hoped would come. To get there, we had to pass through the village of Vieux Dun, and with the utmost care this we did. In the middle of the village we found a house well lighted with long illuminating fingers stretched out across the street from the half-closed venetian blinds, but from the sounds of revelry within we guessed that there was not much to fear from that quarter and slid silently past.

On the DZ we lay together, wrapped up in our gas-capes and watched and waited, waited and watched. Not a plane disturbed the stillness of the night air; even the crickets mocked us with their silence. At 3 o'clock, we abandoned hope and trudged sadly back to our hut. Denby and Gapeau remained at the rendezvous until after 5 o'clock but our secret agent did not turn up. Truly we seemed to be abandoned.

Next morning I was the first to wake and cooked our breakfast in the hut with the last of the concentrated fuel that we had brought. Our supplies were now very low and our position becoming desperate. After breakfast we held a council of war and decided that steps must be taken to contact the French Resistance movement; but as we knew nothing about their activities in this area, the problem of getting in touch with them was no easy one. Ian was the first to give us a gleam of hope, as he found a message scrawled on the wall of a little shack near by and we confidently expected that it would turn out to be a patriots' rendezvous. However, neither his French nor mine was good enough to interpret the jingle and we had to fetch Gapeau. The fact that Gapeau spoke English only with difficulty and that he had been a *curé* before he became SOE rather interfered with the exact interpretation, but the impression we gathered was that it appeared to be rather more like a dirty limerick than a significant message to the patriots!

After a rough lunch cooked in the open and a minor scare when a fisherman came nosing around our hut, we disguised Gapeau in civilian clothes and sent him into the village to see what he could do. All afternoon we waited. We washed, and shaved, and dozed, and we waited and waited and waited. At last

Gapeau returned. With him were two lads in the clothing of peasants. One was a Belgian refugee who also wished to join the Maquis, and the other a farmer's lad who knew where the Maquis could be contacted. I was so overjoyed to see them that I pulled out my much-prized whisky bottle and we drank half of it.

We gathered together our kit and set out on the long trek into the depths of the Maquis-controlled wood. We crossed our rendezvous bridge which spanned the River Cure and skirted the back of Vieux Dun without encountering a soul. We followed rough cart-tracks into the wooded valleys and toiled up steep and winding footpaths into the heart of the wooded hills. My rucksack seemed to weigh a ton and to increase in weight with every step. My raw side ached and my bent back seemed to be permanently arched beneath the burden. I was unutterably weary and could scarcely have walked another step when at last we tumbled over a low stone wall. Our guide told us to wait while he went on with Denby and Gapeau to contact the chief of the Maquis.

I dropped to the damp ground, pillowed my head on my rucksack and fell into a weary doze. Ian and Centime were not feeling much better. The Belgian looked on. We waited perhaps an hour. At last we heard French voices echoing among the trees. The men of the Maquis had arrived.

Looking back on it, it is evident that we took over-elaborate precautions to avoid being seen by the French, but it must not be forgotten that we were an advance party and therefore it was important that our presence was not reported to the Germans. Furthermore we had no idea of the strength of the German garrisons in the neighbourhood, nor of the feelings of the French civilian population. Indeed, we had been told that there were no known Maquis operating in the area and the French members of the SOE were far more distrustful than we were of their own countrymen.

CHAPTER III

With the Maquis

Then they appeared. They were young lads, mostly in their teens, and were dressed in rough peasant clothes. One of them carried a Sten gun, the rest were unarmed. Our guide was with them and he pointed out the way. The young Maquisards picked up the heavier items of our kit and we followed our guide on and on, up and up, along the narrow mountain trails. Soon I judged us to be in the depths of the wood known as Bois de la Reine, to the south-west of Vieux Dun.

Suddenly, at a fork in the tracks, a figure appeared and beside him stood another. In their hands they held serviceable Stens, and pistols were stuffed roughly into their belts. They recognised our companions and motioned them to pass. They shook us warmly by the hands and taxed my poor French to the limit with the effusion of their welcome. They were older men and more experienced. They wished us 'Au 'voir', and we continued on our way.

Soon, through the trees, I could see the white gleams of parachute silk and the duller white of canvas tents. The Maquisard with the Sten whistled a low lilting tune and we moved on into a little clearing. As we came to a standstill, people came running from all corners of the wood. They pumped our hands until we were weary and Ian had parted with his last cigarette. It was still light and the crowd began to drift away. We had more time to look around and get our bearings. The clearing was dominated by a large beech tree. At the base of the tree many bicycles were propped and on the edge of the clearing more bikes could be seen in rough wooden stands. All around, in the depths of the foliage, tents and makeshift parachute coverings showed the living quarters of the men. Close beside the beech a mountain stream bubbled down between muddy banks, eventually emptying into an artificial pool beside which a rough wooden shelter was erected. This was the cookhouse and already the appetising smell of roasting meat and boiling coffee assailed our hungry nostrils.

As though reading our very thoughts, the Maquisards led us to an open space in front of the cookhouse where rough tables and benches made from lashed saplings were driven into the ground. There we were made really welcome. We did our best to talk in our pidgin French. The few men who knew a little English aired their small knowledge and we devoured a delicious meal.

There was a thick, meaty potato soup. There were thick red steaks done to a turn, a plate heaped high with steaming cauliflower and sour brown bread, so new that it was almost warm, with tasty goatsmilk cheese; all washed down with hot sweet coffee made from roasted barley, but prepared as only a Frenchman could prepare. As a special treat, a little Cognac was produced from a jealously guarded bottle. We all drank long life and continued prosperity to our friends of the Maquis.

As we sated our appetites, I had more leisure to study the men around me. It was hard to tell what they had been before the German labour laws threw them all together in the depths of the wild woods. Some had been shopkeepers, artisans, young sons of wealthy parents. Others were scum of the gutter and many were soldiers. Now, however, all were much the same. All wore the clothes, and many still the wooden clogs, of peasants. Some lucky ones had scraps of uniform and British battledresses, but predominantly their clothes consisted of drab coloured shirts, blue overall trousers and German field boots, whose owners no doubt had ceased to require them for obvious reasons. They wore neither brassards nor regular uniform of any kind. The only distinguishable difference between the men of the Maquis and the men of the country from which they had sprung was the pistol cocked aggressively from the trouser tops, the rifle on the shoulder, the Sten on the back or the string of grenades depending from the belt.

I was immediately struck and greatly surprised by the neatness of the camp area, the clean-shaven faces of the young men, and their generally tidy appearance, for it is not easy to keep clean in the depths of the woods.

After our enormous meal we felt an urgent need to sleep, but the problem of regaining contact with the Regiment was still before us and we prepared a message for Denby which was just about completed when he returned.

Denby and Gapeau had been taken to the head of the Maquis, a tall, slim lawyer, who always wore a Luger stuffed into the top of his high riding boots and was known as 'Grand Jean', the Maquis itself being called Jean after him, as was the custom. Jean, not entirely convinced of their story, had taken them by car to a distant château, where a man who claimed to command the Maquis of the whole Nièvre *département* was in residence. Denby was much shaken to find a couple of pretty girls there with Sten-guns on their knees doing guard duties. However, he duly met the great man himself, who was known as Lemniscate; and having satisfied him as to our bona fides, he had obtained permission to make use of his wireless to get our message through to London.

Thus at last, the first part of our task accomplished and our message duly sent, Ian and I retired to snatch what little sleep we could in a small tent, leaving instructions that we were to be awoken at 11.00 and requesting a couple of the Maquisards to accompany us to the DZ to act as guides.

The place was reached without difficulty and one of the men dispatched to bring us a bottle of wine from the village. For three hours we maintained our vigil, drank the good red wine and talked in low voices. Our French was pretty bad but we did not have a great deal of difficulty in getting ourselves understood. Our system was rather a skilful combination of our respective talents, for though Ian spoke it quite well, he was a bit diffident about using it, while I spoke the most execrable French but dived into it with all the joyful abandon of a seal after a fish. The result was that I would run merrily on until hopelessly stuck, then Ian would explain what I was getting at. A truly noble example of co-operation.

Two of our companions, we discovered, were important men in the Maquis, and were really fine fellows. The senior was 'Camille', a tough little Frenchman of about thirty-five with big spectacles and a jaw like granite. He had broad shoulders and a broad grin. He was Jean's right-hand man and second-in-command of the Maquis. The other was a tall, swarthy, good-looking fellow from Algiers. He was known as 'the Moor' and was an absolute expert with the knife. I should have hated to try conclusions with him.

We learned much about Maquis life from these two, for both had been fighting the Germans for a long time. Camille, in fact, had been a corporal in the war of 1939–40 and had taken to the hills rather than surrender. We were told that in this war the Germans were known as the 'Shleuh', after the North African Berber race noted for its cunning barbarity. He also told us something of the methods that the Gestapo used in the occupied territories – stories that would curdle the blood and put the more official atrocity stories into the shade for vicious inhumanity and lust for torture.

As the night wore on, we became more and more depressed, for the plane did not come and a light rain started to fall. Eventually it had grown so late that it was useless to wait longer and accordingly we set off to return. It was pitch black now, for the dark storm clouds covered what little moon was left and in the depths of the wood and along the forest trails the darkness was even more intense. We walked for what seemed an age, our Maquisards conferring now and again in low voices and the water dripping unpleasantly off the leaves above us. At last, after an hour and a quarter, the leader admitted what we had already guessed; somewhere in the middle of the labyrinth of small paths we had got lost. We were cold and wet, but daylight was not far off, so building an enormous fire in the thick of the wood, we curled up around it and slept until dawn.

As soon as it was light, the Moor cast around, and after picking up first one trail and then another, he at last led us into the camp in time for *petit déjeuner*, which for us famished wanderers included an enormous omelette. At breakfast we met Denby once more. He had manned the RV by the bridge and once more our Foreign Office agent had not turned up. Our luck seemed still to be holding bad.

Ian and I turned in once more and slept the sleep of the utterly weary. We woke in time for a late lunch in the middle of the afternoon and tried to find out whether any message had come in reply to our wireless call of yesterday evening, but there had been no acknowledgement and we doubted whether it had indeed got through. During the afternoon there was much bustle in the Maquis camp and many new tents were erected and shelters put up. In the evening the reason became apparent when swarms of new faces began to appear, among them a number of women. The staff and bodyguard of Lemniscate were moving into the Maquis for safety.

Later, the high, sparsely wooded ground at the back of the camp, where it was possible to erect wireless aerials and contact with London was not too bad, became a hive of activity, as set after set was erected and transmissions began. Denby had managed to borrow a set and tried again and again to get through on the emergency frequency to repeat our message, but without result. That night a Maquis party went off to blow up some lock gates in a nearby village and we watched them depart, all armed to the teeth, carrying explosives and wearing old French steel helmets and as many official accoutrements of war as they could muster. I never heard whether they were successful or not.

During that night, 10 June, as Denby with four men of the Maquis manned the DZ, a plane flew over low; he signalled frantically with his light but it did not appear to notice and continued on its way. Denby watched at the bridge again but still no one came. We began to feel that at the War Box, our pin must have fallen out.

In the early hours of the morning we heard the single crack of a pistol fired in the dark. When daylight came we found that our friend the Belgian refugee was no longer at the breakfast table. His antecedents had been checked; he was proved to be a Gestapo agent. No one dared take chances. He was made to dig his grave and shot in the back of the neck.

Sunday, 11 June was a more exciting day. At 10.15, I was taken up a long twisting trail to a place where a little road ran through the heart of the woods. It was well guarded, and hidden in the thick undergrowth on either side were many cars of all shapes, makes and sizes: the garage of the Maquis.

Three Maquisards escorted me and we mounted a Sten-gun to fire through the windscreen. Apart from this we had two rifles, my Colt and a couple of grenades. We were off to the place at which I had landed to retrieve our parachutes and other abandoned kit.

It was an incredible experience to drive through a country theoretically occupied by the enemy, in a car full of civilians who were soldiers of France, on a drive of at least twenty-five miles, which was to take us through many towns and villages.

To keep up the impression that it was merely a Maquis car, I removed my red beret and at a distance the loose camouflaged smock that I wore was very similar to the dirty blouses of the peasants.

Our course led out of the woods to the west, and skirting it to the south we passed through the suburbs of the town of Dun-les-Places, up through Vieux

Dun and back along the trail that we had marched arduously so short a time before. We detoured to the north and passed through the town of Quarré-les-Tombes, where we pulled up and the men went into the local grocers, their weapons held conspicuously in front of them so that their friend the shopkeeper could not be accused of voluntarily giving his aid to the 'terrorists' from the woods. I got out of the car and idly covered the curious crowd that gathered in the square, for being Sunday, the good people of the town were just strolling back from church. They displayed a quietly neutral interest in the whole proceedings and the potential threat of my gun kept them at a safe distance.

When my companions had returned to the car we set off once more, following the good second-class road through St Léger-Vauban to the neighbourhood of Rouvray. I searched around quickly and soon picked up my bearings. I led them to the wood where we had harboured throughout my first long day in France and without difficulty I picked out the poorly camouflaged mound of earth in the depths of the wood where all our unwanted accoutrements were hidden. We dug them up and loaded them on to the car. I was amazed at the brazen effrontery with which they piled the parachutes openly into the carrier on top of the car's roof.

Next, we contacted some good friends of the Maquis in the area, where the latest news of German troop movements and intentions was passed on to my fellow travellers. From there we went to a little farm on the outskirts of the village of Bussières, where we hid the car and went in for lunch. Here, where the farmer and his wife were staunch supporters of the Resistance and my hopeless French betrayed the country of my birth, all pretence was thrown aside and the good people shook me warmly by the hand. We were given a typical lunch of bacon omelette, with bread and cheese, washed down with red wine and water. The daughter of the house, however, who did the cooking, almost spilt the omelette she was making, her hands were shaking so much, and who could blame her? She knew that if the Germans ever discovered the nature of her clandestine visitors, every person in the farm would be mercilessly shot.

Our meal completed, we thanked our hosts and took our leave, returning by the same route as far as Quarré-les-Tombes, where we branched away to the west and stopped along a secluded stretch of road, hooting three times. Almost immediately a red-faced little man in greasy blue overalls climbed out of the ditch and with a few gruff words of French, handed a knobbly brown-paper parcel to the driver. It was the foreman from the local garage, delivering much-needed spare parts to the Maquis mechanics.

Soon we were speeding through the woods once more and the car was sending up clouds of dust as it wound along the forest roads. Now all of a sudden we dived into the thicker woodland and at each corner the driver tooted a signal upon his horn. At last a bunch of Maquis sentries peered at us from the depths of the shrubbery, from which the wicked barrel of a captured German Spandau could be seen protruding. It was 6.30 and we were home.

After another excellent meal with Ian at the Maquis, we prepared to set out for the DZ for yet another arduous vigil. Ian had waited vainly for a message all day and not a sound had been heard. Just before we moved off, however, Denby came hot-foot from the Maquis headquarters. Word had come at last. Sixteen paratroopers were being dropped tonight but there was some doubt as to which DZ they were coming to. Strong reception committees were sent, therefore, to man the two likely DZs. The parties had already set off by car to take up their positions and nothing remained for us to do but sleep and wait. We slept.

The morning of the 12th brought nothing but disappointment. No para-troops had appeared at either of the DZs and not a plane had been heard. No messages came all day and attempts to get through on the SOE emergency frequency were once more unavailing. The agent still had not materialised. Nevertheless, I decided to search for a possible camping site for the Squadron, so that I could provide Bill Fraser with as much information as possible when he arrived. So I disguised myself as a man of the Maquis, in my torn corduroy trousers and my khaki shirt, borrowed a carbine and set out after lunch with Camille to look for a site in the Bois de la Pérouse, back on the east side of the River Cure.

The weather for once was beautiful and the bright sun warmed us as we climbed down into Vieux Dun, crossed the valley and toiled up into the *bois*. Up in these very hills, Camille had lived for three years and the little clearing that we found at the top of the hill of the Pérouse had been the DZ at which he had received his first supply of arms.

As we came down the hill in the late afternoon, we found the lovely beauty spot of the Roches, where we could look down into the valley of the Cure and out across the mountains of the Morvan towards the Montsauche country that I was soon to know so well.

Back in Vieux Dun we stopped in the little *estaminet* of Madame Lamoureux, where we were able to buy strong white wine out of her cellars and ate a supper of omelette and cheese. We were back at the Maquis camp before dusk.

During the day there had been strong rumours of German troop movements in the vicinity and a fairly heavy scrap had taken place between a Maquis near the town of Lormes, twenty miles to the east, and the Germans. After darkness men from the Lormes Maquis, mostly without arms and equipment, began to drift into our camp.

That night Ian and I almost gave way to despair. There was still no news and for a week we had been in the depths of enemy-held territory waiting for the rest of the party and for at least a few orders, which never came. We were less than 100 miles from the Swiss frontier and we began to consider seriously the possibility of making our way out by this route, for we were beginning to fear that we had been given up for lost and that the main recce party was being put down in a different area. We certainly felt that there was no point in continuing to man a DZ that should have been used at least three nights previously and which we were beginning to feel was unlikely ever to be used at all.

This was our first dark hour before the dawn. The next morning brought us the glimmering of joyful tidings. A message came from the Maquis Bernard in the Bois de Montsauche, twenty miles to the south of our camp, that they had been in contact with British parachutists of the SAS the previous day and intended to bring them in that night.

Lemniscate was, that very morning, going over to the Maquis Bernard to have a conference with his military rival in control of the Maquis, a Colonel Du Pain, and Ian and I were allowed to squeeze into the back seat with Lemniscate's aide-de-camp, while Grand Jean himself drove the car.

We made out way along trails that I was later to know like the back of my hand and finally swept up to an aged railway station, standing beside a line that had long since had its rails ripped up for scrap. Here, more Maquisards challenged us and we knew that we had reached the guardroom of the Maquis Bernard.

Our car was driven under cover and camouflaged, for every evening, with clock-like precision, a German recce plane would fly over the Maquis-held woods, searching unavailingly for the campfire smoke.

For two miles we trekked up a long steep trail with woods on one side and an open stump-studded valley on the other, until, turning into the depths of the woods, we came to a group of well-made wooden huts sunk well into the ground, fitted with loopholes and surrounded by a stockade. It was the Maquis Bernard, one that prided itself on its military traditions and over whose camp fluttered bravely the Tricolour of France, with the blood-red Cross of Lorraine. It was here that I met many new friends and many men who were to be my comrades in adventures then unthought of.

There was old Bernard himself, the grizzled gendarme, with dirty broken teeth, who carried his long pistol swinging by the muzzle from his hand and was the acknowledged chief of the Maquis in the Bois de Montsauche. There was small dark Josef, his deputy. There was Georges Brûlé, a young ex-medical student and lieutenant in the French army, who spoke English fluently. He was the leader of the brave men who had followed him from Paris and was responsible for the military training of the Maquis. There were André Bouche-Pillon, Roger, Jacques, Meurice and many other grand fellows among his men. There were Paul and Alexis, two Russians, soldiers of the Red Army who had escaped from prisoner of war camps in Germany and who were still on probation in the Maquis, partly, I think, because they hardly spoke a word of French between them, though I must admit that I liked them instinctively.

At the conference which Ian and I found ourselves forced to attend, we met

Colonel Du Pain himself, a fat red-faced little man with a bristling white moustache. He looked like a cross between Colonel Blimp and Adolphe Menjou. He talked incessantly and very fast, blowing raspberries every now and again as he spoke. We were introduced to the man they called Le Four, his aide-de-camp, reputed to be one of the richest men in France, a one-time game-warden in French Equatorial Africa, whose mother was English and who dressed very much like an Englishman. He spoke our language well and we were grateful for it. Here also, we met wise old, white-haired Colonel Dubois, military adviser to the Maquis Bernard, a man who stood outside the sordid politics that clouded the Du Pains and the Lemniscates of the Maquis.

We were all treated to a most admirable lunch, washed down with quantities of red wine and afterwards had to endure the interminable political arguments of Du Pain and Lemniscate, which neither Ian nor I were able to understand.

By judicious enquiries from the people not too deeply engrossed in the wordy battle that raged all afternoon, we discovered that a Lieutenant 'Coopah', whom we recognised as Johnny, had been met the previous night by a small party from the Maquis Bernard, and that night they intended to send out a thirty-two-seater bus with an escort to bring him and his men in to the Maquis. I decided to accompany the bus.

When at last the political struggle had abated without any compromise being arrived at, Ian and I parted. I remained at the Maquis Bernard to join with Johnny Cooper. Ian returned to the Maquis Jean, where a surprise was in store for him.

CHAPTER IV

Reunion

Now we must return to SAS headquarters in London and follow the march of events. Within two hours of Johnny Tonkin's drop he had been in touch with headquarters by wireless, aided by the Maquis reception committee which had guided him in and met him on the ground. For two whole days after we had dropped there was nothing but silence, and when on the evening of the third day our message at last came through, it was somewhat garbled in transit and difficult to follow. Nevertheless, it was decided to send in the main reconnaissance party at once and messages were sent to us acknowledging our own and giving us all the details for the drop of this party. These messages we never received and consequently remained completely in the dark.

It was in the dusky twilight of 10 June that two Stirlings, loaded down with the main recce party, taxied into position on a runway somewhere in southern England, prepared for the long flight through the pitch dark to a DZ, which they confidently expected to be manned by the advance party. Just before they took off, however, an urgent message was received that they were to be dropped that night at all costs and that anywhere within a radius of ten miles of the DZ would do. As the powerful engines roared to their crescendo, the huge planes lumbered across the field and slowly lifted into the darkening sky.

The party in the first aircraft was commanded by Bill Fraser himself. With him was Tom Moore, of the Royal Corps of Signals 'Phantom' patrol, with a wireless set and team of signallers; his batman Furness; troopers Babbington and Kennedy, with a Eureka radar-beacon; SOE Colonel Hastings, who went by the name of 'Isaac'; and an SOE sergeant signaller with another wireless set. They took off at 10.30 and soon the hostile battle-line was far below them, lit up in lines of fire.

Twenty minutes later the second aircraft took off. Johnny Cooper was commanding this party and with him were SSM 'Reg' Seekings, SQMS 'Mac' McLennon, Sergeant Zellic, (a Jugoslav of the 3rd French Parachute Battalion, attached as interpreter) and twelve men, two of whom were signallers, with yet another wireless set. Each man was armed with a Colt, and about half had carbines. They carried grenades and a little explosive, but their arms were miserably inadequate for a fight if they bumped into any sort of trouble.

· It was shortly after 2 o'clock in the morning, when the action stations was given. There was no sign of a reception committee and the pilot judged himself to be within the ten-mile area. The green light came on and the stick was gone.

47

As the plane roared homeward it passed over the DZ, where Denby and his faithful Maquis waved their lights, but being empty, it continued on its way. The other plane never even came near our lights.

By 3 o'clock in the morning, Johnny had managed to contact all his men except for Zellic and troopers Docherty and O'Neill. They found a small wood and harboured there until daylight. At 11.00, Johnny managed to make contact with Zellic and O'Neill and, when satisfied, approached a farm and made arrangements through the farmer to get in touch with the local Maquis. He also managed to get a bit of extra food to supplement the unappetising emergency rations.

The wireless set was in good working order and contact with London was successfully established. All day the party lay up quietly in the woods and waited for dark. Zellic established their position and found that they had been dropped close to the farm of Les Hâtes, close to the village of Fétigny, some ten miles to the south-south-east of the Vieux Dun DZ, and about nine miles to the north-east of the Maquis Bernard in the Bois de Montsauche.

Darkness fell. A small truck from the Maquis Bernard arrived; it brought a little food. The Maquisards satisfied themselves as to the bona fides of the party and promised to return at 11 o'clock the following evening to collect them.

During the next day Docherty turned up. He had got caught in a tree on landing and had found considerable difficulty in disentangling himself. However, once on the ground, he had managed to reach a nearby farm and had at last made contact with the rest of his stick.

Wireless contact with London was kept up all day but the position was somewhat obscure. The first plane had evidently also failed to find the proper DZ, and the exact position at which the stick had had to bale out was uncertain. Tom Moore's wireless was also in contact with London but apparently he had lost touch with Bill Fraser. Brigade HQ wanted to get the main party in as quickly as possible and asked Johnny to look for a suitable DZ in his area. During daylight, Johnny, Reg and Zellic searched for one and found it in the marshy valley of Les Valottes, a couple of miles to the south-west of Fétigny.

As soon as it was dark the party lay up in their original area and true to their word, 11 o'clock, found the thirty-two-seater bus of the Maquis Bernard duly arriving to pick them up. The bus was well manned by the better trained men of the Maquis and was commanded by our good friend Georges. Aboard it, well disguised as a Maquisard in a borrowed overcoat against the cold, was half of the advanced recce party, to whit myself.

I was very glad to see them all and Johnny and the boys were pretty surprised to see me. There was still no news of Bill and all searches for him and his party in the area were unavailing; so it was decided that Johnny, with Reg, Zellic and the signallers should stay by the new DZ while the rest of the party , under Mac, should return with me to the Maquis and prepare for the coming of the rest of the Squadron. Johnny would wireless back for the survivors of the first Stirling to rally on him at the DZ, and we would accept the Squadron on the Les Valottes DZ the following night.

Slowly we returned in the bus to the Bois de Montsauche, stopping on the way to try to get further news of Bill and once being brought bottles of wine by a patriotic farmer. Each time that the bus stopped, the men of the Maquis tumbled out and took up defensive positions around it, being recalled by blasts on the whistle when we were ready to move off once more.

Eventually, just as dawn was breaking, we got back to the guardroom in the disused railway station and I left Mac and the men there to sleep while I went up to the Maquis and curled up in a borrowed parachute in one of the barrack huts. We had been very lucky, for hardly had the bus been safely hidden away before a German motorised detachment passed down the main Montsauche road on its dawn patrol.

I woke early, having slept only a couple of hours, and after a hearty breakfast got Bernard to show me a good spot in the woods where we could set up a camp for the Squadron. He led me deep into the heart of his forest domains, along small disused bullock trails, to a small mountain spring, with a slope beyond, where the trees thinned out a bit and the ground rose steeply above the trail. The woods swept away for at least a mile in every direction and such a maze of old trails led past the place that it was virtually impossible to find unless one knew the way. At the same time, with an eye to the distant future, I could see that all these bullock trails could be negotiated by a jeep and there appeared to be at least three feasible exits for wheeled transport with a reasonable cross-country performance. The most direct way into this corner of the wood lay straight past the Maquis Bernard. I was assured that the extreme southern end of the Bois de Montsauche was occupied by the Maquis Serge. This appeared the ideal site for our camp in this area.

I also arranged for Bernard to provide us with fresh beef and a little bread and sugar and paid him from the wad of notes that I had been given before I left for just such a contingency. After this, I collected a few men from the Maquis who were not otherwise engaged and returned to the guardroom where I collected Mac and the boys and, aided by our Maquis friends, lugged our kit up to the new campsite that I had found. I showed Mac the jobs that I considered required doing most urgently, particularly the digging out of a washing place below the spring, and after arranging for the men to have a good breakfast I left them to it and went to the 'officers' mess' of the Maquis to get my own lunch.

One of the officers there was a young captain of the French Tank Corps, named Jean-Paul, with whom I talked a great deal, harking back to my own tank regiment days. Jean-Paul professed to speak no English but he had for the past four years listened so regularly to the English broadcasts of the BBC that he could understand slow-spoken English very well. It was while I was talking

to him over the lunch table that Denby arrived with orders for me. To
understand these we must retrace our steps to the previous afternoon, when Ian
left me to return to the Maquis Jean.

Ian had returned to the Maquis Jean with the intention of retiring to his bed.
But he got there to find, to his surprise and joy, that Bill Fraser was fast asleep
on it. It was a happy return. Bill, it appeared, had dropped with Kennedy as
numbers one and two. They had been dropped from well over 1000 feet so that,
drifting down through the cloud, the stick had got badly separated. Bill had
dropped into a tree and was so suspended that he was just able to reach the
ground with his tiptoes. Lighting a cigarette, he had slid lightly out of his
harness and stepped to the ground. He quickly found Kennedy but an all-night
search failed to produce any signs of the rest of the stick, who, it turned out
later, had landed on a ridge of high ground over which Bill and Kennedy had
just drifted.

Kennedy had been carrying a Eureka radar beacon in addition to his own kit,
but the rope on his kitbag had broken and Eureka and kit, carbine and all, had
been lost. Bill himself, having left his receiving set with his batman, was now
quite cut off from the rest of the Squadron. They had lain up till dawn,
however, and when there was still no sign of the rest of the stick, they had crept
out of the woods towards a large village, which they took to be Bonnaret, just
south of the proper DZ. Enemy transport, however, was seen to be passing
through the village and the voices of German troops could be heard among the
houses. A few minutes later a field gun was seen and more troops seemed to be
arriving every moment. Bill and Kennedy returned to the area of their drop and
after a further fruitless search and an unpalatable meal off the emergency
rations, they slept in the woods all night.

Next morning they once more moved forward towards the village for a quick
recce, were able to identify the place as Lormes and realised the extent of the
error in navigation that had put them there. Hardly had the full truth dawned
upon them than heavy rifle and machine-gun fire broke out in the streets and
the echoing explosions of hand-grenades quickly followed. A minor skirmish
with the Maquis was in progress and as bullets began to whistle unpleasantly
close among the trees, Bill set off as quickly as possible towards the Vieux Dun
DZ. That night they had lain up in the Bois de St Martin and early next
morning they met an old woodcutter to whom they explained their predicament. The old man gave them food and guided them to the Bois de la
Chevrière, behind which towered the hill of the Bois de la Reine. He explained
to them the route up to the Maquis Jean and wished them good fortune, so that
by the time Ian returned, Bill had consumed a really excellent Maquis repast
and was sleeping off the results of his adventures.

Later that day, Colonel Isaac and his sergeant arrived at the Maquis Jean. He
had landed safely with Tom Moore and the rest of the stick but as food had

been low they had agreed to separate for travelling and thus the colonel also had ended up in the Maquis Jean.

The next morning, at about the time that I was looking at the new campsite in the Bois de Montsauche, Bill held a council of war and decided to send orders to Johnny and me to return to him at once in the Bois de la Reine. Denby was dispatched as messenger and came across in a Maquis car, which unfortunately he immediately sent back. These new orders placed me in an awkward position, as I had no way of getting in touch with Johnny. We had great hopes that Tom Moore would be able to contact him that afternoon and we expected the bulk of the Squadron to arrive at Les Valottes that night. So I decided to go first to the rendezvous and try to find Johnny; thence I hoped to be able to go on to Major Fraser and persuade him to let the Squadron come in that night, bringing him myself to meet them in. I also wanted to tell him about the new camp in the Bois de Montsauche, which I thought very much more suitable than the Maquis Jean, or the campsite that I had recced in the Bois de la Pérouse. This, however, was easier said than done. Denby now had no car. All the petrol-driven cars of the Maquis Bernard were out at the moment on various missions. The lorries were too big and slow to risk in daylight and this left only two slow charcoal-burning delivery vans, both of which would require quite a long time to warm up. Undeterred, however, Denby and I, with Georges and a couple of other Maquisards, trekked down to the Maquis car-park to get one of the vans going. Eventually we set off at a good pace down the first hill.

I was sitting on the floor with my back to the engine, when suddenly there came a violent jerk and I found myself being flung around by the uncontrolled bucks of the car. There was a splintering crash and we were on our side in a ditch. We were all unhurt, but the laborious job of warming up the second charcoal burner had to begin all over again.

We were now running very late. The task of warning the foreman of the local power plant, whose son was in the Maquis, that he would have to switch off the current that night on the stretch of power line that skirted Les Valottes, was delegated to a man on a motorcycle and at last we set out, doing a good 25 mph down hills and dropping to an excruciating crawl up steep inclines.

Our first call was at the rendezvous and though we shouted for Johnny and his men by name and whistled loudly our pass-tune of 'Sur le Pont d'Avignon', we could get no reply. We scoured the woods around the rendezvous as long as we dared, but without success, and turned sadly to the long trail up to the Maquis Jean.

Our car was going slower and slower and at times it was scarcely able to keep up enough speed to breast the rises at all. A quick calculation of our speed and the distances before us told me conclusively that we were attempting the impossible. We could not hope to get to Major Fraser and back to the Maquis Bernard in time to keep our appointment with Johnny and guide in the

Squadron. The only thing to do was to return at once to Bernard and make fresh plans.

Back at the Maquis Bernard, I got a bite of supper and found to my annoyance that Mac and his working party were three parts drunk, thanks to the exuberant hospitality of the Maquis and the unexpected strength of the good red wine.

Our new plans were quickly formulated. Mac, with his men and an escort of the men of the Maquis, would take the thirty-two-seater bus to the rendezvous and prepare to receive the Squadron. If it appeared that more men were coming, a further lorry could be sent for to carry them. Meanwhile Georges, Bernard and I would go in one of the fast petrol-driven cars, which had now returned, to pick up Bill and bring him to the Les Valottes DZ, where he could welcome in the Squadron and make his decision regarding the new campsite. Denby remained with Mac, so as to be able to cope with the language problem.

Twilight was already deepening as we set off for the Maquis Jean. The situation was in no way eased by the fact that Bernard had only once previously been to the Maquis Jean and the route was tricky, even in daylight. It was pitch dark by the time we reached the area of the Bois de la Reine and we were soon hopelessly lost. Suddenly, the lights of another car swept down on us through the gloom. We were pretty unsure of ourselves and fingers tightened instinctively on the triggers of our guns, which were poked out of the windows at all angles. The other car, however, was equally hesitant, and as it drew level we were relieved to see a swarthy face peering at us dubiously over the top of a Sten-gun. It was a returning car from the Maquis Jean and as soon as Bernard had made himself known they were glad to guide us back to their garage.

It was after 11.00 as I hurried down the roughly beaten track to the Maquis itself, and Bill was in his tent when I arrived. He welcomed me warmly. I gave him all the latest news and told him of the arrangements that I had made. He agreed to come with me and Ian came along, too. Back we went through the night along unfamiliar roads and again and again we got lost, found ourselves again and pushed on. We had the greatest difficulty in finding the DZ, and I remember most clearly finding a signpost marked 'Montboblin', a place that neither then nor at any other time have I ever been able to find on any map or on the ground.

At last, however, in the distance we picked out a glimmering of light and were finally able to make out the sidelights of our bus parked into the side of the road and screened by trees. As we drew up, Johnny Cooper came to greet us. The drop of the Squadron had been postponed until another night, but Johnny and all his boys were here. With the exception of the little body of men still with Tom Moore, the whole recce party was reunited.

CHAPTER V

Paving the Way

The big bus made its way slowly back to the Maquis Jean, stopping for a while at a rendezvous that had been given to Tom Moore and where we searched for him without success.

At Maquis Jean, we carted most of our kit into the trees and slept on the ground close by. Next morning, we slept late and the Maquis fed us at lunchtime.

During the night, a party of the Maquis had been out receiving a *parachutage* of supplies for themselves at a DZ to the north. Camille had been in charge of the party and by great ill luck they had been ambushed on the way back by a party of Germans hidden in the hedgerows. The Moor, badly wounded, had returned with the tale but nine of the Maquis were known to have been killed in the encounter and Camille had not returned. An aspect of the situation that shocked us was that four of the dead Maquisards had been wearing loose jumping-jackets that we had given to them, thus causing the Germans to identify them as 'British parachutists' at a time when we hoped that our presence was undetected. Worse still, when the Maquis recovered the bodies it was found that two of them had only been slightly wounded and in spite of, or perhaps because of, the assumption that they were British soldiers, had been beaten to death.

During the afternoon we made a dump of the kit that was too heavy to carry and set off with our most immediate needs on our backs to go to the camp that I had originally recced in the Bois de la Pérouse.

It was a long hard climb up to our new camp and it was getting late before we finally reached a little copse near the clearing at the top where we cooked our dinner and slept the night in our sleeping bags under the stars. We were woken twice by the sound of rifle and machine-gun fire in the neighbourhood, but we were not discovered.

The next morning we moved the camp again into a deeper part of the wood and I went the odd four miles back to the Maquis Jean to arrange for our kit to be transported by lorry to our new camp. The increase in enemy activity had somewhat alarmed the Maquis and they refused us the transport, so that I had to return empty handed, and after lunch Mac took a party of the men across to collect the last of the kit and carry it by hand across to the new camp. Food was running pretty low and I went down to the old rendezvous by the Cure bridge, where men from Maquis Bernard were supposed to meet us at about 2 o'clock. I waited until nearly 5.00, when at last they turned up and I guided them up by the road route to the environs of our camp, for normally we approached the camp by forest trails. They brought us a certain amount of food, though not very much, and offered us any assistance that we wanted, but at present there was nothing that they could do for us.

The new location proved quite impossible for our wireless set and no radio connection with London could be obtained at all. That night it started to rain. It rained in torrents and sleeping as we were in the absolute open we were soaked to the skin through a miserable night.

The next day saw a comparative lull and we did the best we could to improvise rough shelters out of boughs and to dry our clothes. In the late afternoon we received instructions over the radio that three planes, with most of the rest of the Squadron, were coming in to the Les Valottes DZ that night. I went across to the Maquis Jean and asked Denby to request the Maquis Bernard to lay on a reception committee for them, which he did; meantime I managed to get the Maquis Jean to give me a car for Bill. While I was getting it filled with oil and petrol and learning how to drive it, Bill, Ian and Reg Seekings arrived and I drove them down to the Les Valottes DZ, just as it was getting dark. Ian did the navigating and we again encountered the Montboblin sign but had the greatest difficulty in finding the DZ. Furthermore, it was pouring with rain.

At last, somewhat dispirited, we stopped by the roadside to consider our next move. All of a sudden we heard the sound of a heavy vehicle and coming down the road behind us was the light of an enormous truck. For a dreadful moment we thought that it was a Boche patrol and my passengers baled out into the ditch. I was well jammed behind the steering wheel and unable to move. I expected a quick burst in the back at any moment, then as the car drew abreast, I recognised, with a sigh of relief, the thirty-two-seater bus with the DZ party and that more by good luck than good judgement we had arrived at the right place after all.

The DZ fires were arranged and we waited eagerly for a sign of the longed-for Squadron. The rain increased, a low fog gathered over the DZ. In the distance the sound of engines could be faintly heard. The fires were lit.

Distantly we heard the three planes circling around. One of them roared over very low. Dimly through the mist and the rain we could make out the silhouette of a Stirling. Then the roars of the engines died away. The planes were making for their base once more. One of those Stirlings failed to return and Les Cairns and sixteen of the best and bravest men we had were never heard of again.

We waited cold and disconsolate on the DZ until all hope had gone. We waited in those dripping woods until the last dim echo had passed into nothingness and then at last we turned our cars for home.

Denby travelled back with us to the Maquis Jean and as we raced along the narrow country lanes, our headlights only with difficulty piercing the driving rain, we had one of those encounters which can be so comic or so deadly tragic.

As I turned a corner I was suddenly confronted by the looming bulk of a German truck. There was no mistaking the brown and black markings of the camouflage or the cut of its lines. It was a Boche. Never in all my experience have I ever changed direction so fast. As my feet practically pressed the brake through the floorboards, I smashed the gear lever into reverse almost before the wheels had ceased to turn, backed away from the truck which completely barred our path, and flicked off the headlights. At the corner I drew to a standstill and as I stopped, Ian, Bill and Reg dived for the ditch. Denby and I, wedged in the narrower space of the front seats, were forced to stay put, he covering the back of the truck with his carbine, though there was not a sign of life.

When I had disengaged myself from the steering wheel I got out and weighed up the chances of turning round. Bill whispered that they were going to creep up to investigate the truck and told us to keep it covered. Nothing loath, Denby and I did so. Minutes crept by like hours. Suddenly a light appeared at the back of the truck and the low murmur of voices could clearly be heard. A torch played over the tailboard and a figure could dimly be seen beside the back of the truck.

'There they are,' said Denby. 'I wonder if it's a truck that the Maquis have captured. I don't suppose that they can make themselves understood. I'd better go and give them a hand.' So saying, he stepped out of the car and began to walk up the centre of the road towards the truck. From the ditches Reg, Ian and Bill had watched the light with deep concern. It was not they who had reached the truck but a group of men who had emerged suddenly from the depths of the wood on their left and were as surprised to see Denby as he was to see them. For a long minute there was one of those awkward, pregnant silences that might as well have been broken by the crack of a gun as by peaceful words. But cool heads prevailed. Denby spoke to them in French; the men replied in the same language. The truck belonged to a small Maquis which frequented the neighbourhood. The situation was saved.

We dropped Denby off at Vieux Dun, where he could make his own way up to the Maquis Jean. We took our car back to the wood by our camp and camouflaged it in the undergrowth.

The next day was spent in eating and sleeping. The food situation was bad and by lunchtime there was not a bite of any description left in the camp; however, both Maquis Jean and Maquis Bernard brought us a little food and a sheep we had procured through Maquis Jean was slaughtered.

It continued to rain almost continuously and only the fact that Zellic managed to steal a couple of tarpaulins from a nearby farm saved us from another night of utter misery.

Tom Moore had turned up at the Maquis Jean the previous evening and been redirected to our camp in the Pérouse. After his arrival, he managed to get wireless communication with London re-established. The main hold-up appeared to be the lack of a Eureka beacon without which it was definitely hazardous to send the entire Squadron, complete with all its equipment, at what was maximum range for these short summer nights.

At the same time, Bill sent off a long message explaining the local sabotage situation. He pointed out that there was very little work within the reasonable range of foot parties and anyway that small-scale sabotage was much better carried out by the Maquisards, who had local knowledge, local contacts, were indistinguishable at a glance from harmless natives and were the only people with transport capable of getting them somewhere near a decent target. He suggested that we should be given more offensive arms , such as Bren-guns, mortars, jeeps and possibly 6-pounder anti-tank guns, so that we could operate as a Heavy Squadron to the Maquis, giving them a strong backing in the assault and guaranteeing them a safe base of operations. The reply that he received was not encouraging, though by the end of August he had been proved absolutely right, and that was indeed the role into which we were forced by pressure of circumstances.

That night, the Vieux Dun DZ was manned by Ian with a few of our men and a party from the Maquis, but no planes came.

Next morning, we were awoken by whistles and shouts and firing in our wood. I went out to investigate. It proved to be Denby, who did not know the way to our camp and had a message for us from the other Maquis.

It rained all day and was thoroughly miserable. The food situation again became somewhat depressing and there was no indication of any planes coming that night. In the afternoon the doctor from Maquis Bernard, Martell by name, came to see us and Docherty, who had been suffering severely from a badly septic arm, was given a rough operation in the open wood, and conveyed to the Maquis hospital at the Château de Vermot, on the eastern side of the Bois de la Reine.

At our cold and hungry camp we were pretty dispirited, particularly as there was news of further German troop concentrations against the Maquis. The Bois de Saint Martin was now being occupied by the Germans and fresh troops of Cossack 'free' Russian cavalry were supposed to have reinforced the garrison of Château-Chinon, some twenty-five miles to the south. Furthermore, we were completely isolated, being cut off by the River Cure from any hope of Maquis assistance, and most of us were only armed with our Colts and our knives. We had a few carbines but nothing bigger, and the danger of an attack was felt to be unpleasantly great.

That night we did not man a DZ, but shivered in the dripping woods. The next day it was decided to begin operations even without the support of the rest of the Squadron and accordingly bicycles were borrowed from the Maquis Jean and our explosives were reallocated and prepared. Before we had time to set out, however, the long-awaited message arrived that the Squadron was coming at last.

It was now the night of 20/21 June and men from both Maquis manned the Vieux Dun DZ. I was ordered to bring the car along but what with a treacherous ditch on the darkened trail, a punctured tyre and a slipping clutch, we had to abandon the car and walk. The Maquis Bernard had brought several water-bottles and big flasks full of red wine and we were in high heart as we awaited the drop. As the night wore on, the whole prospect became less auspicious. It was a lovely night and the stars twinkled brightly from the clear sky. Towards 2 o'clock we began to drink the wine that we had brought for their reception and at 3.30, weary and dispirited, we had at last to abandon our vigil.

The next morning, an even more disturbing thing happened. A woman from the town of Quarré-les-Tombes arrived, demanding the tarpaulins that Zellic had taken to give us shelter. It was obvious to all that if a woman who had lost a tarpaulin could track us down and reach our camp unobserved, so could a German patrol, and in our comparatively defenceless state we dared not remain so isolated any longer. Accordingly, that afternoon, we began to shift our camp to the wooded valley behind Vieux Dun, where there was a convenient stream and where we were less than half an hour's climb away from the Maquis Jean.

During the morning we had done everything possible to repair our car and all the heaviest items of equipment were loaded on to it. At lunchtime a wireless message came through stating that the Squadron was definitely coming in tonight. Two planes were scheduled to drop men and supplies at the Les Valottes DZ and three were to drop at Vieux Dun.

I drove our rickety car down to our new camp site and, leaving the boys to unload it, I settled down on the roadside near Vieux Dun to intercept the truck that was supposed to be coming from Maquis Bernard to find out the possibility of a drop tonight.

As the afternoon wore on into evening, most of the Squadron HQ men toiled past along the dusty road. I dozed in the sun. I waited and waited, but the truck never arrived. It was now 5 o'clock and the truck was two hours overdue. At last Bill himself came striding along the road. The Pérouse camp had now been completely cleared, but the Maquis truck still was nowhere to be seen. Bill himself decided to stay and wait while I went to collect our practically useless car and bring a bit of supper back.

Our car was now so low in petrol that it was evident that I would be unable to get as far as the Maquis Bernard and I sent Zellic and two men up the dreadfully long trail to the Maquis Jean's garage to collect the fuel. Meanwhile I ate a bite of supper and collected eggs and sandwiches for Bill. After what seemed an age, Zellic at last returned. With practically the whole of the party pushing, we managed to get the car up out of the valley and I picked up Bill.

Johnny Cooper and Ian Stewart were arranging with the Maquis Jean to man the Vieux Dun DZ, but the truck from the Maquis Bernard had still not materialised and the matter was becoming most urgent. Darkness was beginning to set in.

With the clutch slipping worse than ever and the last of the light starting to fade from the sky, Bill and I started a crazy ride.

At the best of times I cannot pretend to be a good driver, but on little known roads in the fading light, with the possibility of enemy patrols and a clutch slipping so much that I dared not drop my speed for hills or corners, I was abominable.

It grew dark. As we approached the Maquis Bernard we were passed by a car which swept into the maze of small tracks ahead of us. We followed and when it stopped we drew up behind and got out. Immediately a Sten-gun from the other car covered us and a man came round the back towards us. 'C'est le Lieutenant Gremlin,' I said and Bernard's husky voice answered me from the shadows.

Quickly we explained our mission and quickly Bernard got to work. A message was again dispatched to the foreman to switch off the power that skirted the DZ and we were guided up to the Maquis where feverish preparations for the coming operation were put in train. The men had to be roused from sleep and had to dress. The charcoal-burning bus and lorries had to be warmed up and got out of the awkward dead-end which formed the Maquis garage. We were given a good supper and in a fever of excitement waited for all to be ready.

At last we trooped back down the long trail from the Maquis and waited for the bus to arrive. We waited and we waited. The planes were due at about 1 o'clock and we needed to be on the DZ a good half-hour before they arrived. The DZ was many miles away but we waited and still waited. At last a frantic messenger arrived from the garage. The largest lorry was stuck in the only exit and no vehicle could get in or out. They were working on it as hard as they could but it would be a long time before it was freed.

The position was critical. It was already too late for the lorry to get to the DZ in time, even if it was freed immediately and if there were no lights, the planes would go away without dropping their precious cargoes. The car in which Bill and I had come was now quite useless; with a drastic tightening of the clutch it might perhaps get as far as the Vieux Dun camp but it could not possibly be used tonight. The only other car readily available was that belonging to Josef, the *chef de Maquis*, and that had no brakes at all. Desperate situations, however, require desperate remedies. Into Josef's car were crammed Bill, myself and three others to man the DZ lights and also the car batteries and headlights that were going to be used to guide the planes down. Among the lamp-lighters were Georges and Roger, who thus began an intimate association with the Squadron that was to last until our departure months later.

The journey from Vieux Dun to the Maquis had been a nightmare, but it could not compare for sheer horror to the ride that followed it. The roads were narrow and winding, sweeping up hills and down dales. We were grossly overloaded and we knew that there were no brakes; nevertheless speed was essential and at every corner the car bucked and swayed as though it had a will of its own.

At last we arrived at the DZ. We tumbled out of the car and began to lug the batteries into position. Georges supervised the placing of the men and himself operated the centre light. The last light was in position, though Georges had not yet had time to return to his own, when with a dull pulsating roar the first Stirling swept in low across the field and the order 'Allumez' was shrieked from the signal light.

In an instant three headlamps pierced the darkness and played upon the spread wings and deep belly of the leading Stirling. A second plane could be seen following hard behind.

They circled the DZ once and then on the second run in there came the rustle of chutes, the banging of containers and the swooshing thud of a 'roman candle' (a container whose chute has not developed).

Now they ran in for a second time and more containers and a few panniers (big wicker baskets) came fluttering down. The sound of men's voices could be heard floating out of the air. The Squadron had arrived.

CHAPTER VI

Main Party

Back in England the main body of the Squadron had waited impatiently for their orders. The gallant deeds of B Squadron were already beginning to filter through and the difficulties that we were encountering were hard for them to understand. They were warned to be ready night after night, but night after night they did not take off. The unhappy loss of Les Cairns and a plane-load of very fine men cast a shadow over them all and the endless boredom of being continually cooped up in a concentration camp was wearing their nerves.

The night of 20/21 June was so misty and unpleasant that the hopes of taking off were never very high. The next day, however, was more promising and that evening saw five Stirlings ticking over on the runway, the crews already briefed, and the passengers aboard ready for take-off.

The most important part of the Squadron, consisting of Johnny Wiseman with One Troop (the troop to which I really belonged and which included my own operational party), Alex Muirhead with Two Troop, the MO and the remnants of Squadron Headquarters were in the three planes bound for Vieux Dun. This party went off without real difficulty. The planes found the DZ and the men landed fairly well bunched. They collected their kits and were guided by the Maquis to the Vieux Dun camp. There were, however, one or two minor troubles. The first was when a container full of mortar bombs 'candled', and catching fire, began to explode. Ian Stewart, who had retired to bed once the DZ was organised, woke to a noise like a full-blown battle and had visions of being the sole survivor from an ambushed DZ, but all was well.

One of the guides managed to lose his way and kept one stick wandering about the woods all night, but they turned up in the morning, none the worse.

There were a few casualties on landing, a number of twisted ankles, a strained back for Sergeant Chalky White and a badly broken leg for Trooper Bill Burgess.

All day the party worked on getting their kit from the DZ to the camp and by teatime the task was accomplished.

Meanwhile Three Troop under Roy Bradford, with the Padre, was coming in to our DZ near Les Valottes to the south. Their drop, however, was not a great success. In the first place, the pilot insisted of dropping the whole stick of sixteen in one long line, which meant that there was the better part of a mile between the first and the last man. Secondly, he ran up the line of lights in the wrong direction and did not signal the first man to go until he was over the last light. The result was that Roy himself was the only man to land on the DZ, the rest of his stick being scattered for miles among the trees.

The containers from the various planes were pretty scattered, too, and the Maquis were busily engaged in finding them and dragging them to the roadside where they could be retrieved by the lorries that had by this time arrived.

Searches were made for the men and the first half dozen or so of the stick were eventually found and guided to the waiting bus. Sergeant Jeff Duvivier was found precariously perched at the top of an enormous pine tree, and the three headlights from the DZ had to be brought along to floodlight the scene while one of the Maquisards climbed up to give him a hand. I have a very clear mental picture of Jeff hugging the trunk of the pine full in the glare of the headlights like a small performing bear at the top of an enormous pole.

As more and more containers were collected, we began to open one or two, particularly the Bren-guns, which were worth their weight in gold. We were particularly chagrined to find the guns in no fit state to be used as they were still blocked up with packing grease. However, we got a local farmer to boil some water and as the Brens became serviceable, they were sent out to replace the small Maquis standing patrols which were stationed at all the roads leading to the DZ. A kindly farmer's wife also boiled us some tea and eggs.

When it was at last fully light, we organised more extensive searches for the missing men and containers. Parachutes that were seen hanging in trees were retrieved and one of the lorries was sent off with the bulk of the containers.

Luckily there was a heavy ground mist that morning, for a German recce plane was heard circling overhead; but we were invisible in our misty shroud.

I found one chute at the top of a very high tree; the harness had been cut and it was obvious that the man in question had cut himself loose in the dark and dropped a good thirty feet to the ground. Later I found the man; it was Fraser McLuskey, a minister of the Church of Scotland and the finest Padre one could imagine. The nasty fall had knocked him out, he had been violently sick and had wandered around for quite a time before he was picked up by a couple of Maquis boys. Another of the missing men was Ooly Ball, Roy's second-in-command, whom I finally came upon in bed. He had realised that he had hardly landed in quite the right place when, disentangling himself from his harness, he had taken a step backward and dropped down a twenty-foot bank on to a bed of moss. So, deciding to make the best of a bad job, he unrolled his sleeping bag and dozed till dawn.

During these collecting operations, we had another lucky escape. A German patrol passed the bottom end of the road, along which we were working. Fortunately it did not deviate from its route and we continued our work unmolested.

Eventually, when there were only three of Roy's men unaccounted for, we embarked on the bus for our return journey. It was now 10 o'clock, and the peasants were working in the fields and the artisans at their crafts. The dangers of bumping into a German patrol were gravely increased, particularly as part of the journey back to the Maquis had to be accomplished along good second-class roads.

We mounted our Bren-guns on the roof of the bus and on top of the lorries. The major travelled back in Josef's car and I sat myself, grenade in hand, on top of the bus. I thought it a good deal safer than inside.

On the return journey, we had an unpleasant accident, when Josef, worn out with many nights of *parachutage*, fell asleep at the wheel of his car and it turned over in the middle of the road. This caused quite a hold-up at the most dangerous part of the route and Josef's arm was broken, but fortunately none of the other occupants was hurt.

At last we got back safely to the Maquis Bernard and trekked up once more to the camp in the woods, where we were given an excellent dinner and dropped down to sleep.

That evening, just as it was getting dusk, Bill, the Padre and I returned slowly in our damaged car to the Vieux Dun camp. We got there just as darkness fell and after I had had a few words with Fred Hindle, Poland and Glyde, the men of my party, I unrolled my sleeping bag and slept like the dead.

The next morning Sergeant White, who was partly paralysed, was helped into my car. With Poland and Glyde as my escort, we were pushed out of the valley on to the Vieux Dun road and I drove round to the Château de Vermot, where we left White, and I had a look at our other patients who were there.

Thence we continued on our way up to the garage of the Maquis Jean, where we left our broken-down car to be repaired and took over a new Citröen for future use. I returned with this to the Vieux Dun camp, where I picked up Johnny Wiseman and drove him over to the Maquis Bernard where he had liaison with the chefs of the Maquis, got various information that he wanted and arranged the details of tonight's move with Roy Bradford.

While we had been away two of Roy's missing men had been recovered by the Maquis and Roy had been able to sort out some of the stores.

Liaising finished, we returned to the Vieux Dun camp. There I was able at last to draw a carbine and began to feel slightly less unprotected. I also wrapped my toothbrush and other essential articles in my bedding roll as I was going with Alex to the site I had chosen for him in the Bois de Montsauche. I was to act as guide and introduce him to the men of the Maquis Bernard before returning to join my proper troop. My rucksack and the rest of my kit I stacked neatly in my section area.

That night, as it got dark, the men of Alex's troop, with the Padre and Johnny Cooper temporarily attached, made their way up to the village of Vieux Dun. We drank a little of the wine from the *estaminet* and waited.

At 11.30, the Bernard bus rolled sedately into the village. Roy Bradford and his merry men tumbled out and began to unload their kit.

As soon as they had disappeared down the road to our camp, Alex and his boys began their loading. Among the arms that they put aboard with tender care were the two 3-inch mortars which were his especial pride and joy.

Once all were aboard, we began the long slow journey back to the Maquis Bernard. Trapped in that enormous bus, we would have been caught like rats if the enemy had happened to ambush us; but I was too tired to be frightened that night and slept all the way.

At one place along the route, we found a German truck parked outside a small house. The owners were evidently inside carousing. After we were safely past, two of the Maquisards slipped off the bus and next morning the Maquis garage was one German truck to the good.

Arriving at the Bois de Montsauche, we collected our personal kit from the bus and walked up as far as the Maquis Bernard; there we slept the sleep of exhaustion, for we had been going pretty continuously for two days.

A late breakfast was provided for us by the Maquis and while the boys were eating it I showed Alex the site of our proposed camp. After breakfast, the boys got to work settling into their new home, bringing up the rest of their kit and beginning to sort and prepare the ammunition and other equipment from the containers. But work of a more desperate character was in the offing and it was not long before our container sorting gave way to more bloody business.

CHAPTER VII

Baptism of Fire

For some time it had been obvious that the Germans intended to clear this part of the Morvan before it was too late. The Maquis were small, ill-armed and untrained. Before we arrived, the Maquis Bernard had only three light machine guns and only about forty of their hundred odd men were armed. Jean's Maquis was somewhat better, being in more direct communication with London, but it is doubtful whether he could raise a hundred fighting men and his automatic weapons were woefully short. Although full of enthusiasm, none of the Maquisards, even the most military of them, had any idea of true discipline and were liable easily to be discouraged. Their real worth depended entirely upon the capacity of their leader and use of their local knowledge. Faced only by these scattered forces, but fearing a potential rising of the entire French nation, the Germans felt that the time had come to clear out this awkward pocket and make safe their lines of communication. Thus they had steadily built up their forces in the garrison towns around the Morvan and were now ready to strike.

The first active news that we received in the Maquis Bernard was on the morning of 24 June when, wearily sorting containers after our long night's journey, we were suddenly informed that a party of some sixty Germans and Grey Russians (Red Army prisoners of war, who had volunteered to serve with the German army), had passed the head of the valley of the Chalaux, which covered our normal entrance to the Bois de Montsauche, and were taking up position in the flourishing little town of Montsauche itself. We feared that an attack was imminent.

Alex did not wish to commit his trained saboteurs to a guerilla battle of the type for which they were not trained, particularly at a time when they were so newly arrived and comparatively unprepared. However, he was willing to give what assistance he could, and two of our Bren-guns, with a 3-inch mortar to support them, were moved down to the Maquis guardhouse area, from which they could cover the valley of the Chalaux.

I was, of course, a completely spare man, having merely come as a guide and being marooned with Two Troop until such time as Bill should come over and fetch me. However, since I was keen to see action, after my four years of waiting, I rushed around trying to be useful in any way I could.

Although the Germans continued to hold Montsauche in force, Bernard suggested that as they were almost certain to leave the town by the Planchez road, we ought to ambush them on the way out. This scheme was put to

Colonel Dubois, who drew up a plan, and to Alex, who promised the support of two Bren-guns.

Alex ordered two of the Bren crews to report to him at the Maquis Bernard and agreed that I should be allowed to accompany the Maquis themselves to see how they behaved under fire, though I had to promise not to take any risks.

Unfortunately, something went wrong and his orders were never received at the 'Maquis Anglais', as we came to call our new camp. So Alex had to use two Bren crews who had just come up from the valley of the Chalaux, on their way to camp for supper.

Eventually, at about 6 o'clock, the party was organised. The Maquis element, some fifteen men in all, consisting mainly of Georges' Parisians, was commanded by Bernard in person. Among the Maquisards were the two Red Russians, allowed to fight beside them for the first time. Our party consisted of Alex himself, Johnny Cooper and Sergeant Zellic, Sergeant 'Nobby' Noble, Corporal 'Silvo' Sylvester, Trooper Middleton and myself. Owing to the shortage of men, I joined the party as an actual fighting man, but as I had never been in action before and the others were all old soldiers, I told them that for the purposes of this operation, I wished to be treated as a trooper. It was rather a shirking of responsibility, but as none of the men had ever been with me before, even on exercises, it seemed the best solution.

Colonel Dubois commanded the whole force and explained the plan to us all very carefully in French, illustrating it with the stub of a pencil on the back of an envelope. Broadly, the plan was as follows.

The convoy was known to consist of two large lorries, a number of small cars and a motorcycle. The British would be responsible for the head of the convoy and the French for the tail. Everyone would be on the same side of the road and the Bren guns so sited as to be mutually supporting. The signal for the start would be the throwing of a plastic Gammon bomb into the leading truck; after that everything was to open up until not a German was left.

Silvo and I were to keep well away from the rest of the ambush, detailed to kill at all costs the motorcyclist, who would initially be let through, to gain surprise, but on no account allowed to get back to Château-Chinon to report.

At the head of the ambush proper were Nobby and Middleton with one Bren and Zellic and Johnny Cooper with the other. Lying practically side by side and well concealed, their fire was co-ordinated by Alex himself.

From the British Bren position the ground fell away steeply into a little valley where the track from the Bois de Montsauche met the main road. Here the Maquisards were hiding, protected from view and from fire by huge piles of cut timber that were awaiting collection by the roadside. A spur of wood gave them complete concealment and a covered line of withdrawal in case of accidents.

Nearer to Montsauche, there were some open fields running up from the road to the edge of the forest and dominated by the farm of La Verrerie. Here in the wood, not far from the farm, were the two French *fusils-mitrailleurs*, one a Bren and the other a captured Spandau.

It was about 8.30 when we finally took up our positions. Silvo and I were a quarter of a mile beyond the main party and stationed ourselves one on each side of the road. Instead of my red beret, which I thought would make me too conspicuous, I had been wearing a camouflaged veil tied round my head. I now let this down to cover my face and dug my hands into the soft soil of the ditch to dirty their tell-tale whiteness.

For what seemed an eternity, I crouched by the roadside. The sun slid below the fir trees and the flies began to irritate me as they buzzed around my face, sweaty with exertion and excitement.

Minutes wore on. We had expected them to come out at about 7.00, now it was 9.00. We had been assured that the Germans had not yet passed down this road, but perhaps after all they had gone back the way that they had come. Maybe they were going to spend the night in Montsauche, maybe they would go on to Saulieu.

An old man with a bullock cart laden with logs passed slowly along the road towards Planchez. I reflected what would have happened to him had he been going the other way, for we could not have permitted him to pass for fear that he warned the Germans. I kept imagining that I heard the noise of engines; perhaps I did. I wondered what would happen if a patrol came up the Planchez road towards Montsauche and caught our ambush in general, and me in particular, from a most unhealthy angle. I wasn't absolutely sure that I wanted any Germans to come at all. Meanwhile I swatted flies and waited.

Another distant drone – the flies again, or my imagination. No! This time I heard the distinct crash of gears as a heavy vehicle made a noisy change on the incline that led up to the British position. Before I had time to do any more thinking, the hellish melody of chattering Brens shattered the stillness of the evening air. Then, above the clamour, I heard the unmistakable roar of a plastic bomb as Roger hurled his missile into the leading truck.

I crouched deeper into the bank where I hid, clutched my carbine more firmly in my hands, glued my eyes to the corner where the motorcyclist should appear, and waited once more.

The initial crescendo of fire had died away to a series of sharp bursts interspersed with the sharper crack of rifles and the occasional bursting of grenades. I decided that I had waited long enough. Crossing the road, I sought out Silvo and we ran crouching along the ditch to the scene of the battle.

As we reached the corner where the British were stationed, I was able to see clearly down the length of the road. In the foreground, not more than fifty yards away, the leading German lorry was blazing furiously. The windscreen was shattered and the bodies of the men in the cab lolled grotesquely in their seats. It was the first time that I had seen a dead man but I found myself strangely unmoved. Beyond the first truck was a small civilian car. It, too, was stopped and derelict, and a huddled form twitched on the road beside it. Further away, at the next bend, the nose of another lorry could just be seen and I hoped that the French were dealing with it as effectively as our boys had dealt with its leader.

Diving into the wood at Sylvester's heels, I came upon Alex and the gunners as they rose from their positions of concealment and began to move forward, clearing the ditches as they went. Alex told me that the dispatch-rider had turned back at the first shot and returned in the direction of Montsauche. Later we learned that the French had got him.

Now as we approached the Germans, cowering in their ditches, the fire got hotter. Ricochets went whining away through the trees and on the left we heard a German Spandau come into action.

Middleton and Sylvester were like anxious nursemaids with me.

'Take a shot at those Germans in the ditch, sir.'

'Where?'

'There! Look, that one's just popping his head up, sir.' Bang.

'I think I got the bastard, sir. Look, just beyond him, have a go at that one, sir.'

Bang, bang, bang.

'Oh, you missed, sir. Better luck next time.'

And so it went on. With Sylvester on one side and Middleton on the other, I worked through the wood as far as the blazing lorry. Shots were still coming from the inferno, but whether it was a wounded man fighting to the last or ammunition bursting in the heat it impossible to tell. On top of the cab a badly wounded German was writhing in the flames and groaning. Middleton and I emptied our Colts into the side of the lorry at point-blank range and heard a satisfactory yelp. I gave Middleton half my carbine ammunition as it was pretty evident that he was a much better shot than I.

By now we were opposite the ditch in which most of the survivors from the first truck were cowering for shelter. From behind a large pile of stacked timber, I lobbed my grenades across the road, assisted and encouraged by Middleton. My first grenade was hurled too far and burst inoffensively in a potato patch beyond the enemy, but the second fell on the very lip of the ditch and no more heads appeared.

Moving beyond the lorry, we reached the spot where the Maquis track debouched on to the road and here we waited, while Nobby Noble and others finished clearing the far side of the road. At this point I saw our boys do two very pretty pieces of shooting. The first was when a German, crouching in the further ditch, suddenly leapt to his feet and darted across the road about twenty yards from us. We had no time to take aim, but Sylvester, firing his carbine from the hip, hit him in mid-stride and he tumbled in a heap against the wall, mortally wounded. The second occurred a few moments later when Nobby, moving gingerly down the road verge, suddenly heard a movement in a thicket to his right. He fell back on to his haunches in the middle of the road and fired a short burst from his Bren as he fell. The movements ceased and Nobby continued his cautious advance. When the battle was over, I investigated the thicket and found a German corporal there, his arm shattered by Nobby's bullets.

The area of the leading truck was now entirely cleared and the firing had died away. André, one of Georges' officers, came up to us and began shouting in German for enemy soldiers to come out on to the road and give themselves up, we would not kill them. But his harangue did not appear to be very effective, perhaps because all the Germans within earshot were dead, wounded or very badly shaken.

Since Alex did not know whether the dispatch-rider had escaped, he now thought it best to leave the scene of the ambush before any enemy reinforcements put in an appearance and withdrew with most of his men. Because I knew many of the Maquisards and spoke a little French, I remained behind to make it quite clear that the British were not deserting them and to try to persuade them to retire into the woods themselves before any more Boches turned up. At first Sylvester remained with me.

In the woods, the German Spandau was still burping away and there was the occasional sound of a rifle shot, but our own area was quiet. From the burning lorry, shaken, but miraculously uninjured, emerged a grey-haired old Frenchman, who had been taken by the Germans as a hostage and now berated his rescuers for having destroyed his motorcycle which the Shleuh had also shoved into the back of the lorry.

Two more hostages had survived from the second car. One was a middle-aged man, badly hurt, who was carried away tenderly by the Maquis on a stretcher, improvised out of a gate. The other was the young lad who had led the advance recce party up to the Maquis Jean when we first arrived in France. He was overjoyed to see me again, which is more than I can say of him, for white-faced, unshaven and reeking of garlic, he proceeded to embrace me in what I had been led to believe was truly French style.

I was then confronted with the problem of prisoners. It was self-evident that, living as we were behind the lines, it would be impossible to keep any considerable number of prisoners. For this reason, we had been instructed to shoot straight so that the problem did not arise, but naturally this was easier said than done, and as I walked around the wrecked lorry I found several badly wounded men. What was to be done about them? I admit that the idea of shooting them in cold blood did occur to me. I drew my Colt, intending to finish them off; but it was my first skirmish and although I found myself peculiarly unmoved by the sight of blood and the sufferings of the enemy, I still could not bring myself to press the trigger. Some weeks later it might have been a different story, but that night I left them where they lay.

Meanwhile, the Maquisards had been searching the dead, removing the boots of every German in sight and gathering up as much of their arms and equipment as they could find. Two men in German uniform were taken, very frightened but only slightly wounded, from the ditch where I had thrown my grenade, and after being searched were taken, under Maquis escort, back into the woods for interrogation. As I got back to the blackened skeleton of the leading lorry, I found that a 'dead man' had come to life. By his better quality uniform and by his epaulettes I knew him to be an officer; and as a Maquisard dragged him to his feet he began to beg for his life.

'Je suis Anglais,' he cried. 'Je suis Anglais, ne me tuez pas!'

'So you're English, are you?' said Sylvester, coming round the corner of the woodpile, 'Let's hear you speak it.'

The man's eyes dilated with fear. 'No spik English well, Secret Service!' he cried.

'Where are your papers then?' I demanded, joining the knot of men who held him cornered against the stacked timber.

He looked and acted like a trapped rat. His shifty eyes searched our faces and the greenish white of his face and hands were in violent contrast to the deep red trickle of blood that coursed down his soiled grey trousers from a wound in his groin.

'Secret Service,' he said at last. 'No British, Russe!'

Then, warming to his theme, he turned to the Maquisards. 'Oui,' he repeated. 'Je suis Russe.'

From the narrowing circle, Alexis the Red Russian pushed his way forward. He was small, broad and blonde, and his blue eyes seemed to be tearing the luckless officer apart. 'Vous, Russe,' he said in his thick ugly French, and then he burst into a torrent of Russian.

It was the end. The man in field-grey seemed to shrink, withered by the verbal blast. He replied feebly in the same tongue but his answers were unavailing. With some fierce Russian oath, Alexis sprang, ran his fingers over the man's body, drew out a vicious little automatic from the prisoner's inside pocket and handed it to me.

'Pah!' he almost spat as he spoke. 'Russe Blanc!' Then before a soul could stop him, he whipped the binoculars from around the White Russian's neck and, swinging them wickedly, shattered them against the renegade's check. Seizing the wounded man's shoulder, he twirled him round, kicking him with fierce zest up the slippery track towards the Maquis. It was useless to reason with Alexis in a language he could not understand, so we let him go and were rather surprised to find later that he had brought his prisoner all the way back to camp. But in truth he was far too good a soldier to kill an officer who might be induced to give useful information.

The twilight already was deepening into dusk and Sylvester, too, had disappeared. Nothing I could say or do would induce the Maquisards to take the reasonable precaution of withdrawing as soon as possible into their woods and I stayed with them until it was quite dark, helping to collect the enemy rifles from among the dead. At last, knowing that I would have been missed at our camp by this time, I took up an armful of rifles and set off towards the Maquis.

About a hundred yards up the track I found Georges, Roger and a little knot of the Parisians around the still form of Jacques. He had been hit straight between the eyes and most of the back of his head had been blown out. I remembered now having seen four of the Maquisards carrying him away early on in the action, his body slung between them, and hanging down like a carcass of meat. Roger, who was with him, was deaf from the effects of the plastic Gammon bomb which he had thrown so efficiently that he had destroyed the enemy in the back of the leading truck.

Leaving the German rifles with some of the Maquis, I continued up the track alone. At one place I was stopped by a few excited Frenchmen who tried to tell me exactly where the German Spandau, which was still firing sporadically, was hidden. But I found their French too difficult to follow, and not wishing to try conclusions single-handed with an unlocated machine-gun in the half light, I pretended that I could not follow their instructions at all and carried on.

At the Maquis Bernard, I found great excitement. The three prisoners had just been led into the camp and the Maquisards, most of whom admittedly had taken no part in the battle, were celebrating their victory.

I went into one of the barrack huts, where the Grey Russian officer was being interrogated, and I remember very clearly, as I entered, that one of the Maquisards drew off the wounded man's boot and inverted it, so that the blood poured out into a pool which spread slowly across the rough mud floor. Somehow it all seemed natural enough and at the time sickened me not at all.

I could learn little from the peculiar trilingual interrogation that was going on, but having told the Russian that I was a British officer and that he would not be killed so long as he made no attempt to escape, I went on up to our camp and informed Alex that an officer had been taken.

Alex went down to get any details that he could, and after supper I went to bed in the makeshift shelter that Dickie Grayson had prepared for Alex, himself and me.

As a result of Alex's questionings, and of information that came in later from the villagers, we were able in time to piece together more details of the fight. The two French F-Ms had, by bad luck, only fired one magazine each. The first young Maquisard had been unable to clear his stoppage and the other, misunderstanding his orders, had retired into the woods after firing only some thirty rounds. Nevertheless, for the loss of one man killed, we had killed thirty-two enemy soldiers, captured three of them, and released four French hostages, as well as gaining for our own use fifteen German rifles, with ammunition and grenades – this in spite of the fact that it was the first time that most of the French had been in action, and that we were outnumbered about three to one.

I have always been astounded at the large number of Germans killed. It is my belief, though completely unsubstantiated, that the Maquisards were merely waiting for darkness to fall, and for the presumably soft-hearted British to disappear from the scene, before they quietly but effectively butchered the wounded.

The presence of the British and the strength of the Maquis had, it appeared, been a complete surprise to the Germans, and the story of how they came to fall into our trap was ironic.

It seems that the German general commanding at Nevers had sent his son, who was a staff captain, down to Château-Chinon, to teach the new garrison of Grey Russians how to lay ambushes. He had started off by giving them a long lecture, and had then taken them out for a practical demonstration at Mont-sauche. His own demonstration was not conspicuously successful, but the one so skilfully arranged for him by our little party was perhaps altogether too efficient for him to appreciate in its entirety. He was killed by the first long burst from Nobby's Bren.

CHAPTER VIII

After the Ambush

The morning of Sunday, the 25th, was crisp and clear. During the evening there had been two new British arrivals in the area of the Bois de Montsauche. The first had been Trooper Thornton, the last man of the Squadron still missing. He had been sheltering in the farm of La Verrerie during the fighting, and afterwards had been retrieved by the Maquisards. He had dropped deep in the woods and had been assisted by the local peasants until he had found his way across country to the Montsauche area. Maquis patrols had been out searching for him, and it was surprising that he had not been brought in sooner, but now that the whole Squadron was complete, we felt much happier.

The other arrival was Trooper Burgess, with his broken leg roughly set, who had been brought across from the Maquis hospital at the Château de Vermot by Dr Martell so that he could be smuggled into the nearby town of Saulieu in French civilian clothes and be X-rayed. He was kept down in the village of Savelot during the night, and had been fêted and kissed by all the local girls, come to see their first Englishman.

After breakfast Alex, who was expecting trouble, sent Sylvester and myself off to reconnoitre the tracks out of our camp to the south, to ascertain the dangers of being attacked and surprised from that direction, and to seek a possible line of withdrawal if assailed from the direction of last night's ambush, or through the villages of Savelot and Coeuson.

We walked for miles along the narrow, winding trails, using my compass and measuring every step we took so that we should not get lost on our way back. We found evidence of woodcutters at work, and finally emerged from the woods some three miles south of the camp.

We could see a distant road, and a few houses straggling along beside it. Sylvester climbed a tree with my field-glasses while I took compass bearings and tried to determine what course we had taken through the trees. Eventually we decided that this was the village of Poirot and, having got our bearings, we cut away to the east and again traversed the wood. This time we did not have so far to go and emerged into open fields where huge Nivernais oxen were grazing, very white and peaceful. As we skirted their pasture we came upon a road, which appeared to be from Montsauche to Planchez and likely to be pretty unhealthy after yesterday's party.

Thence we struck north once more, eventually joined up with our outward tracks and returned to our camp about lunchtime.

Meanwhile all was far from quiet in the Montsauche area. The Germans appeared to be reacting vigorously. A column of them from Château-Chinon had swooped down on the town once more, passing through Ouroux on the way, and amusing themselves by shooting down a harmless civilian in the streets and tossing hand-grenades into a crowded café. Exactly how many were killed I never learned, but a year later we were shown bloodstained tablecloths and heard most of the tale in all its gory details.

The precise strength of the enemy was hard to estimate from Maquis reports, but we were told confidently that the party was some 200 strong and supported by a tank.

It was during our belated lunch that bursts of fire from the direction of La Verrerie made us fear that a large-scale enemy attack was impending, and soon afterwards a runner from the Maquis came panting up into our camp with a request for assistance from Colonel Dubois.

Apparently the Germans had been investigating the scene of the ambush and were preparing to burn down the farm of La Verrerie as a reprisal, when they had been interrupted by a Maquis patrol, which with more courage than good sense had opened fire on them.

Some half dozen of the enemy had been killed and wounded by this unexpected attack, launched from the shelter of the woods, and one elderly French Bren-gunner had wiped out his mistakes of yesterday by a well-placed burst into their midst. The Germans had withdrawn without completing the destruction of the farm, but not before several more had been hit. However, reinforcements were brought up and it was feared that they would attempt to seize the high ground in the north-east of the wood, and thence sweep down into the Maquis, assisted by their tank. We were asked to hold this high ground, and two Bren-groups, one under Dickie Grayson, and the other under my command, were sent over to carry out this task.

I had Nobby Noble with me, and found him awkward to handle. He had the greatest confidence in Alex, but he did not know me. He had spent nearly as many years' campaigning as I had soldiering, and he felt, perhaps rightly, that he knew all there was to know. Certainly when we received our orders from the French colonel, his requests for more precise information and his decision as to the spot where he proposed to place himself and his Bren were very sound. Without being insubordinate, however, he completely ignored me, which put me in an awkward position as I was not prepared to start a full-blown verbal battle with him in front of the French, and anyway time was short. But to avoid further friction I did manage tactfully to slip him under Dickie's command, which solved my problem for the time being.

We now took up our positions in the woods covering the only possible tracks and open stretches up which the enemy could advance to the attack on the Maquis. The Maquisards themselves were in position around us, and I was pleasantly surprised to see how cool and quiet they were, as many of them were very young, and this was the first time that most of them had actually faced the enemy.

All afternoon the noises of combat rose and swayed along the edges of the wood, the chatter of automatic weapons being interspersed with the sharp crack of the Germans' self-propelled gun (not, after all, a tank) and the bursting of rifle-grenades. At one time I had the gravest fears for Dickie's safety, for he went forward with Bernard to reconnoitre La Verrerie, and I heard considerable firing from that direction. Eventually, however, he returned all right, having lost Bernard, although they had not encountered any enemy.

As evening drew in, reports began to arrive to the effect that the enemy were passing down the road to the south, and I asked the colonel's permission to withdraw my Bren. As the noises were growing fainter southward, he let me go.

That evening I was on guard. We took no special precautions, trusting to the thickness of the woods and our distance from the main tracks to save us from being discovered by the enemy during the hours of darkness. All the same, I think that everyone's slumbers were somewhat uneasy, as there was always the possibility of German fugitives in the woods inadvertently stumbling over our sleeping bodies and attacking us out of sheer terror. Fortunately we were undisturbed, though heavy rain did not add to the pleasures of a lonely night.

The next morning we heard the truth about the day's fighting. Bernard had returned safely, bringing with him a tale of horror that enlightened us as to the barbarity of our opponents.

Baulked in their attack on La Verrerie, the Germans had not, as expected, launched their full strength against the Maquis, but had turned on the town of Montsauche itself. The inhabitants had been ordered to clear out within two hours. Two men who resisted had been shot, and as soon as the houses were empty they had been burned to the ground. Even the church had not been spared. Apart from the gendarmerie and the post office, the whole town had been razed; not a dwelling house remained habitable. It had been the burning and battering of Montsauche that had simulated many of our battle sounds, for the Germans had not dared to enter the woods in force and had merely left a few soldiers to keep us contained.

The battle, however, had not ended with the destruction of the town. On their way back to Château-Chinon, the Maquis Serge, at the southern extremity of the wood, had in their turn sprung an ambush on the retiring Boche and had inflicted seventeen casualties without themselves losing a man.

Again the Shleuh had retaliated against the civilian population. The town of Planchez had shared the fate of Montsauche, although as darkness was falling the job was not so thorough and a number of houses escaped. Taken by and large, it had been a mildly victorious day for the Maquis. They had inflicted far more casualties than they had suffered, but morally the Germans gained much by their savagery. For although they raised hatred against themselves to fever pitch, at the same time the knowledge of these brutal reprisals against the civilians did much to discourage future Maquis activities. Also, the danger of an attack on their camp had come as a rude shock to many who had believed their position inviolable, and the resultant evacuation of the camp by the non-combatants had bordered on the panic-stricken. Even in our camp, we decided to pack our most vital necessities into escape haversacks as a precaution against a determined enemy attack. This feeling of insecurity remained with us for a long time.

During the height of the fighting along the eastern side of the wood, Bill Fraser had slipped in from the west. He brought news that enemy concentrations seemed to be building up all around the Maquis Jean and heard from us all the details of the fighting. The Russian officer had talked freely and it was hoped that it might be possible to induce the Russians in Château-Chinon to surrender, a task that was entrusted to Zellic, for which he was granted a temporary acting unpaid captaincy and transferred to Bill's headquarters.

Bill also arranged that I be permanently transferred to Alex's troop, for which in some ways I was very grateful, but which left me still with the problem of leading very touchy troops who did not know me. However, I did much to ease my mind by having a long talk with Nobby, telling him exactly what I thought of his attitude and explaining my own point of view. From then on I never had any bother with Noble and found in him a most loyal friend.

Bill left us again within the hour and the next day we began to hear rumours of a big attack on his camp and the Maquis Jean. In the lull following the storm of Montsauche and Planchez, I went on another reconnaissance with Sylvester into the southern part of the wood; this time we were joined by Alex, who wanted to find a good site to lie up if a large-scale attack did take place. He found such a spot close to the road, whence we could sneak across under cover of night if the necessity ever arose to abandon the Bois de Montsauche.

After lunch we took the whole troop down through the woods to see the RV where we were to hide if the worst happened and we returned to camp about teatime.

Next morning, we received news of the most unpleasant kind. Doc Martell, who had decided that things were now a bit too hot to risk smuggling Burgess into Saulieu, tried to take him back to the Château de Vermot under cover of night. He had got as far as the high ground around the Dun-les-Places–Brassy road, when he had been startled to see a great conflagration flickering and dancing among the trees in the direction of the castle. Being alone in the car with his patient and his chauffeur-nurse, he had decided that to carry on would be suicidal and had driven back. The idea of the Maquis hospital in flames was not pleasant for any of us to contemplate, and sounded even worse on top of the rumours that had been floating about the Maquis.

During the morning, I went on another exploratory trip through the wood to the south-east, in an attempt to find the Maquis Serge, supposed to be covering this side of the wood, but which we knew only by repute, without any contact.

As companion, I had a tall, swarthy Lancashire lad, 'Swag' Jemson. He had been with the Parachute Regiment in Italy and had joined the SAS about the same time that I did, in company with his pal Charlie Worn. Swag was a most cheerful and pleasant character and this was the first of many expeditions that we made together.

The reconnaissance, however, did not achieve its objective. We found a small three-field clearing in the middle of the wood and saw smoke rising through the trees on the far side of the clearing; but we were unable to get round to the fire and returned to our camp for lunch. It may have been fortunate that we did not find the Maquis Serge, for at that time the presence of Britishers in the Morvan was still a bit of a myth and the Maquisards were notoriously quick on the trigger.

Serge, a small, somewhat chubby man, later became a good friend of mine. Everywhere he went he was accompanied by his tough, battle-scarred body-guards, and the fact that his Maquis was Communist in sentiment made it much distrusted by the other Maquis in the area. In civilian life he was the leader of a dance band and his more evil-looking henchmen turned out to be first-rate saxophonists. He was reputed to have successfully hijacked all the arms from Bernard's first *parachutage*. I don't know whether this was true or not, but he certainly succeeded in making effective use of the arms that he did get. The next year, after the liberation, I was to be Serge's guest in Autun and at the *amicale* of his Maquis at the Lac des Settons.

When we returned to the Maquis Anglais, we heard still more rumours of the position to the north. They grew more and more alarming as the afternoon wore on and at one time it was estimated that 1500 Germans supported by tanks and artillery were engaged in an out-and-out assault of the Maquis Jean. The British were said to have been fighting like devils and to have inflicted 300 casualties. But what in fact concerned us much more than all these alarmist rumours was the practical question of what was happening to the wireless sets. For although every officer and almost every sergeant had his own listening set for tuning into the BBC to hear our coded messages and our SAS news, there were only two transmitting sets with which we could demand supplies or send back vital messages. Both were in Bill's camp. Colonel Hastings and Lemnis-cate also had sending sets, but these, too, were at the Maquis Jean. We were haunted with visions of the Maquis being dispersed and ourselves cut off from all possible communication with our resupply service from England. So when, in the evening, the Maquis Bernard announced that it was going to try to send a party through German lines to find out what had happened to the Maquis Jean, I was sent with them by Alex to find out what was really happening to Bill Fraser and his boys.

CHAPTER IX

Dun-les-Places

The party which set out in Martell's car at about 7.00 that evening consisted of Martell himself, Meurice and Petit Jacques (two of Georges' Parisians) and myself. The car, which was neither large nor powerful, was run on a species of wood alcohol, giving it an abominable smell and detracting much from what little strength and reliability still remained in its aged engine.

The original plan was that the car should merely take us down the old oxen trail out of the wood and down the valley of the Chalaux as far as the Montsauche–Clamecy road, after which we felt that it would be more prudent to proceed on foot. For this reason we travelled very light and had only my carbine, one Sten-gun and a number of grenades between us.

The sun was shining for once and the shadows of the trees dappled the little Renault saloon and threw pretty patterns on the rough track, as some of the men of the Maquis put their shoulders to the frame and began to manhandle our *camion* along the path till the motor broke into fitful life.

We all piled in and I sat in the back, on the side nearest the verge, feeling that a hasty exit was always liable to be an important item on the itinerary. We jerked and jolted through the woods and eventually emerged in the little village of Savelot. Thence we headed down the valley until we reached the main road. No Germans had been heard of in the area that day and so, with typically French preference of taking risks to taking exercise, the party decided to continue at least a little of the way by car, intending to hide it in some field when we got close to the danger area and proceed from there by foot.

As we dipped down off the Clamecy road and swung once more on to the third-class roads which the Maquis could call their own, the sun was setting redly on our left and the church on the hill overlooking Savault was silhouetted against the ruddy glow of the sky.

In Savault village, we stopped and Martell asked again if there were any Boche about. The villagers told us that they had seen none all day and that the next village had been clear all afternoon, so once more we pushed on.

Our next stop was at the village of Bonin, where the road bifurcated towards Dun-les-Places to the east and Brassy to the west. Here the villagers warned us that the enemy had been up to some devilry in Dun and that they were probably still in the area, but accurate details were lacking and they assured us that none had penetrated as deep as Bonin itself. Except that it had moved, the Maquisards had no idea where Jean's camp was. Our own camp was on the

77

other side of Dun-les-Places and we felt that the locality was hardly likely to be healthy. However, having come so far by car, the French considered it would now be a pity to walk, so I volunteered to guide them to our camp, skirting Dun-les-Places and not passing straight through it.

Accordingly, we turned off on the road towards Brassy and then, bearing right-handed at every occasion, we struck the main Dun-les-Places–Brassy road opposite the village of Vermot, though hidden from it by a slight rise. Now we turned completely east and raced along the road towards Dun as fast as our car would let us.

I liked to sit in the back, carbine between my knees and with one hand on the door handle, so that in the event of being ambushed I could throw the door straight open and dive into the ditch. The French, however, preferred to have every available weapon poking out of the windows so that they could reply at once to any hostile fire. To save argument, therefore, I followed the French example and hoped for the best.

As we approached Dun, we noticed that the streets were deserted. Even the ubiquitous chickens seemed to have fled the town. On the outskirts, we stopped and asked at a house for information of German movements, but were met by weeping and almost hysterical women who could only tell us that many of the townsfolk had been shot, that much of the town was in flames and that the *curé* had been hung from his own belfry and cut down into the courtyard which fronted his church. Women had been molested and the whole town was still in the hands of the enemy.

It was too late to turn back now and with our guns held firmly in our fists we carried on.

Before one gets to Dun-les-Places proper, there is a narrow rocky lane which cuts across from the Brassy road to the Vieux Dun road. I had discovered this side track, which bypassed the whole centre of the town on the day that I had taken Chalky White to the Maquis hospital, and now it stood me in good stead. On entering the town, we found that smoke hung low over the roads and the smell of burning was heavy on the nostrils. As we bucked down the back track, we could see the wanton destruction all around us and it was with thankful hearts that we climbed back on to the Vieux Dun road and began to make for Bill's camp with all possible speed.

Our luck held good and without incident we bumped into the rough roads that dropped down behind Vieux Dun to the valley in which the major had his camp. We went as far as we dared along the tricky boulder-strewn path and then, leaving the Maquisards in the car, I went on alone to find the camp.

I crossed the little river at the bottom of the valley and walked along the grassy path towards the camp whistling 'Sur le Pont d'Avignon', so that they would know I was SAS. The first shock that I received was when no sentry challenged me as I approached the camp. The stillness of the place was eerie. The black waters of the lake gave not a ripple, the leaves and the grasses not a sigh. It was that last moment of the day as the afterglow fades imperceptibly into night and all the last long shadows seem alive, yet all is quiet. The silence was utter and intense. My harsh whistling jarred the air and only silence answered it.

I mounted the steep grassy bank that masked the camp and a scene of desolation, accentuated by the deepening shadows, stopped me in my tracks. Everything was in disorder. Rucksacks were lying abandoned in the long grass. The ashes of the dead fire lay heaped around the cooking utensils. Empty container cells were scattered in every direction and some cells, still neatly stacked, could be seen half camouflaged in the undergrowth beyond the cookhouse sites. I called out softly, more in hope than in expectation, but the silence mocked me. I shouted again, but nothing answered save a breath of wind stirring the silent trees. I moved gingerly into the camp area, but stopped dead, as I saw a box of chocolate lying open and inviting in a clearing. This, I thought to myself, is too good to be true. This, I told myself, is a booby-trap. I knew that Alex's intention had been to booby-trap everything in the camp if he found it necessary to leave it and I guessed that Bill would have done the same thing. It was now almost completely dark and the fact that the camp had been deserted was only too evident. I could gain nothing by staying any longer in the vicinity and any attempt to salvage anything the others had left behind was likely to end with me springing a trap left for the Boche. So, with a confused and heavy heart, I returned to my companions.

Back at the car, we held a council of war. It was very difficult to say where the Maquis Jean would be found, but one thing was certain: if things had got so bad that the British had had to clear out, it was evident that Jean's Maquis would not be in its old location.

One of the Maquisards, however, had an idea of a possible hiding place to which Jean might have fled, and this meant a return via Dun-les-Places. There seemed to be no alternative, so we had to take the risk.

We pushed the car up out of the valley and, before embarking on this perilous adventure, decided to try to obtain more first-hand information. With this in view, we knocked on one of the doors in the village of Vieux Dun. Panic. Terror. Abject fear. I have never, either before or since, seen anyone so utterly frightened as the good lady of Vieux Dun. At first she could not speak. As soon as she realised that we were of the Maquis and not Shleuh, she gained her tongue, but only to beg and implore us to go away. She said that there had been Germans in the village all day. That they were still there. That if she spoke to us she would be shot. Oh, would we, please, please, go away.

This hardly seemed helpful, particularly as this was the second time that we had passed through Vieux Dun and it was evident that if there were any Boche here they were lying remarkably low. Well warned, however, that there were Germans about, we proceeded with rather more caution.

As we approached Dun-les-Places for the second time, we halted the car at the junction where a few hours earlier we had joined the Vieux Dun road, and here dismounted. The doc remained in the car to drive while the rest of us, keeping well in the shadow of the walls, moved silently up the street towards the centre of town, grenades held ready and revolvers cocked.

It was a fantastic advance. The smoke cloaked our movements, the crackle of the embers and the occasional crash of a falling beam served to cover the noise that we made, while the dull glow from the fires that still burned in the gutted houses helped to light us on our way.

Step by step we approached the turning where we hoped to be able to skirt the town once more. Fifty yards behind us the car crept in our wake. At last, unchallenged and unseen, we reached the corner, and turning down it to the left, we whistled up the car and leapt aboard, retreating rapidly from the fatal church. But in a matter of moments we realised we had merely turned up a cul-de-sac.

We stopped at a house. One of the Maquisards banged upon the door and another terrified old women came to answer it. The news she gave us was grave in the extreme. We had indeed run into a dead end; the road we wanted, leading out over the River Cure towards Saulieu, was on the other side of the church. We had been wrong, however, to assume that because we had succeeded in reaching the centre of the town unchallenged that there were no Germans in it. It was full of the Boche.

Meurice gave a low whistle and muttered 'Oooh la-la!' In my view this hardly began to express the situation.

We turned the car around once more and, sticking our weapons out of our windows, trusted to luck, roaring at top speed down the main street, across the front of the churchyard and swinging sharply down the road towards the Cure bridge.

Not a shot was fired, not an alarm was raised. We tore down the gentle slope leading out of the martyred town and hardly checked our speed until we had bounded over the bridge and turned northward once more into the maze of forest tracks where we were unlikely to encounter the enemy. It was a narrow escape, for it was only later that we learned that the bodies of the murdered townsfolk had still been piled in the courtyard of the church and that the Germans had mounted sentries over the dead throughout the night.

From now on, I am very hazy as to what happened. I had no map, nor any clear idea of where we were trying to go. The tracks that we followed were narrow and hedged in by tall trees. It was a night as dark as pitch and although the stars twinkled far above us, their light barely penetrated the thick foliage of the pines. I believe we ran far to the north, bypassing Quarré-les-Tombes and going through Marigny-l'Eglise. I recollect we asked many times for pointers as to the position of the Maquis and that more than once we had to turn back upon our track. But above all I remember that, with freezing hands, I held the carbine out of the window and began to pray as I had seldom prayed before.

Luck was with us, for shortly after midnight, on a forest track, we picked up the tail-light of a car bumping away ahead of us. We followed it doggedly, always in danger of being taken for Germans by the Maquis, or discovering that the car we believed to be Maquis would turn out to be German. At last, the car halted on a narrow wooden bridge over the Cure and, heavily covered by Maquis Brens, we drew up behind it. It turned out to be Grand Jean himself, returning to his new Maquis, which in the morning we found to be situated on the west bank of the Cure in the woods around Les Isles Menéfrier. I must admit that I was mighty glad to see him.

From him we learned a little about the great fight at Vermot, and he led us into the forest where the mobile tents of his Maquisards had been pitched and where already they were operating their wirelesses. Denby, Gapeau and Centime were still with the Maquis, but they could give me very little information of the exact whereabouts of Bill or the details of the part that he and his boys had played in the battle. They lent me a single blanket and I curled up with it under the trees, sleeping exhausted until dawn.

The next morning found me up and about early and after breakfast Gapeau and I set off on foot to try to locate Bill's new camp, which we believed to be somewhere to the west.

It was a hot day and we were soon sweating profusely as we toiled across country, trying to keep direction through thick woods, skirting deep and reeking bogs and trying to avoid anything that faintly resembled a main road. About midday, we halted in a meadow on the outskirts of the little village of Mazignien and ate the bread and cheese that we had brought with us for lunch. Afterwards, we entered a lonely farmhouse on the edge of the village, where the lady of the house gave us a little wine to drink and some of the good strong ham of the Morvan.

After lunch, we struck south, crossing several main roads and searching everywhere for signs of the British. Here and there we did come across the distinctive sole-marks of the rubber-shod SAS boots, but all efforts to follow these traces proved in vain, as they always petered out when the tracks reached hard ground and we were unable to pick them up again. We followed diligently all signs of smoking fires and came across many charcoal burners at work, but still without finding any of the men of the Squadron.

We climbed to the summit of a hill which commanded much of the valley of the Chalaux and with field glasses swept the whole countryside from the top of a prominent rock, but still without success. All day it stayed hot and we were tortured with thirst. Some of the charcoal burners sent their boy away to fetch us water, and on another occasion I dipped my beret into a little mountain spring to get us a drink. Nowhere did we see a camp.

At last we returned towards Mazignien, and in a narrow valley just below the village we found evidence of many British boot-marks going in all directions in the soft ground. However, not far from the stream, the terrain gave way to great boulders and tangled undergrowth where the tracks were impossible to follow. Here we shouted and sang and whistled, using all the pass tunes that we could think of, and hoping against hope that a voice would reply, but no answer ever came.

Finally we gave up and ascended the hill to Mazignien, only to be caught in a shower of torrential rain as we reached the top. Soaked to the skin, we entered the nearest house for shelter, hoping for a little wine, for we were parched with thirst and pretty hungry. However, the old man of the farm did not welcome us, taking us, I think, for Germans in disguise. He would give us nothing but plain water but let us shelter until the worst of the rain had subsided.

Eventually we moved on once more and were lucky to encounter some Maquis boys in the village who brought us to a farm where we were given cakes and a little Marc. This fierce brew of the Nivernais and Burgundy, distilled from the pressings of the grapes, has the taste, colour and characteristics of low-grade petrol.

After saying goodbye to our latest hosts, we continued on our way towards the camp, where we arrived just as supper was being served, and I was ready for it.

I was disappointed to find that the others had left without me in order for Doc Martell to look at the patients in the new Maquis hospital, now a deserted house in the depths of the wood. However, they had promised to come back for me, and I paced moodily up and down by the bridge waiting for the car to return. They had expected to be back by 7 o'clock but by 9.00 I was alternately a prey to the gravest fears for their safety and furious that they should keep me hanging about so long.

At last they turned up and as darkness began to fall we set off on our journey back to the Bois de Montsauche, where we arrived without incident at about 11 o'clock.

Taken by and large, my expedition had been most unsatisfactory for I had entirely failed to locate Bill. The Maquisards, however, had at least found the Maquis Jean and before I left I had been able to arrange provisionally through Denby that supplies and arms for them would be parachuted to us at Montsauche.

I was very pleased with one bit of news, namely, that Camille, whom I had last heard of as missing after the German ambush of the Maquis on 14 June, had turned up all right, though wounded and suffering severely from his exertions.

That night I spent with the Maquis in one of their barrack huts, wrapped up in a parachute. But I did not sleep very well and was up early. After a quick omelette, I made my way back to Alex's camp and gave him all the news that I could.

While I had been away, Alex had taken the opportunity to dig many trenches, carefully noted on a plan that he and Dickie kept, in which he buried every bit of food and ammunition that was not in immediate use. In the event of an unexpected attack, the trenches could be covered over and we would at least stand some chance of being able to recover our stocks later.

On the afternoon of the day on which I returned, Colonel Isaac, or Colonel Hastings, as we knew him, arrived at the Maquis Bernard. He had left the Maquis Jean on the 27th, immediately after the battle, and with his small staff he had crossed to the Bois de Montsauche, carrying his transmitting set and travelling all the way on foot and mostly by forest paths. We later learned that he had had one exciting brush with an enemy patrol in the woods and had been lucky to escape without casualties or loss of equipment.

We were very pleased to see his wireless and asked him to send a message for us demanding specific supplies of various things that we required most urgently. We had now found an excellent DZ on an open stretch of ground in the middle of the Bois de Montsauche and close to a little lake on the edge of the trees which made a good marker for the pilots. We referred to this as the Montsauche DZ and it had the great advantage of being within the defended area of the Maquis so that it was unnecessary to mount guards, lights could be flashed at random and there was no absolute need to clear it by daylight. However, it was to be some days before we were able to make use of it.

The day after I returned to the camp, Alex arranged for road watches to be mounted on all the important roads in the area and we had high hopes of learning something more of the strength and activities of the enemy. However, when evening came and all the watchers returned, we found that the sum total of traffic seen on all the roads in the area throughout the hours of daylight was one gendarme on a motorcycle. A distinct disappointment.

The next day we heard by wireless from London that the authorities took a good view of the suggested attempt of Sergeant Zellic to get the White Russians to desert and he was told to do what he could to get in touch with them.

In the late afternoon of that day, 1 July, Ooly Ball and Docherty came into camp. They were very weary and had had a most arduous journey over from Bill's new camp. It was now a week since there had been any direct contact between the two halves of the Squadron and we listened eagerly to everything that they could tell us about the battle of Vermot and all that transpired after it, though it was not until I returned to England that I was able to piece together the whole story in detail.

CHAPTER X

The Battle of Vermot

Squadron HQ and the other two troops had in the meantime been involved in no mean measure of excitement.

On the morning of the 24th, the day after Roy Bradford's troop had arrived at the camp behind Vieux Dun, and the day that we mounted our successful ambush on the Montsauche road, the Maquis Jean had a minor panic. All roads leading into the Maquis were heavily defended with Bren-guns, both the British and French camps holding themselves in a state of readiness.

The next day the 'flap' continued, and it was in no way reduced when Major Fraser returned from his visit to us with the news of our two-days battle, nor as the rumours of the burnings of Montsauche and Planchez gradually began to filter back to the Maquis.

The night, however, was quiet, and nothing untoward occurred during the morning of 26 June, although at about lunchtime the Maquis reported strong rumours that an enemy force was passing through Dun-les-Places and requested that the British cover the Vieux Dun road. Accordingly, Roy Bradford and his troop were sent out to hold the village of Vieux Dun, and the rest of the Squadron remained quietly in their camp.

The next incident to involve the British occurred several miles away on the other side of the Bois de la Chevrière, where at 6.00 in the evening, Chalky White was lying comfortably in his bed in the Château de Vermot. The first thing that Chalky knew about the impending hostilities was when a burst of Spandau fire entering by the window embedded itself in the wall just above his head and showered him with plaster. The German attack on the Maquis had begun in earnest.

With great gallantry, the Maquis staff of the hospital, aided by all the walking wounded, managed to evacuate the stretcher cases into the woods immediately behind the château, and at the same time the men of the Maquis opened a heavy fire from the woods on to the advancing Germans, one lad particularly distinguishing himself by knocking out the leading enemy lorry with his Piat.

The battle around the château was short-lived. As soon as the Maquis positions were pinpointed, the Germans opened fire with mortars and rifle grenades, which burst among the trees along the edge of the forest and forced the Maquisards, who had never before had to face an attack of this nature, to take cover in the woods. The Germans themselves were unwilling to engage in close fighting in unfamiliar country and did not enter the forest, so that for the moment the battle became a stalemate, leaving the château uncovered for the Germans to enter at their leisure.

The château was an obvious hospital. The clean white beds in their neat rows, the surgery with instruments fitted out in racks and cupboards, the reek of ether, the rows of bottles, all proved beyond a doubt, even to the most casual observer, that this was no Maquis HQ but a well-appointed hospital. This, however, did not in any way influence the enemy. With cool deliberation, they smashed every bottle. With complete and painstaking thoroughness, they broke every instrument. Having made completely sure that nothing of value could possible escape, they gave the lovely old château over to the flames.

Meanwhile, the Maquis had requested that the British strike from the camp at Vieux Dun, around the shoulder of the hill on which the Maquis stood, and across the rear of the German line of advance, while the Maquisards endeavoured to hold the enemy with frontal fire. To do this, Major Fraser had sent off Captain Johnny Wiseman with Reg Seekings and One Troop to move across in a short left hook against the German flank while Bill himself, with the rest of his HQ, took a much wider swing.

It was a soaking wet day, and movement through the undergrowth was a slow and miserable process, so that it was getting on for 9 o'clock when Johnny's party suddenly found themselves within fifteen yards of the Vermot road and face to face with an enemy patrol.

'Look! Germans!' exclaimed Reg, stating the obvious, and falling forward with a bullet through the neck. The rest of the party, warned by the sergeant-major's fate, sank quietly into the bushes. A brief and indecisive action ensued in which Lance-Corporal 'Pringle' Gibb greatly distinguished himself by his quick and accurate work with the Bren. The SSM, swearing profusely, was successfully extricated, and sent back to camp. Johnny withdrew to a low hill from which he could cover the road and there he remained in the fading light, soaked to the skin, until darkness had fallen, when he too returned to camp.

Bill's party, however, was much more successful. After an even longer and possibly wetter march than the Wiseman party, he arrived on a small feature overlooking the village of Vermot, and saw quite clearly a little group of Germans sitting at the roadside. Something made the major think that these fellows must be waiting for something, and so, positioning his Brens as carefully as he could, he waited and watched.

After a few minutes a number of other soldiers joined the originals and then in ones and twos, little by little, an entire enemy platoon, complete with a heavy mortar and a number of automatic weapons, was assembled in the street below. At last an officer appeared and gave the order to fall in. It was the last order that many of the men ever had the chance to obey, for on a signal from the major, the combined murderous fire of four well-handled Bren-guns was poured down upon them. In an instant, all was disorder. Cries of the wounded and hoarse orders mingled with the wild racket of the Brens, and in the narrow streets there was little chance to get any cover, or put up an adequate reply, against the unseen marksmen.

For several minutes the slaughter continued, and then as quickly as it had started, the fire slackened, and Bill, well satisfied with his evening's work, led his party back to the camp. It is hard to believe that more than a handful of the enemy could have escaped uninjured from the shambles in the streets of Vermot.

That night was spent quietly in the British camp. Bren positions were sited, guards doubled and preparations made for a hurried departure if the need arose, but nothing happened to cause undue alarm, though sleep was quite impossible, owing to the continuous fusillade that was kept up by the Maquis, and a few odd German patrols all along the Vermot front throughout the night. Next morning showed many bullet-scarred trees on both sides, but a depressing absence of bodies.

With the rising sun came a more determined enemy attack, and the Maquis, with a small number of casualties, were pressed back deeper and deeper into the woods. The Germans followed them up gingerly.

Colonel Hastings (Isaac) who was still with the Maquis at this time, once more asked for British assistance against the enemy's rear, but when Bill sent a runner up to the Maquis camp to get a more accurate picture of what was going on, the man returned with the unwelcome news that the whole Maquis had cleared out, bag, baggage, tents and all, and that the enemy appeared to be engaged in destroying those cars that the Maquisards had been unable to remove.

With this sudden defection of the Maquis, Bill decided that the safest course was to withdraw his camp into a safer neighbourhood; accordingly, he abandoned all the kit that could not be carried, and set out on a long and tiresome trek to the north-west. As darkness was falling, they ended up in the area of Mazignien where they established their new camp. All day it had poured with rain, making the jungle paths wet and slippery underfoot, and the dripping trees a shroud of misery through which they had had to struggle. It had been a most unhappy day.

Meanwhile, the Germans, who were only about 250 strong and largely composed of Grey Russians, having destroyed the garage, pushed out their patrols to the old Maquis camp and even penetrated as far down the hill as the outskirts of our deserted camp, though never actually finding it. Their movements were watched by a number of small patrols that Bill had left behind, one of which had a short and noisy encounter with the enemy in the neighbourhood of the still smouldering château, but no casualties were suffered by either side.

Once more, baulked of their revenge on the Maquisards, the enemy wreaked their fury on the civilian population. In the village of Vermot every house was burned to the ground, six men were shot or brutally beaten, a fourteen-year-old girl was raped, and other women suffered further indignities.

On returning to Dun-les-Places in the afternoon, the enemy claimed to have been fired on by civilians from the church tower. This was demonstrably untrue, as every civilian who was armed was with the Maquis, and there were no Maquisards in Dun that day. Nevertheless, on this pretext, the *curé* was taken up to his belfry and there pushed out with a rope around his neck so that he was hung in full view of the whole village. When he was dead, the rope was cut and his body fell sickeningly on to the very porch of the church.

In Dun-les-Places there had been a French Gestapo agent. He knew that the patriots of Dun had been helping the Maquis and the English. With the aid of a list that he had compiled, the Germans were able to seize every able-bodied man in the village who sympathised with the Resistance and to crowd them into the church. Then, driving them out into the courtyard in front, the Germans shot them down where they stood. Even a year later, their blood and the bullet holes in the door of the church remained as a memorial of this evil deed. The bodies of the dead, which included all the most prominent men in the town, were then mutilated with hand-grenades, and a guard was mounted over the carcasses of the murdered men for two days to deny them decent burial. Today, no less than twenty-seven graves stand in the little cemetery of Dun, an ever-present reminder of this martyrdom.

Still unsatisfied with their butchery, the Boche then proceeded to burn the houses of those who had helped us. Thus on that very evening I twice passed through Dun-les-Places in flames and missed Bill Fraser by only a few hours.

The next day I was to miss him by an even narrower margin, for the soft ground by the stream where we stopped and shouted so loud and long was the watering place where they bathed and shaved. Their camp had been less than a hundred yards from where we were calling and it was a piece of inexplicable bad luck that they never heard us.

The next day, 29 June, Bill learned from London that there would be a *parachutage* of jeeps in another night or two; so he sent Ooly and Docherty to find us, give us this news and reveal the location of the new camp.

While Ball was making his arduous two-day journey, Bill and his boys were beginning to suffer severely from lack of food. The sudden move and prolonged bad weather had made resupply impossible for more than a week, and being out of touch with the Maquis made it difficult to obtain supplies locally. However, on 5/6 July, there came the most momentous *parachutage* since the Squadron arrived.

That night three Halifaxes came over and dropped Tony Trower a couple of fitters and three jeeps on a makeshift DZ near Mazignien. One of the jeeps fell into a forest of small trees and forty of them had to be cut down before the jeep could be extricated, but all arrived undamaged.

The next morning, Johnny Wiseman, with Tony Trower, Sergeant Jack
Terry, two corporals and a trooper set off in one of the jeeps to begin operating
in the Dijon area. That afternoon the two remaining jeeps, with Bill Fraser and
the Padre, ran over to call on Alex's troop and took Ball back to the HQ camp.
Neither party encountered any enemy on their routes. The crisis was over.

In the three days of battle in the heart of the Nièvre, we had successfully
repulsed the enemy. His attempt to destroy the Maquis before they were too
strong had failed and it was not until forced into the area by their panic retreat
in September that the Germans came again in force into the Morvan strong-
hold. At the time, of course, we did not realise the magnitude of our success.
Indeed, we continued to live in constant dread of large-scale reprisals by the
enemy in a grand effort to regain control of the area, but it never developed. We
had inflicted upward of 150 casualties – a very high percentage, considering the
number of troops engaged – and we had won for ourselves a breathing space
during which it was possible to recruit, arm and train many more Maquisards.
Thus they presented a force of real strength when their next trial came.

I have always considered that this was our greatest single success throughout
the time that the Squadron was in France, for had the enemy succeeded in
breaking up the Morvan Maquis and our own ill-equipped forces, the whole
history of the SAS and Maquis in that part of France would have been ter-
minated.

SAS Brigade, however, took a different view. 'Well done', came the reply to
our message of victory, 'but refrain from engaging in Maquis battles, get on
with cutting the railways.'

As one-third of the railway lines that Brigade had given us as targets turned
out to have been taken up by the French government before the war, as most of
the others were no longer in use, as the Maquisards themselves were making a
much better job of cutting the remainder than we could ever hope to do, and as
the arrival of jeeps was opening up new vistas to us, it can well be guessed with
what feelings we received these orders. But at least we were now reasonably
settled in. Two troops had been deployed to their operational stations and
contact between all parts of the Squadron had been re-established. Our firm
bases were never again to be short of food or ammunition and indeed now we
were set to begin our operations against the enemy in earnest.

CHAPTER XI

Camp-life in the Woods

From the arrival of Ball at Alex's Two Troop camp on 1 July to the arrival of the jeeps a week later, very little happened. During that quiet week, and on occasional peaceful days when we were not engaged with *parachutages* and operations, life in the camp followed a set routine. The day began at about 6 o'clock, when the last man on guard would stoke up the remnants of the previous day's fire and fan it into life. As it was nearly always raining, this was not an easy operation, although last thing each night the glowing embers would be covered with a container lid as shelter from the wet. At first, we tried to keep dry sticks for starting up the fire but we soon discovered that a little plastic explosive will burn quite fiercely for several minutes; and as there was never any shortage of plastic, we normally employed this method.

An hour later, when the water was boiling and quite a lot of wood had been gathered, the guard would wake the cook and the real task of preparing the breakfast would begin.

'Mickey' Flynn, a cheerful Irishman, and a very long-standing member of the SAS, was our usual cook. He was helped by various different people, and the cookhouse fatigues, such as potato-peeling and wood and water collection, were done on a voluntary basis, the officers joining in with the men. At first we were handicapped by having no real cooking utensils, but cans for boiling water and brewing tea were improvised out of parachute containers and empty biscuit tins, and to the end of our stay in the woods we continued to cook over open fires with these makeshift pots and pans. Our fighting knives came in very useful for cutting and for opening tins, and clean or not-so-clean sticks were used for stirring. Our single genuine cooking implement was a jealously guarded ladle, which someone procured for us from Ouroux.

Somewhere between 8.00 and 9.00, depending on what the weather was like and how the fire was going, breakfast would be served. This usually consisted of a generous portion of tinned sausages and bacon, or fried bread and beans. About twice a week, when we were lucky, we enjoyed fresh eggs, which we swapped from the local farmers for chocolate and sweets, the normal rate of exchange being four eggs to a bar of chocolate. This was followed up with bread, bought from the Maquis, margarine and jam, the whole being washed down with a pint of tea made from a concoction of powdered milk, sugar and tealeaves which came in tins. After successful Maquis raids on German food convoys, we scrounged sugar from them, which was a welcome though rare supplement.

Breakfast was normally eaten in our 'pyjamas', that is to say our sleeping-kit, which varied according to individual taste from completely clothed to near naked. I used to sleep in a pair of gym shorts, with a flannel pyjama top, and keep my gym shoes close beside my bed. After breakfast, if the weather was more miserable than usual, and there was nothing else in view, a return to bed was the rule.

The normal work of the day consisted mainly in cleaning weapons, fetching water up from the spring at the foot of our hill and cutting wood for the fire. Once a day, a party of men with the cook would walk the mile or so to the Maquis and see what they could scrounge in the way of bread, fresh meat and vegetables, but there was not much else to do. After the jeeps had arrived and when we had a few requisitioned cars to work on, we busied ourselves with maintenance and used the vehicles for fetching food 'and water.

Tiffin, eaten around midday, consisted usually of something cold, with biscuits and margarine and cheese or jam. This too was finished off with tea, or when this was short, with ersatz coffee bought from the Maquis. We also got a ration of sweets and chocolate after this meal. It worked out at about a bar of chocolate and a dozen sweets every other day, non-smokers getting about 50 per cent more than smokers. The smokers got a steady ration of about eight cigarettes a day but this was a major hardship, because when there was nothing much to do the cigarette consumption tended to be much higher. In theory there should have been regular drops of NAAFI issue cigarettes and also of gift cigarettes from the Squadrons still in England, not to mention the duty-free cigarette packages sent by friends. But in fact these additional sources were not a great success. Two NAAFI packs 'candled' (i.e. came down with closed chutes). The packers in England seemed to imagine that there was a much closer liaison between the four troops of the Squadron than there actually was, and tended to send the whole cigarette issue to one troop for distribution. Cigarettes being in short supply, both in England and in France, great temptation was put in the way of packers at home and Maquis collecting parties, who helped on the DZ. I do not think that the boys themselves ever stole from one another because under such cramped conditions any such theft would soon have been discovered; but we often found cigarettes filched from containers.

In the late afternoon, there would be a cup of tea or cocoa and biscuits, to last us until dinner at about 7.00, which was our big meal of the day. This was basically a tinned repast straight out of the compo ration packs, but it was augmented with fresh food whenever possible and was most filling. After dinner we would usually sit round the fire and talk, as the embers died, and then turn in at about 10 o'clock.

Later, when we knew the countryside better, the men would go down to the villages in the evenings and drink in the *estaminets*, or take their girls for walks through the sweet-smelling meadows. But at first we had to keep very much to the woods in our spare time.

After the jeeps came, we managed to get the occasional barrel of wine up from the Maquis, but it was very raw stuff, and not popular with the men, though the French lapped it up. Rum, occasionally dropped to us in *parachutages*, was a rare treat, but we did have several rum parties about the evening fire.

During the night a guard was always mounted, but as we were so deep in the woods, and as the Maquis were all around us, this was more of an alarm clock than a serious fighting proposition. At first the guard mounted with a Bren-gun on the main track up into the camp, but later the Bren was discarded in favour of a two-man standing patrol. Finally, when André formed his Maquis and moved up beside us, we booby-trapped the camp, and mounted a joint Anglo-French standing guard on the main track, with one man from each camp. Officers and men did equal share of guard duty and I have many recollections of cold nights of misery beneath the dripping trees in company with some morose lad from the Maquis André. And I remember well the bitterness of one night, when I returned from a soaking vigil only to find that my tent had leaked and that all my bedding was soaked through. I spent a very chilly morning, wrapped up in a damp parachute on a wet floor.

We had a lot of fun setting the booby-traps. Worn and I did it together and we devised many ingenious little trips, which we connected to detonators, leaving slabs of plastic explosive close at hand. Normally, we connected up the wires every evening just before it got dark, but planned never to fasten the plastic round the detonator unless we were expecting an attack. Thus the detonator made a most efficient alarm signal without ever endangering the life of any innocent Maquisards lost in the wood.

Once, after the jeeps had arrived, I altered one of the traps without telling Worn, who was out with a jeep party that night, returning at about 10 o'clock, by which time it was quite dark. Instead of calling for the guard to clear the traps, Worn said, 'OK, I know where it is', and leapt out of the jeep, groping for the hidden switch. Before he reached it, however, he trod on my new wire. There was a sharp crack. Worn jumped a clear foot off the ground with the shock and the things he said about 'officers mucking around with bleeding booby-traps' had to be heard to be believed. Some weeks later, Sylvester walked on to one of his booby-traps when going the rounds and had his face cut by the blast of the detonator, but we never had any fatal accidents.

During our first week in the Bois de Montsauche, we received certain additions to our strength from the Maquis. The first man to throw in his lot with us was Georges Brûlé, known by the *nom-de-guerre* of Dubroy, who came to us with his sergeant, Roger Eté, shortly after our first ambush. He came with the full approval of the chiefs of the Maquis as interpreter officer to Alex's troop. Both proved themselves excellent fighters, as well as *agents de liaison*.

Georges, who I have already mentioned as a soldier, was a natural leader. Roger was a tall, handsome fellow with wavy brown hair, and a scar running down his left cheek. He had been a skating instructor in Paris before the war, and had captained the French ice-hockey team. He was very tough in his own inimitable way, and was always cheerful. But he was a lazy linguist, refusing to learn any English, although he clearly understood it when we spoke to him. He did, however, accumulate a large number of English slang expressions and swear-words, which he would suddenly produce at the most devastatingly appropriate moments.

Another Frenchman who attached himself to us, at first largely against our will and against the wishes of the Maquis, was Fernand Ravassat. He was a local lad, from the town of Ouroux, who had worked for *wagons-lit* and had been for some time in their English office. He spoke excellent English but had done no military training and did not seem to be much of a soldier. In the end, however, after he had come up to our camp many times, we let him stay, and he proved very useful with his local contacts in arranging laundry, and getting extra food. Later he proved a brave man and good battle-comrade, eventually going on into Belgium with C Squadron after we had been brought back to England.

The two Red Russians, and a Czech from the Maquis, also joined us. They were not happy with the Maquis, whom they despised as civilians lacking true military training. The Russians could speak nothing but their native tongue, but Zellic spoke enough Slav to be able to make himself understood. Nevertheless, the language difficulty always stood between us and a close understanding of them.

For a short time we had yet another addition to our numbers in the shape of a woman-doctor from Paris, who was a friend of Georges, and who had only escaped from the Gestapo after being tortured for several days. Having no MO at our camp, and finding Martell at the Maquis Bernard a bit far away, we welcomed her presence and she took time to look at my foot which still troubled me a little since I had twisted it on the night that I landed. But later, when the Maquis André moved up near us, she shifted over to their camp to be nearer her countryfolk.

Owing to the safeness of our location, Two Troop became the holding unit, as it were, for all our wounded, whom we had to look after, feed, clothe and make as comfortable as we could. This, too, put a strain on our organisation, for even at our strongest, and including all the people attached to us, we never numbered more than forty and often sank as low as ten or fifteen.

Our shelters became more elaborate as time passed. At first we laid our sleeping bags on the ground, draped or slung a ground-sheet so as to catch the worst of the wet and left it at that. Then we began making a framework of wood, covering it with branches and laying the waterproof on top of it. The parachutes that we were able to salvage from our earlier *parachutages* eased the situation and several layers of parachute silk proved as efficient as a ground-sheet. Some of us continued to use this type of shelter to the end of the operation.

As we came to have more spare time, plus an unlimited number of para-chutes, the parachute tent was evolved. The credit for this invention must go to our Red Russians, but soon it was the normal pattern tent throughout the area. The Maquisards even adapted it to a 70-foot jeep chute and used it as a headquarters tent. In its final form, as erected by the newly constituted Three Troop when it set up its own camp towards the end of August, it was like this.

A pole was slung between two trees about 15 feet above the ground. From the centre of the pole two parachutes were hung by their tips, the one inside the other, and the vent at the top tightly tied. The outside chute, which was normally khaki, green, or some other inconspicuous colour, was then stretched taut and pegged out by the rigging lines in such a way that the edges of the canopy were about 2 feet off the ground; and an opening about 4 feet wide at the base but closing altogether about 6 feet up, was left on one side. This outer parachute formed a camouflage and a rain-break, but when thoroughly soaked it could not prevent splashes of moisture coming through. The second or inner parachute was usually white, gaudy yellow or sombre red, depending on the character of the owner. It was also stretched and pegged like the first, but it touched the ground all round except at the opening, and hung clear of the other parachute so that it only had to contend with the fine spray of moisture that came through the rain-break. Even in the worst weather, these two parachutes, each of double thickness owing to the doubling back which was necessary to leave an entrance, proved completely waterproof.

Within one of these parachute tents, the earth floor would be thickly strewn with bracken and covered with a parachute of the same colour as the inner wall. In the centre of the tent, a bed for two or three men, according to the number in the tent, would be made from a stout framework of wood, raised on empty jerry-cans and carrying a mattress of interlaced parachute cords. On these cords lay more bracken, covered once more by parachutes to make a comfortable bedding, and on to this bedding was laid the boys' sleeping-bags. When the weather got colder, more parachutes could be added to the sleeping-bags for warmth.

Along the side of the bed, makeshift tables and cupboards were made from empty containers and the whole made a very comfortable home from home.

I myself lived in a rough shelter with Alex and Dickie until after I returned from my first operation. After that I shared a parachute tent with my driver Middleton until we left the Bois de Montsauche.

Clothing was another problem, which we also solved, to some extent, by parachute. My own difficulties started early when I lost my pips. These had been sewn on sleeves which could be slipped off and on my epaulettes, so that I could conceal my officer identity if I fell into enemy hands. However, within a few days of landing, the heavy wear and tear of forcing my way through thick undergrowth had ripped both sleeves off and I never found them again. I had landed in thin ginger-coloured corduroys which had belonged to my father. Within a few days of landing they had been ripped to ribbons and I was very lucky to get a pair of battledress trousers which had been dropped to us to equip the Maquis. By the time I left France I had worn two pairs of battledress trousers to shreds.

The next difficulty was at the ankles. I had landed with short puttees, which were both smart and effective for about ten days, until one night on a *parachutage* a puttee came unwound in the dark and I had nothing to keep the bottoms of my trousers from fraying. Here we took a leaf out of the Frenchmen's book, threading boot-laces through the cuffs of our battledress trousers to tie them tight at the ankle. This prevented the cuff from trailing on the ground, but it did nothing to avoid water getting into the boots.

Boots, too, were a difficulty, for we had no repair facilities and in the wet woods the leather was always damp. We had extra boots dropped to us and wore our plimsolls as much as possible around camp, but the one pair of boots with which I returned home was worn right down and rotted along the seams.

Shirts became frayed and were not renewed; and although we got our clothes laundered in the village, if Germans were rumoured in the area our washing would be weeks overdue. So we persuaded the local village girls to make up shirts and underwear from parachutes, and very smart they looked too.

Berets, collars and ties easily became lost on operations which took place at night, and we soon adopted the Maquis habit of knotting a piece of brightly coloured parachute around the throat and another around the head.

I always carried two large squares of silk parachute, one white for social occasions and one black for fighting. I never actually lost my beret, but in the woods by day I preferred to tie my camouflaged face veil around my head rather than sport the conspicuous red beret.

One item I always wore was my Dennison smock, and I made a point of always keeping my escape pack and maps in this useful and well-camouflaged piece of uniform, so that whatever happened I had the bare necessities of life and a fair chance of escape. In the pocket I had sewn inside the smock, I always carried the little hand-painted ivory miniature of my wife Margot, in the blue plush and leather case which she had given me before I left.

The Maquis, with a similar problem, equipped themselves from time to time with items of British uniform dropped at the *parachutages* and with clothing taken from the dead Germans. Good boots were prized above all else, and it was said that there were more fights to capture dead men's boots than to rescue injured comrades.

By the time that we left the Morvan, it was almost impossible to tell the SAS in their stained and ragged uniforms, with their gaudy parachute scarves and ill-assorted boots, from the Maquis, whose newer battledresses looked sloppy but whose choice of bright scarves was unimpeachable.

In the matter of sanitation, we did not follow the books at all. We quickly noticed that the Maquis habit of digging latrines in the woods, not very far from their camps, led to evil-smelling holes and an abundance of flies. So, in the absence of chloride of lime, and knowing that we had miles of wood around us, we used to leave a spade and supply of paper close to the cookhouse. Each man would then dig his own latrine at least 150 yards from the outer perimeter of the camp and fill it in again after use. This system was used without trouble throughout the summer, although the disposal of cookhouse refuse and empty tins did provide another problem, which was only solved by the continual digging of pits and burying of scraps.

We were seldom bothered by animals, though sometimes on sentry duty one could hear the wild boars grunting and scuffling near the camp, and we often came upon their rootings in the soft ground. Cows were sometimes a nuisance, particularly at Bill's camp where they used to set off the booby traps regularly, but this was only a minor worry.

Strangely enough, despite the continual rain, the complete lack of decent bathing facilities and the irregular life that we were leading, there was virtually no sickness of any sort in the camp. Our worst troubles were boils due to dirty clothes and lack of fresh vegetables. Apart from this, we enjoyed remarkably good health throughout.

Our bathing facilities, such as they were, consisted of a pool, which we hollowed out below the spring where we drew our water, and the lake near the DZ, which although very pleasant on sunny days, lost much of its popularity after one of the Maquisards drowned in it. We used to get enough hot water off the kitchen fire to shave two or three times a week and, soon after we had settled into our camp, Johnnie Cooper and I started a moustache-growing contest. He lost heart after a couple of weeks, but I kept my facial fungus to the bitter end, by which time it looked very fine and fierce in the sun, but had a tendency to droop dreadfully in the normal showers of rain, giving me an air of deep depression. I swore to shave it off when France was free again and did not in fact keep it for many weeks after the final German capitulation.

Now and then the recounting of amusing incidents would relieve the monotony of camp life. One, probably apocryphal but too good to omit, concerned the Colonels Isaac and Dubois. Bound from the Maquis Bernard at one end of the Bois de Montsauche to the Maquis Serge at the other, they decided that the main road was too risky and determined to travel through the woods.

Colonel Isaac was at this time suffering somewhat from rheumatism, and was using a donkey-cart for local trips. He had a small Maquis lad acting as his donkey-boy, while Dubois had a young boy as his batman. Accordingly, the party set out with maps, field-glasses, compasses and the boys as guides.

It was afternoon when they started. By evening, despite their route-finding equipment, they were hopelessly lost. Eventually the colonels dispatched the boys to find the right road, while they remained waiting with the cart.

The boys found the Maquis Bernard all right, but as it was now getting late, they spent the night there. Meanwhile, the colonels, bitterly cold and very rheumatic, were huddled in the cart for warmth, having let their donkey out of the shafts to graze.

In the morning, wet, weary and even more rheumatic, the colonels found to their horror that the donkey had disappeared. They searched but could find it nowhere. Soon the boys, after a comfortable night at the Maquis, reappeared and Dubois suggested that they all walk back to the Maquis Bernard; but the English colonel was feeling far too stiff for so long a walk and insisted that the donkey-boys be harnessed into the shafts to drag them to their destination.

All went well until just before reaching the Maquis, the road passed through a shallow, rocky ford. Here by mischance, the leading lad slipped and fell. His companion tripped over the prostrate body in the water and let go the shafts of the cart. The result is better imagined than described. The shafts dug into the bed of the stream, the tail of the cart tipped up. The two colonels were shot as from a catapult, over the front of their vehicle and into the bubbling stream.

Thus it was that nearly twenty-four hours after they had set out, the colonels, very wet, very hungry, very tired and extraordinarily rheumatic, arrived back at the camp from which they had so gallantly set forth.

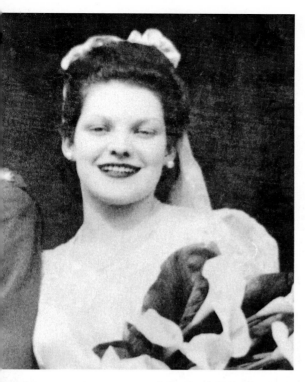

Margot, Ian Wellsted's first wife, whose miniature he often used to establish friendly relations at the farm houses that he and his men visited.

(*Left to right*) Sergeant Ken Sturmey, the proprietress, Roger Eté and a peasant farmer with one of the parachuted jeeps outside the *estaminet* at Ouroux. (*Tom Rennie*)

Burnt-out house in Dun-les-Places, still abandoned in August 1945. This was on the corner opposite the church, round which Wellsted and the maquisards crept during the night of 25/26 June 1944 while the twenty-seven civilians massacred by the Germans lay in the churchyard, their bodies guarded by German sentries. (*Author*)

Ian Wellsted mans the jeep's twin Vickers while Captain Alex Muirhead drives. (*Alex Muirhead*)

Ian Wellsted at 12,000 feet in the Alpes Maritimes on patrol with the Chasseurs Alpins, March 1945.

(*Left to right*) Roger Eté, Lieutenant Dickie Grayson and Trooper Collison with their requisitioned vehicle. (*Tom Rennie*)

(*Left to right*) Sergeant Ken Sturmey, Dr Georges Brûlé and Meurice, a Maquisard, in another requisitioned car. (*Tom Rennie*)

A Maquis hospital, and a bullock cart towing the SAS six-pounder anti-tank gun. Chalky White has his arm in a sling; Ancona is astride the barrel of the six-pounder. (*Eric Adamson*)

In the cemetery in Grain, at the graves of Captain Roy Bradford and Andy Devine, killed in the encounter with the German convoy at Lucy-sur-Yonne on 20 July 1944. The men behind the graves are (*left to right*) Ian Wellsted, Dr Georges Brûlé, Lieutenant Tony Trower, Sergeant Tom Rennie, Roger Eté and Trooper Bill Brown. (*Author*)

Ian Wellsted lays a wreath on Roy Bradford's grave. (*Author*)

The Anglo-Maquis cemetery as it was in 1946. (*Alex Muirhead*)

Ian Wellsted in late 1945 just before 1 SAS w
disbanded.

Ian Wellsted and his second wife, Diana,
their wedding, 20 December 1947.

CHAPTER XII

Parades, Parachutages and Preparations

The one really precise operation which was carried out day after day with unfailing regularity was the wireless watch. Three times a day with our little receiving sets we tuned into the SAS station and heard the signature tune of 'Sur le Pont d'Avignon' tinkling out those first few bars in endless mournful procession. We came to hate that tune, and even now I cannot hear it without my mind harking back to a small damp shelter, amid the high wet trees, listening for that far-off call against the dismal patter of the raindrops.

The most vital messages usually came through on the 7 o'clock broadcast in the evening, and we would all set to work decoding furiously to get the latest news. Sometimes it would be orders for a *parachutage*, occasionally it would be operational orders, most often it was information of German troop movements, and possible intentions.

There was an SAS News in clear, too, which began each broadcast of code messages. 'HULLO ROMO ... HULLO ROMO ...' a voice would repeat and repeat endlessly. 'After the news I have messages for SABU 10, SABU 12, SABU 14, and SABU 19. Here is the news ...' Then it would come, all the latest information of the battles still swaying back and forth on those Normandy beaches 400 miles away, but upon the fate of which our whole future depended.

Meanwhile, night after night, we listened to other news, and when traffic was not too heavy we received messages from wives and sweethearts at home. During the three months that we were there, we, in turn, were allowed to send one wireless message home; it was a great event, and we were glad of the chance.

On several occasions, we had special broadcasts from Paddy himself, the brigadier, or one of the senior officers still left at home. These had an intimate touch that we greatly appreciated, making us realise that whatever else was happening, we were not forgotten.

Church parade was another welcome reminder of home. Using a variety of vehicles, but with amazing regularity, Fraser McLuskey toured from troop to troop, with his basket of library books, his packet of army hymnals, his SAS altar cloth of pale blue and maroon, and his collapsible wooden Cross. Week after week he held his voluntary church parades, which everyone attended irrespective of nationality or denomination, and which brought spiritual comfort where it was sorely needed.

On sunny afternoons, with the sun filtering between the leaves and dancing in patterns on the pine-matted earth, he would lay his altar cloth on a derelict pannier, and set up his Cross. In ones and twos his congregation would wander up, dressed more like buccaneers than worshippers, and carrying containers on which to sit.

Then the hymnals would be issued, the prayers would be said, the psalms shouted, and Fraser would make his sermon, short but appropriate. The communicants would stay, the rest would drift away among the trees and for a few moments on the damp pine needles he would hold Communion.

Throughout our stay, and afterwards when he joined C Squadron, the Padre held his services as often as he could, 'singing the hymns louder or softer according to the situation'. Never did he carry a gun, though always in the places of utmost peril, and his quiet calm was an inspiration to us all. He even held Confirmation classes when there was no work to be done, and it seemed a pity that we had to leave France before all his candidates were prepared. The library that he administered was a godsend in the boring hours of waiting, and the way that he could handle a jeep, when he found himself inadvertently driving in an unexpected road-strafe, had to be seen to be believed. For his work in France he got the MC and richly deserved it.

Towards the end of our stay in Montsauche, we had to bury the crew of a British bomber which had crashed near Gouloux. It was a simple but impressive ceremony. The eight neat white coffins were piled high with flowers, and for once a kind but watery sun was shining through the trees. The grave was lined by a guard of honour from the Maquis André on the left and by eight of Alex's men under my command on the right. A Roman Catholic priest from Ouroux chanted the service in Latin for those of the crew who might have been Catholics, and the Padre read a short English service for the rest. The Maquisards presented arms, smartly now, for by this time they were well trained, and we fired three salvoes from our carbines over the open grave. It was sad, yet very sweet, and the pile of flowers was high and very fragrant.

The airmen were laid to rest in the same little cemetery in the Bois de Montsauche in which Jacques was buried three days after the ambush. Alex and Johnny had attended this funeral, and had been most impressed by the efforts that the Maquisards had made to give their comrade a truly military send-off. Draped in parachutes, his coffin lay in state all morning, with flags dipped around the spot; and when the cortège moved down from the Maquis to the cemetery, hardly a soul had remained in the camp.

*   *   *

It was about a week later that we had our first *parachutage* on the new

Montsauche DZ. Bearing in mind that procedures for these drops tended to be very similar, this detailed description is therefore applicable to them all.

At about 7 o'clock our coded message warned us that the *parachutage* would be that night, and we at once warned the Maquis and requested their assistance. Around 11.00, lightly armed, we set off in long single file down the slippery forest paths to the Maquis, one torch to every six men, leaving as few people in camp as possible. After joining the Maquisards we carried on along more muddy paths to the open stretch of ground, where the lake shone coldly in the moonlight.

Skirting the lake, we took up our position on top of a bare little hill from which by day one could see as far as Ouroux. Here on the edge of the Maquis Bernard car-park, stood the first light. Across a potato field and a high hedge, there was a second light; and a third light was positioned in some open marshy meadow about a hundred yards beyond it. The lights were all the head-lamps of old cars, with newly charged batteries. At first there was one Maquisard and one SAS man to each lamp, but after a time we began to man them exclusively ourselves. Beside the first lamp was a man with a torch; and on occasions when we were using an Eureka this would also be here, and both torch and Eureka would flash the code letter for the night.

Now, with SAS and Maquisards divided roughly into parties half-a-dozen strong, we waited for the arrival of the leading plane. This vigil was the worst period of the whole drop, particularly when, as happened so often, there was a light drizzle. Eventually we developed the technique of sending down the lamp men well beforehand, and only bringing down the search parties at the last moment.

After one or two false alarms, the dull drone of a distant engine would grow louder and louder, and as Alex shouted 'lights', or Georges cried 'allumez', the Stirling thundered into sight, a darker shadow against a cloudy sky. At once the torch began to signal frantically, and all the headlamps to light up, illuminating the plane as it passed low across the DZ. Now swinging in a wide circle, the Stirling swooped in once more. This time it was lower than ever, and as it passed the first light there came a swish and crack of opening chutes, and a clang-clang as the containers bumped together. Sometimes there was a long swish and a dull crump, as a container candled, and at other times there was a dreadful clanging and bumping as several containers fouled one another and fell together; but generally they survived the initial hazards of the descent and with a soft clanking laid themselves gently on the turf or swung suspended in the trees.

Almost as the Stirling cleared the DZ, we would see two panniers tumble from its ample belly and go floating away on the wind. Panniers were the bane of our existence; they always contained the mail, the secret documents, the specially important items that we had asked for and they were always the last released. Then, too, being lightest, they drifted furthest, and gave us more trouble to find than all the other containers put together.

Hardly was the first plane clear of the DZ, than a second swooped in. This one would perhaps run straight across the lights and, without checking position, let go, so that although most of his stick was not too far from the middle light, the end containers and the invaluable panniers would go drifting away into the forest.

Now there might be a lull, but as the search parties set out, when least expected, a third plane would roar into sight, coming in high, so that for a moment we would wonder whether it was one of theirs or one of ours; but as soon as it saw the lights it would veer towards them and, without either checking height, direction or speed, release its containers and turn for home. This stick was scattered over half the mountain. The dispersed, drifting containers took an age to collect, but the job had to be done.

Searching for and collecting the containers was a hard night's work. When they were found, they had to be freed from entanglements, cut loose from their chutes, and dragged by their rigging lines or carried on poles to dumps set up among the trees. It might be well after 4 o'clock before the last reasonably accessible container was found and brought in. Then we would rest until dawn, curled up in a pile of parachutes as some sort of protection from the falling dew. As soon as it was light enough to see, we would start a fresh search in the surrounding country, while other parties began to pack the chutes back in their bags for camouflage and easy transportation. Around 6 o'clock the local peasants arrived with their ox-carts to carry our containers up to the camp or to a central dump in the thick gorse close to the Maquis garage.

How we relied upon these sturdy hard-working folk and their heavy oxen, who used to pull overloaded wooden carts up the deeply rutted tracks into the heart of our woods. None of them ever betrayed us. One old boy, whom we all knew as Charles Laughton, was a great character, always smiling and alternately swearing at his team and calling them his little ones, his pretty ones, his darlings.

Usually it was midday before we had finally cleared the DZ, and after a hearty lunch we would spend the afternoon sleeping off the exertions of the night.

On the morning of 5 July, while clearing the DZ, after a particularly bad drop, Trooper 'Paddy' Kennedy and I worked down as far as the Montsauche–Clamecy road, and hearing a number of vehicles, we crept forward to watch them. We reached the road too late to see the cars, but as we lay there we heard the roar of other engines, and a trio of aged Messerschmidts swept up the valley. However, the DZ had been well cleared, and they did not appear to notice anything unusual.

Occasionally, supplies for the Maquis and ourselves were dropped on the same night, and neither we nor they were over-scrupulous when it came to 'accidentally' collecting one of the other's containers. However, our differences were usually settled amicably on the DZ before anyone came to blows.

One day in early July, Lemniscate, now adopting the rank of colonel, came down to the Maquis Bernard, looking like a mushroom, beneath a parachutist's enormous steel-helmet. He made a speech congratulating all the Maquisards for the ambush on the Montsauche road, and presenting Georges and Roger with the Croix de Guerre. It was a typically French ceremony with everyone kissing everyone else. The decorations were well merited but I could not help laughing a little as I watched, and felt that we were well out of it.

The day after Major Fraser's visit with the jeeps, I had another taste of the difficulties of coming as an unknown officer to an SAS troop behind the lines. I took a party of the men under Sergeant Sturmey down to the DZ to bury the stores left over from the *parachutage* of the previous night. I wanted them to work as hard as they could so that we could get back to the camp as soon as possible, but they adopted a go-slow policy and I was completely impotent. It was in this contretemps that I ran foul of Lance-Corporal Cave for the first time, and started an enmity which lasted for well over a year. The whole situation depressed me, and I began to feel pretty useless, wishing heartily that I had never changed troops.

That afternoon two of the jeeps were to come back, one of them becoming the permanent property of Two Troop, for it was intended to commence operations with a sally by Johnny Cooper against Autun. However, as we were having our tea, one jeep, alone, came tearing up into the camp, bounding violently along the rutted way, and we heard the nasty news that the other jeep had crashed.

Ancona had been driving much too fast and in taking a corner near the Maquis Bernard's guardroom, he had overturned the jeep. The MO, who was travelling in it, suffered severely from shock and there is a libellous story that he walked round for several minutes asking if there was a doctor about. But far worse was the state of Corporal Adamson, whose pelvis was fractured and who was condemned to live for the next nine weeks in great pain and subject to the crudest and most insanitary conditions. That he survived the ordeal at all is due entirely to the excellent surgery of Martell and the tender care of Madam Martell the Maquis nurses.

The jeep was badly damaged and although it was salvaged, eventually becoming my own and doing yeoman service throughout the campaign, it never really recovered from this initial wreck. For the rest of its days its two front wheels wobbled with an independent air and its steering was always erratic.

Throughout that day we and Maquis mechanics worked on the damaged jeep, for Bill took the good one back with him. But by the evening it was quite evident that tonight's expedition must start jeepless, and Johnny and Georges set off for Autun in a civilian car.

By lunchtime the next day, the jeep was ready at last, and I was sent out with it to convoy a Maquis lorry loaded with ammunition and stores for Bill's new camp. I took Swag Jemson as gunner and Peter Middleton as driver. The journey was uneventful and the weather was kind. At Bill's camp we unshipped our load and with their help cached it in the woods. On the way back we sank the empty containers in a lake.

This was my first chance to see Bill's new camp. It was in a deep rocky valley, well-strewn with bushes and trees and easily approached down a couple of long boulder-covered tracks. It was a pleasant location with a southern aspect, not very far from the village of Mazignien. Water, however, had to be carried up the hillside and was not very plentiful if the weather should turn dry.

At this camp I saw Tony Trower, just back from Dijon for the day to collect more of the men of Johnny Wiseman's One Troop. It was the first time that I had seen him since we left Darvel, where he had nearly been returned to his unit, after an exercise in which he had had trouble with his men. I confided my own misgivings and we commiserated.

After saying my farewells to Bill and Tony, I escorted the lorry back to our wood. There were no signs of the enemy, and the peasants, beginning to recognise the red berets, waved to us as we passed.

Curiously, all the time that we were in France, we were known as 'Les Canadiens'. There was no reason for it that we could see except that perhaps the logical French mind felt that if British troops were parachuted into France, they ought to be bilingual Canadians.

As soon as I got back to camp, I handed the jeep over to Dickie Grayson and after dinner he loaded it and set off on a fighting reconnaissance mission for La Charité with Collison and 'Lofty' Langridge, while Sturmey and someone else actually manned the jeep. He took plenty of ammunition, some food and a little explosive. The jeep returned next morning, having left Dickie at a Maquis close to La Charité.

That afternoon, Johnny and Georges got back. They had not done any damage, but a careful reconnaissance had disclosed a synthetic oil plant at Autun which could easily be attacked by night and Alex set to work to develop plans for the expedition.

That night, as darkness fell, the jeep once more crept out of the woods. This time the crew was Middleton and Sergeant Rennie, carrying my own small party. It was my first operation.

CHAPTER XIII

First Operation

The task entrusted to me was one almost as old as the SAS itself: the destruction of planes on their airfields, but the journey to it was the longest that the Squadron had yet undertaken in France.

Fifty miles as the crow flies, south of Montsauche, on the very borders of the old unoccupied zone, lay the valley of the River Bourbince. This area was flat, open and only lightly wooded, and it was well out of the areas controlled by the Maquis of the Morvan. At the point where the Bourbince flows into the Loire lies the town of Digoin, and some twelve miles to the east, where the valley swings suddenly northward, is Paray-le-Monial. Just to the north of this town, on a piece of high ground overlooking the length of the valley, is the airfield of Volesvres; and eight miles south of Digoin, along the banks of the wide swift-flowing Loire, well within the old unoccupied zone, lies the satellite field of St Yan. Both were clearly marked on our maps and both were believed to be in operation. It was up to us to destroy every plane that we could find and report on the conditions of the fields.

As my companions, I took Swag Jemson, Grady and Jean-Paul. Grady was a Yorkshire lad with a French mother. He was well educated, spoke a certain amount of French and German and was an expert with explosives. Jean-Paul, as already mentioned, was the tank captain of the Maquis Bernard, who, due to a political difference of opinion with certain of the Maquis colonels who were now beginning to infest our wood, was at present somewhat out of favour with his compatriots. He volunteered to accompany my party, and though purporting to speak no English, read our maps with uncanny accuracy.

For supplies, we took only our sleeping bags, ground-sheets and rucksacks, with the barest minimum of spare clothing. We carried 75 lb of Lewis bombs, a mixture of thermite and plastic explosive, primed with gun-cotton and Cordtex and done up in 2 lb calico bags. We also carried a large supply of two-hour time pencils, one or two even longer delays, a number of miners' instantaneous igniters, a supply of fuses, detonators and adhesive tape, and a few assorted booby-traps. This we deemed sufficient to put paid to nearly forty aircraft, and make ourselves a nuisance in other ways.

For arms we had our Colts and a few grenades. I took the .22 automatic, which had belonged to the Grey Russian officer, instead of my Colt. Jean-Paul and I had carbines, Grady had a Tommy-gun and Jemson a Bren. Our ammunition, however, was very limited.

111

For food we took enough twenty-four-hour ration packs to last us four days and a certain amount of compo ration in addition, though not enough to make a decent meal for a further day. So, as we intended to be away at least a week, it was evident that we would have to watch our grub.

We included my small wireless receiver in case of messages, although in fact we hardly found time to use it at all.

The afternoon of Sunday 9 July was spent packing and preparing our kit and loading the jeep. Jeeps are officially two-seater vehicles with an eight hundred-weight carrying capacity in the back. Our jeep, however, when it set off down the rugged trail, which would have been sufficient alone to break the springs of most cars, carried six men. In addition to all our kit it mounted twin Vickers-K machine-guns in swivel mountings fore and aft, carrying eight pans of ammunition for each pair. With this load of death and destruction to act as our seating accommodation, and considering the steep and tricky trails we followed, it was hardly surprising that we looked forward to our journey with some trepidation.

The first leg of our journey lay down the good second-class road past ruined Planchez and along towards Château-Chinon, as far as the little village of Fretoy, where we branched off and dived into the Forêt d'Anost. Here we wound in and out among the straggling houses of Lavault-de-Fretoy, and came unexpectedly upon a party of Maquisards from a group that I had not hitherto encountered, who were working on a car at the roadside. Fortunately both sides were too surprised to fire.

As we climbed the long winding hill out of Lavault, we were again disconcerted, on the edge of the forest, to find a wooden barricade barring our path and to hear the shrill cry of 'Qui vive?' It was the Maquis Socrate. This Maquis which we were soon to know well, was another group of Communist leanings, but the bandit-like leader Socrate was the finest guerrilla in the Morvan, and a good friend to the British. In later days I often met him, stripped to the waist and working with his men. Young and good-looking, he was worshipped by his followers, and feared by the Germans, gallant in action and cunning in defence.

This was our first encounter with the Maquis Socrate and we were at first viewed with suspicion. But Jean-Paul explained us and our mission and we showed the Maquisards our guns and equipment to prove our bona fides. The guards gave us swigs of wine from their flasks, wished us Godspeed and cheered us on our way.

Along the forest trails we saw signs of Maquis life and at one place passed the Socrate car-park; but soon, having passed beyond another road-block, we found ourselves once more in undefended country and pushed steadily on.

At the little village of Bussy in the forest, somewhat unsure of the way, we drew up beside a prominent house, with light still filtering from half-closed shutters. Jean-Paul leapt out and rapped on the door. There was a moment's silence and then a quavering voice enquired, 'Qui est là?' 'Résistance,' replied Jean-Paul, in a ringing tone that would have done credit to any spy-thriller.

The door opened half an inch and a nose peered out. Jean-Paul asked the way.

Scarcely had we learned the route and returned to the jeep than we saw the headlights of a powerful car sweep round the corner and bear down upon us in the narrow street.

Who it was, or what it was doing, we neither knew nor cared. I covered it with my carbine from the ditch, the others swung their guns towards it but held their fire. The car raced past, accelerating down the street, and disappeared. No one fired a shot.

Soon after Bussy we approached the main *route nationale* which ran from Château-Chinon to Autun, and which was in constant use by the Boche. We had to follow this for about two miles, and so, with all lights doused and fingers gripping our triggers, we raced at top speed down the dimly moonlit road. We all heaved great sighs of relief as we roared through Le Pommoy and swung off right-handed into the Forêt de Glaine. Now we were driving deep into the beautiful country of the Haute Morvan, and even in the glare of our headlights the scenery was savage and wildly picturesque. Through the small town of St Léger-sous-Beuvray we ran, with the peak of Mont Beuvray towering on our right and Etang de Poisson stretched out before us, shimmering in misty beauty.

Now the *route nationale* from Autun to Moulins barred our way and beyond it the Autun–Nevers railway with level-crossing gates. It was one of the trickiest places along our whole route.

A short dash down the broad highway and the *route nationale* was safely passed. As we approached the railway barrier, the jeep halted and Jean-Paul went forward alone. I covered him from a short distance behind with Grady's Tommy-gun. Behind us in the shadows the jeep stood ready for a quick get-away, its guns covering my cautious advance.

As Jean-Paul crossed the lines, I saw the hooded lights of a nearby station, from which came the noises of men singing.

'Ouvrez la barrière, s'il vous plaît, Monsieur!' Jean-Paul's voice rang out clearly across the width of the railway. There was an ominous silence as the singing suddenly stopped and a couple of guards tumbled lazily on to the platform beneath their swinging lamp. The moment was tense, and then, with a creak, the heavy wooden poles began to rise. Behind me I heard the engine of the jeep rev slightly and the clash of engaging gears. As the barrier rose clear above the road, the jeep swept forward. Jean-Paul and I leapt aboard and the game little vehicle tore off once more into the darkness of the night.

From here, we ran due south along quiet country lanes along the bank of the River Arroux and for fifteen miles our journey was without incident, except occasionally when Jean-Paul stopped to study the map, or with a sharp exclamation of 'Merde!', halted the jeep, turned back a few yards and set us once more on the proper route.

The Arroux itself was our next obstacle – a deep, swift stream best crossed at the German garrison town of Toulon-sur-Arroux. Here we entered warily and as we approached the bridge, I dismounted with most of the men and went ahead on foot. Close to the bridge was a big barrack hut from which issued the grunts of sleeping men; and it was with the gravest trepidation that we turned our footsteps down the long straight road that led to the bridge.

The bridge was high, wide and completely open; and to our fevered imaginations it seemed to have no end, tapering away into infinity. At any moment we expected a guttural challenge from the farther bank. There was nothing to do but walk quietly and pray fervently. I did both, and my prayers were answered.

As we reached the eastern shore, the jeep, which had been creeping along in our wake, leapt once more into noisy life, and pausing only a moment to gather up all its passengers, it hurried at top speed away from the incalculable dangers of the bridge. So fast, however, did we hurry, diving into narrow side streets and twisting through a labyrinth of small passages, that we soon knew we were lost. Huge, hostile houses towered around us and at any moment we risked encountering a German street patrol or passing a building with an enemy guardroom outside. We stopped for a moment in a large tree-filled square and as there were no signposts in sight we crept from corner to corner hoping that the street names might give us some clue to the best way out of the town. At last Jean-Paul made his decision but, to our horror, after a few moments of meandering through a maze of crooked alleys, we found ourselves back in the square again.

Our second cast, however, proved more fortunate. To our unbounded relief, the rows of houses thinned out and the *route nationale* beneath our whirling wheels soon carried us clear of this dangerous town.

The next part of our course lay for three miles down the wide first-class road towards Gueugnon, where there were elements of a German Panzer Brigade, and Digoin, with its garrison of Grey Russians. Well might Middleton coax on his jeep at its very fastest.

After we had turned safely off this *route nationale*, we passed through the pretty Bois de Beaumont, whose thick woods and leafy foliage encouraged thoughts of a hideout where we could arrange our rendezvous. I decided to push as far south as I dared, because the farther I made the rendezvous from the targets, the less time I could actually afford to spend in the target area.

We crossed the second-class road from Gueugnon to Montceau-les-Mines without mishap and came out on another from Gueugnon to Paray-le-Monial at the little hamlet of Clessy.

Beyond Clessy our minor road forked and a small trail, not much more than a cart-track, led through the Bois de Clessy towards the village of En Vevre. We were now getting very near to the edge of the hills, where they dropped down to the open plain of the Bourbince, and so, turning along the track, we halted at about 4 o'clock in the centre of the wood and unloaded the jeep.

As soon as all our kit had been pulled off the jeep, it ran down the track as far as the outskirts of En Vevre so as not to display the exact spot at which it had stopped. Then, waving us farewell, Tom Rennie and Peter Middleton bumped off into the night on their long and arduous journey back to base, promising to rendezvous with us between midnight and 5.00 on the morning of Monday 17 July. We were left to our own devices.

According to the map there should have been a stream a few yards off the track, but in the dark I couldn't find it. So, gathering all our equipment, we pushed into the wood on the southern side and curled up in our sleeping-bags, to see what the morning would bring.

We slept until 9.00, when the sun stood out bright in the sky and I discovered to my horror that we were still visible from the track. However, after a quick reconnaissance of the area, I found the stream for which I had been looking last night and moved our camp down beside it. Here we were sheltered from anyone passing along the track by a thick screen of briars.

We ate a small breakfast consisting mostly of tea, which Swag brewed up for us, and leaving the other two to guard the camp, Jean-Paul and I set out to recce the airfield at Volesvres. The direct distance from our camp to the aerodrome was only about six miles but it was six miles of cross-country going and we wanted, as far as possible, to avoid being seen.

At first we moved with the utmost caution and it was not until we were well away from the Bois de Clessy that we began to take fewer precautions against casual peasants. Jean-Paul was dressed in civilian clothes and looked a normal Frenchman of the better class so that he did not excite suspicion. Accordingly, whenever we were forced to approach buildings, or cross main roads, he went ahead, while I covered him from the ditch or hedgerow. I was wearing my Dennison smock and red beret, and I carried our field-glasses and a gas-cape in a small pack on my back.

The sun shone and after the dripping, all-enshrouding woods of the Morvan, the open country and wide fields, with well-bred horses cropping the smooth turf, was a real tonic.

About 2 o'clock in the afternoon we got close enough to be able to distinguish the tall hangars of the airfield, perched on the edge of a gently rolling down. I climbed a tree and studied the area through my glasses. It was not possible to see the ground itself, but the hangars and other buildings in the vicinity, which I took to be messes, seemed strangely deserted.

As I continued to scrutinise the landscape and tried vainly to pick out any planes upon the 'drome, I was suddenly startled to hear Jean-Paul speaking to someone on the ground just below me. It turned out to be an intelligent-looking, brown-faced peasant lad, in soiled blue dungarees. He realised that we were of the Resistance and very readily gave us all the information that we required.

His news was by no means welcome. The airfield at Volesvres had been turned into allotments. It had not been used for the past two years but the Germans had been working on the satellite station at St Yan, and this was believed to be in use, though not flying off more than three or four aircraft a day. We had a long trek ahead of us.

On the trip back to the camp we moved even more openly, stopping at one farm for a quick omelette and some rich garlicky ham, with good red wine. We stopped for a while in the fading sunlight to admire a lovely old château and got back to our camp about dusk, where we ate an evening meal and slept soundly. We did not bother about a guard, as we were too few to provide one, and the chances of our being discovered were very slight.

Next morning we were woken early by the tooting of a tram service serving the villages to the west, and after Swag had made the breakfast, we reallocated the kit.

First, I prepared all the bombs with their pencils for immediate use and packed them all into one rucksack, which when it was finished weighed about 80 lb. In addition to this we packed a little food and our ground-sheets with one or two articles of warm clothing into a second rucksack. The rest of our kit we carefully hid in the undergrowth close to our camp, and then started out on the long road to St Yan.

We set off about midday and at lunchtime found some cherry trees, all well in fruit and very appetising. We stopped there for a long time, knocking down the ripe juicy cherries and eating till we nearly burst. The sun was warm, the fruit was good, and bees hummed cheerfully among the clover fields. The war seemed – as indeed it was – hundreds of miles away.

Throughout the afternoon we made our way slowly and carefully through the woods and along the hedgerows until at last the woods ended and the ground fell steeply away towards the river, the canal and the railway, which marked the boundary of old Vichy France.

We had been warned that as a check-up on movement in the country, the Germans still maintained their old frontier patrols along this line; and as the canal could only be crossed at a single place in the whole stretch from Digoin to Paray, we had grave doubts as to whether or not it would prove possible to cross this formidable barrier.

Luck was with us, and while we waited on the edge of the wood we noticed two old peasants and a young lad working in the fields. With great show of force we approached them, and once we had explained who we were, they were delighted to see us. The lad, who was about eighteen, was a well-educated young Parisian, working as a labourer to avoid being called up by the Germans for labour service. He wore the Cross of Lorraine carved into a ring on his finger and he promised to give us all the help that he could in exchange for our offer to get him accepted into a Maquis.

He told us that the Germans no longer patrolled the frontier, though they occasionally kept a watch on the railway line. The enemy in the area did not appear to be very high-class troops and he agreed to bring us food at dusk and guide us across the frontier.

For the rest of the day we lay at the wood's edge and surveyed the workers in the fields below. We watched the sun set westward in ruddy splendour, and as twilight faded from the sky, the young lad arrived with a basket of bread and cheese and two bottles of first-rate wine, pinched from his aunt's cellar. As we ate our frugal meal we were tormented by big flying beetles from the trees. They swarmed around us and although they did not sting or bite, they became a dreadful nuisance.

When it was quite dark, we set off. I carried the explosives, Jean-Paul navigated and carried the clothing, while Grady and Jemson carried their Tommy- and Bren-guns respectively. With sure foot our young guide led us down through fields and along hedges until at last we emerged on to a fairly good-class road. This we followed, turning right-handed at a fork which led down to the bridge over the Bourbince.

The guide went first and then, at a distance, Jean-Paul. I followed with the others at my heels. There was no disturbance. The stone bridge lay quiet in the starlight and the river flowed past with a sluggish gurgle.

On went the guide along what was now a hedge-topped causeway over the marshy ground, until he reached the tow-path which ran alongside the canal. Here there was a long, sturdy bridge with iron railings, very open and vulnerable, but as the two Frenchmen got across unchallenged, we followed them slowly. Now the road passed through a bit of a cutting and began to rise sharply to the level-crossing over the railway track. The barriers were down and indeed we had seen several trains pass while we had been waiting for the sun to set. We let ourselves through the wicket gate and crossed the lines. A couple of hundred yards beyond the level-crossing we came to the broad *route nationale*, which was the Paris–Lyon trunk route, and with a whispered farewell to the lad, we cut across it, trudging steadily down the dusty road to Vitry-en-Charollais.

The night's journey is somewhat of a blur in my mind. My load was appallingly heavy and the roads and tracks down which we were led by Jean-Paul seemed interminable. I remember well the way that the dogs pinpointed us wherever we went, starting to bark when we were about fifty yards short of a farm, and continuing their yelping until we were the same distance beyond it. Luckily, after about 1 o'clock, most of the brutes seemed to go to sleep and as we neared the danger zone around St Yan, we were grateful to find that our approach had ceased to be advertised with such fervent canine vigour.

The airstrip at St Yan, according to our maps, occupied the southern half of an island formed by the River Loire, the swift Arconce stream and the marshy land to the south of L'Hôpital-le-Mercier. It was my original plan to cross the Arconce by a track marked to the north of St Germain-des-Rives, and harbour in the woods at the extreme northerly tip of the island. My intention was to spend the next day in reconnaissance and launch my attack the following night. But as so often in war, my plans were soon most rudely shaken.

As we turned down the track towards the Arconce, we suddenly came upon a big sign in German hung on the gates of the manor of Bécheron. And on the other side of the track opposite the gates, and in just the position where one would expect the guardroom to be, there was a wooden hut. Beneath the door of the hut a crack of light showed and chinks of light gleamed from the badly blacked-out windows. It was after 2.00 in the morning and peaceful citizens should all have been abed; here we could discern the low murmur of voices and felt safe to assume that this was a German guard. Fortunately it was not a very alert one.

We returned to the St Yan road and dumped our packs in the shelter of some convenient trees. Grady and I went forward to recce the crossings of the Arconce, while the others remained behind to guard the explosives and cover our retreat.

Back down the track we passed the guardroom and found a narrow wooden footbridge across the river. On the further bank, however, there was a small shed, which might well be a sentry box, although the sentinel appeared to be asleep, I did not feel inclined to risk this crossing place, so carried on down the track. About 150 yards further on we found the ford, but the river was in spate, and a welter of foam was creaming over the roadway, so that in our heavily laden condition I felt that the footbridge would probably be the lesser of two evils.

Returning to the bridge, I slung my carbine and, covered by Grady's Tommy-gun, crept across, knife in one hand, grenade in the other. My rubber-soled boots moved silently over the planks and the roar of the water below drowned the creaking boards. As I approached the sentry box, I was keyed up to the finest pitch. The last few yards seemed to take hours. Then I reached it.

At first I could see nothing, but in a moment I realised that the shed was rather bigger than it had appeared from the other side. I stepped in, dreading the awful moment as I was silhouetted against the light. No shot came. Nothing stirred. I hooked my grenade on to my belt and pulled out my torch. For a brief instant I flicked it on and flashed it rapidly about me. Nothing but a few empty sacks and a pile of fishing gear met my searching eye. I switched off the torch, collected Grady and returned to the clump of trees where we had left our kit and our companions.

We shouldered our burdens again and one by one tiptoed past the guard-room across the unguarded bridge. On the far side of the stream, the footpath ran across open meadowland, and it was not until we had gone some 200 yards that we sighed with relief at the shelter of a friendly hedge.

We were now on the island and well north of the airstrip. Nothing remained for us but to find a safe hide-away for the following day. Taking up our loads once more, we continued along the track, only to be brought to a dead stop a few yards further on by a large notice in French and German nailed to a tree.

It is absolutely forbidden to trespass on this aerodrome,

Signed, The Commandant.

This shook us considerably. Either we were far south of where we thought we were, or the airfield was far north of where it ought to be. The track now branched right and left and we decided to follow the fork that appeared to be skirting the aerodrome northward. But we had scarcely begun our move before I was halted in my tracks by a great mass towering to the left of us, silhouetted against the misty sky.

'Christ! A hangar,' I exclaimed, and we retraced our steps to the signboard.

I dropped my pack there and Jemson and I went forward, climbing up out of the sunken track on to the surface of the airfield itself. Right at our feet I found a German aerodrome defence position covering the track up which we had come. Luckily it was not manned and while I was examining it, I suddenly heard an urgent whisper from Jemson.

'Look at all them bleeding aircraft,' he said, and I followed his pointing finger. There, about fifty yards away, shrouded and distorted by the morning mist, were four large machines lined up.

This was too much. We were right on the aerodrome itself and had had no opportunity either to make reconnaissances or to prepare a plan. We were dead tired after a day and a night on the march and we had no escape organised. I decided that we would make one more attempt to ensconce ourselves at the northern end of the island and then get out.

Accordingly, I sent Grady and Jean-Paul down to the Arconce, to follow it round until they reached its junction with the Loire, or found a suitable spot to lie up. They returned within quarter of an hour. The German outbuildings reached right down to the Arconce just ahead of us. Nothing remained but to retrace our steps.

As we recrossed the footbridge and crept back past the guardroom, the boys wanted to toss in a grenade. But I could not allow this as we did not want to stir up a hornets' nest before we had done our work. We regretted afterwards that we had not brought back the 'No Trespassing' sign, but it would have been a deal of unnecessary weight.

Once back on the St Yan–Digoin road, we set our faces to the north and began to plod back the way we had come. When we judged that we had gone far enough to be opposite the northern tip of the island, we turned west, and finding a small overgrown island in the Arconce close to the junction with the Loire, we made camp. Swag brewed some tea and as dawn began to lighten the eastern sky we rolled up in our ground-sheets and slept the sleep of exhaustion.

We slept until 9 o'clock, when I was woken by the cold, the damp and the mosquitoes. I woke Jean-Paul and we began to recce the area in which we had spent the night. We found a farm close at hand and while I kept watch Jean-Paul contacted the farmer. He returned with a little food and a bottle of wine. He also arranged to use the farmer's boat to row us across to the island airfield.

After a quick meal, and with the sun now growing stronger in the sky, Jean-Paul and I crossed the Arconce and began to recce southward. We carefully avoided all buildings and at last arrived on the edge of the aerodrome proper. It was very much larger than we had been led to believe, but from our point of vantage in the woods we could see only one aircraft and this was of very aged design. We observed a few lorries and signs of constructions still in hand, though there was no one at work that day.

I hid myself in the woods, while Jean-Paul went forward in his civilian clothes to talk to the peasants who were still tilling their land along the edge of the airfield.

I slept in the sun until his return, and he did not bring good news. The airfield was certainly big, but it was not finished. It was very seldom used and the only aircraft on it was the very old model we had already seen. The 'hangar' and 'aircraft' of the previous night turned out to have been nothing more than a huge pile of sand for concrete mixing and pieces of airfield construction equipment distorted by the mist. The Todt workers who had been carrying out the work had been taken away some time before, but there was still a German army garrison of a platoon strength stationed at St Yan to guard the airfield.

One of the peasants had agreed to feed us after dark and apart from this our information was entirely negative.

Back at the camp we found that the farmer's son had come with his father to visit the camp and had been engaged on the construction of the new airfield. He was an intelligent lad and Jean-Paul worked out a very accurate plan of the airfield with him, showing the location of the barracks, the dumps and the dispersal areas. He also told us of the existence of two other new strips that the Boche had built in the area, giving us their length and location. He confirmed, however, that nothing ever seemed to use the fields and added that the dumps, though built, contained neither bombs nor petrol.

I decided that the one obsolete aircraft was not worth the trouble of attacking, particularly as an assault on the airfield at Auxerre had been mooted and there seemed to be no point in giving away the fact that there were aircraft destruction units operating in the region. Regretfully, we thanked the farmer for all his assistance and prepared to depart at dusk. My first operation was accomplished. Not a fighting aircraft remained on either of the aerodromes I had set out to attack, but it was little thanks to me.

CHAPTER XIV

The Fourteenth of July

As the sun dipped, we hid our loads, and borrowing the farmer's boat we all crossed once more to the islands. The sun was setting in a haze of smoky red and purple fire across the wide Loire when we rendezvoused with the old peasant in a field beside the river. He brought us a bottle of wine and as darkness closed in, to cover our movements, he took us into his house and gave us a fine omelette and good home-cured ham.

Back across the Arconce for the last time, we took up our rucksacks and began the endless march to our camp in the Bois de Clessy. We stuck to roads most of the way and traversed the frontier again without mishap, crossing the quadruple barrier of road, railway, river and canal unnoticed. In the distance we heard the roar of motorcycles but we encountered nobody.

As soon as we reached the first crest of the hills overlooking the Bourbince, we found a small thicket below the village of Vigny and dumped the explosives, hiding them carefully in the undergrowth. With this weight off my shoulders and our camp not so far away, we felt new vigour, and as the dawn was breaking over the woods we found the camp, just as we had left it.

We were too tired for breakfast. Swag brewed up some tea while we unrolled our sleeping-bags and after a few biscuits we curled up and slept like the dead.

We slept all that day and it was not until dusk that we packed our beds, caching them in the underbrush before setting out on a new expedition.

The failure to find suitable targets on the aerodrome had left me with a problem. How was I to use my explosives to best advantage? I had seen the trains along the Paray–Digoin line and had heard the tram serving Gueugnon and Toulon. I decided that a really good wreck on the railway could seriously embarrass the efforts of the enemy to withdraw their Atlantic Coast troops by this route, and I hoped to follow it up by a daylight hold-up of the tram. I did not want to derail the vehicle, as it would be carrying civilian workers, but I felt that we were strong enough to stop the tram, turn off the civilians and kill any unsuspecting Germans whom we found on board. We could then, at our leisure, burn the tram and destroy the single-line track on which it ran. This would have no very great military value but it would hinder the movement of munition workers and might prove a nuisance to the garrisons of the three towns it connected. However, first we would deal with the main line.

As soon as it was dark, we went up to an isolated farmhouse and asked for food and information. Our method of approaching these suspicious peasants was always the same. We would choose a farm which had no telephone and was far enough away from other buildings for it to be difficult for a traitor to give us away. Then, Jean-Paul would go alone to the house, knock on the door, see if there were any enemy about and ask for us to be fed. At first he was always distrusted because the peasants feared a Gestapo trick. Then he would produce the letter which I had been given for my advance reconnaissance, but never used. It was written in French and in English and signed by General Koenig himself, Commander of all the Forces Françaises d'Intérieur. It asked that loyal Frenchmen give us all possible assistance and guaranteed our bona fides being countersigned by myself. Mine was No. 11. It was a pity that I never retrieved it from Jean-Paul; it would have been a marvellous souvenir.

After they had seen the letter and we had been called forward out of the shadows, the French would become less suspicious, though still a bit wary. Our next move was to talk as much as we could among ourselves in English, so that they would realise that the language we were speaking was certainly not German. I would try out my best French, in which my appalling English accent stood me in good stead. Next we would show them our weapons, which they could see for themselves were of British or American design. We also made a point of being as clean, well-shaven and smart as the situation permitted.

The final step in establishing friendly relations would come when I pulled out my miniature of Margot and passed it round to be admired. Margot was of a type much admired by the French and the portrait was well done and very beautiful. Scores of rough, toil-stained hands passed that miniature round with a tender care and many were the compliments showered upon it. It was always the passport to their friendship.

Then we would sit around the table and a meal of ham, eggs and good brown bread would be served to us with fresh milk or watered wine. Swag Jemson always waited until about the end of the meal to burst into French. He would speak slowly and ponderously with a Lancashire accent that could be cut with a knife.

'Après la guerre finie . . . ' Then he would forget the rest and grin all over his face at the resultant applause. It became a part of the approved ritual. I still wonder how the sentence was meant to end, but I never did find out.

After we were all replete, Jean-Paul would make excuses for us and we would leave regretfully, begging the good folk not to tell their neighbours that they had been visited by British parachutists. This, of course, was asking too much of human nature, for soon the whole countryside was buzzing with rumours of our presence, though I do not believe that any of them gave us away to the Hun. As a precaution, however, we always concocted a story for our hosts which suggested that we would be leaving by a route quite different from that which we intended to follow.

We offered to pay for any food that we consumed but this was always refused and we seemed to leave friends wherever we went. Only once were we turned away from the door by an old lady, because all the men of the farm were working in the fields.

On the night of 13/14 July, after we had finished our meal, we moved down to the wood where we had dumped our explosive. Leaving Swag and Grady there with all the kit that we did not require, Jean-Paul and I walked down to the bridges and made a recce for the next night's work. We found a good spot on the line not far from the level-crossing where we hoped that a derailed train would cut up both tracks and the carriages would get whipped over the embankment into the canal. We tried to find alternative means of crossing the canal, for it was 100 feet across and very deep, but found that the lock gates had been destroyed by the Maquis and there was no possible way across except by the bridge.

We then returned to the wood below Vigny and spent the rest of a cold night trying to sleep on the hard ground, curled up in our Dennison smocks. I did not find this altogether satisfactory.

At dawn we found that our thicket was in a rather exposed position, so we moved into a thicker wood a bit further back from the road. There we prepared breakfast and spent most of the morning sleeping in the sun.

In the afternoon, Jean-Paul went down to the house where our guide had lived and the rest prepared the explosives for that night.

We removed all the time-pencils from the Lewis bombs and strung them out in pairs along a piece of detonating Cordtex, so that they were ready to lay along the lines, two to a sleeper. We reckoned that this would blow about fifteen yards of track, with enough left over to put a small charge on the other track, in case it was not uprooted by the wrecked engine. This took up about half our explosive.

To initiate the charge we had two alternative methods. We had a four-hour time-pencil, which would blow the whole charge at about dawn if no trains had passed, and we had fog-signals. The saboteur's fog-signal, just like the commercial railway fog-signal, is activated by the train passing over it. It differs, however, in being connected to a detonator so that the flame from the fog-signal detonates the Cordtex and sets off the charge at the moment that the engine passes over it. The fog-signal has this unfortunate disadvantage. A train fitted with a small scoop can flick it off the line without exploding it. To overcome this drawback we fitted instantaneous detonators to a couple of hand-grenades and connected them up to our charges, arranging to fasten them under the rails by a piece of adhesive tape to the fog-signals on top. In this way the lever of the grenade was pressed against the rail. Thus, when the safety pin was removed, there was nothing to prevent the lever flying up and exploding the grenade, except the piece of tape holding it tight against the rail. Now the charge could be set off either by the normal pressure of the engine on the fog-signal, or by the flick of the scoop breaking the adhesive tape and allowing the grenade to explode. This had the additional advantage that if the charges were spotted before dawn by a railway patrol, the grenades acted as a very convenient booby-trap if anyone tried to remove the fog-signals.

While we were thus engaged in completing our neat little instruments of destruction, Jean-Paul returned. He had been successful in contacting our friend and had learned that the Germans were passing many troop-trains down this length of line, but that the last time the line had been blown there had been severe reprisals on the civilian population. I toyed with the idea of leaving a trademark to show conclusively that it was army work, but in the end I decided against it for fear it was used to track us down with dogs.

Anyway, the lad had agreed to go round by the level-crossings in the morning and see what damage we had done. He would meet us the next night in the village of En Vèvre and was coming back with us to Montsauche.

The rest of the evening was spent sitting around our little fire, chatting. Far away in the woods we heard the sound of a rifle. It was a German officer shooting game. The boys were all for kidnapping him but we did not want to disclose our position prematurely.

I remember that we talked about music and the moral justification for blowing a trainload of troops to Kingdom Come. Our language was peculiarly bilingual. Jean-Paul had blossomed out into a veritable linguist, speaking English almost as well as Georges. Grady and I spoke very slowly, so as to be well understood, and occasionally, when we did not seem to be getting our meaning quite clear, we broke into French, and became utterly unintelligible. Only Jemson seemed unable to get his ideas over very well, but after he had had his leg pulled unmercifully about his habit of punctuating every other word with a swearword, he too began to be understood. Indeed, by the time we finished the operation, Jemson had stopped blaspheming, Jean-Paul was speaking excellent English and I was swearing like a trooper.

The sun set at last and we moved down to the cache where we had originally left the explosives. There we made a dump of the explosive that we were not requiring that night, of our extra clothing, and of a bottle of wine that Jean-Paul had brought back from our friend the guide. We then set off to seek a dinner.

It was the night of 14 July – the great French national *fête*. The farm at which we stopped was just finishing its annual feast, but there was plenty left for us to share. We had a thick vegetable soup, with cabbage swimming in it. There was omelette and mutton and ham. There was a dish that I have never had any-where else, of new potatoes served in their jackets and eaten hot with a thin runny cream cheese: a really excellent mixture. We ended up with jam, a great treat, not spread on bread but eaten like a sweet with a spoon. Throughout the meal we had more wine than usual and to top it off we were given a swig of Marc which burnt our throats but warmed our innards.

At last, in a most merry frame of mind, almost singing as we walked, we set off down the road to the bridges.

As we approached the Bourbince bridge, we found a house with no blackout. Its windows were all ablaze and it was very difficult to pass by it without being silhouetted against the light.

We arrived at the bridge without trouble and crossed it safely. At the end of the causeway, at the spot where our road met the towpath, I left Swag Jemson in the right-hand ditch, his Bren-gun covering the open canal bridge. His orders were quite clear.

'You are to lie there,' I said. 'Whatever happens. And you are not to fire until someone else fires, even if Hitler at the head of a Panzer Division comes marching across this bridge. If there are enemy about, we will lie doggo until they have passed. If we are spotted, we'll make our way down to the bridge, and shout when we want to cross. We will run across along the left-hand rail and you can shoot anyone who tries to follow us. If anything goes wrong, we'll meet back in the Bois de Clessy.'

With that, I left Swag to his lonely vigil. The rest of us crossed the bridge carefully and turned off the road to the left in the field between the canal and the embankment along which the lines ran. I wanted particularly to avoid the small house by the railway crossing, as I had been warned that a collaborator lived there. Making as little noise as possible, we climbed up the embankment in a long steep line, at a place where trees grew thickly between the railway and the canal. At the top, we crept quietly under the signal wire, which ran along the side of the line, but could not help touching it occasionally. Each time we caught it, it seemed to twang like a crack of doom.

We walked quickly and noiselessly along the line as far as the spot that Jean-Paul and I had chosen for our blow. I took off my rucksack and we lifted out the long string of Cordtex with the Lewis bombs dangling from it like some hideous fruit on a fantastic vine.

Jean-Paul at once set to work forcing the plastic 4 lb slabs firmly into position between the sleeper-ties and the body of the rails, while Grady concentrated on the intricate task of setting up our ingenious little contrivance with the grenades. It only needed one false move on Grady's part and the whole operation would have ended then and there with one big bang, but Grady knew his job.

I contented myself with running the small charge across to the other set of rails, where I wedged the plastic well in between the ends of the rails and the fishplates. After this I attached the time-pencil and came back to help Jean-Paul finish his job.

Suddenly Jean-Paul held his finger to his lips. 'Attention! Did you hear that?' he whispered. I had heard nothing but the sluggish rippling of the canal water, and the sigh of the wind in the trees. I listened carefully, but not an unnatural sound broke the stillness.

'Rien!' he remarked, and we continued with our deadly work.

Soon we were finished. I picked up the now empty rucksack and slipped it on. I forgot the mess-tin in which we had carried the fog-signals for safety and left it lying beside the track. I walked over to the time-pencil and waited for Grady to finish.

'OK!' he said in a low voice, straightening up from his task. 'Carry on,' I replied. Easing the pins out of the grenades, he walked back along the track to join Jean-Paul. I pulled the pin out of the time-pencil and crushed the little phial of acid with my teeth. In four hour's time that pencil would complete our work if nothing else had.

I joined the others and we walked back slowly along the permanent way.

'Très bien!' said Jean-Paul, and smiling broadly in the dim light, we shook hands.

Not wanting to make more noise than necessary, we kept straight on along the embankment, clearly outlined against the sky, until we were opposite the field beside the bridge. Then, stepping over the wire, we slid quietly down the gravel slope to the level of the field.

'Did you remember my mess-tin?' asked Grady.

'Damn! I forgot!'

'OK, I'll get it,' he replied, and disappearing behind the trees, he began the slow ascent of the embankment.

Minutes passed. We heard the pad of his feet as he came back along the top of the embankment. We saw him clearly silhouetted, the mess-tin swinging by the handle in his left hand. He stepped over the wire....

In front of us, with a vicious rattle, three Schmeissers opened a devastating fire. Angry hornets whipped by my head. Three dark shapes in the blackness along the canal bank became twinkling lights of stabbing fire. Grady gasped suddenly and came tumbling down the embankment between us.

I turned to Jean-Paul and murmured, 'I'm awfully sorry, old chap!' There really did not seem much else to say.

CHAPTER XV

Dispersed

Exactly why the German commander opened fire when he did, I have never been able to decide. On one side of the bridge he had two Spandaus, on the other he had three Schmeissers. If we had been in the middle of that long open bridge, we would not have stood a chance. But hold his fire he could not, and at least we knew where we stood. All I can think is that having seen the three of us descend the embankment and waited for us to appear on the bridge, he failed to see Grady go back for the mess-tin. By the time Grady reappeared, the German thought that we must be creeping away from the scene of the crime by another route, and believing that he had now missed us irrevocably, he decided to make sure of getting Grady.

Whatever his motives, however, our situation was by no means cheerful. Only ten yards away, between us and the only way back to our own side of the canal, were at least three Germans with automatic weapons, and between us and them was the doubtful cover of a few tall sunflowers. It was definitely unhealthy.

As the first burst of enemy fire rang out, we heard Jemson come into action and soon the sky was lit with the flickering fires of red and green tracer. But with bursts of fire coming from all directions and the occasional crash of bursting grenade, everything was far too confused for us to gather anything like a reasonable picture.

My first reaction was to unsling my carbine and blaze back at the enemy. I struggled to get it off my back but for some unaccountable reason it appeared to have stuck. I lay on my back cursing silently and trying to understand the babble of urgent French which Jean-Paul was whispering in my direction. I couldn't follow a word he said and replied in English, which at this moment of crisis was equally unintelligible to him.

At last I found the cause of my difficulty with the carbine. I had put the rucksack on over the top of it and naturally could not pull it round. By the time I had wriggled out of the rucksack and got at my carbine, another thought had hit me. I was damned if those confounded Jerries were going to undo all our good work. So, dropping the carbine beside the rucksack, I drew a grenade and wriggled off into the undergrowth beside the embankment. As soon as I was reasonably out of sight of the Boche, I scrambled up to the top and paused for a second on the edge of the track.

It was the first and only really brave thing I have ever done, because I honestly expected to be met with a hail of bullets as soon as I appeared on the track. Doubled up, I darted across the lines to where our handiwork was still clearly visible, the Cordtex gleaming whitely through the dark. Not a shot came in my direction, though all along the line of the canal the firing never diminished.

In my pocket I had a miner's igniter with a thirty-second fuse. It was a matter of moments to knot it into the system. I pulled the pin and let it go, there was a most satisfactory fizzing noise and I knew the time had come to move quickly. I moved!

Down the embankment I charged, as though my boots were winged. Along the bottom I dashed, as far as I dared. Then, barely with a second to spare, I flung myself flat on my face, cupped my hands over my ears, opened my mouth against the blast and waited.

BLAAAM! It was the loudest single noise I have ever heard. I had a momentary vision of the whole top of the embankment glowing and pieces of molten metal flying across the sky, then a silence fell.

I rose gingerly to my feet. I was untouched. At that moment the pieces of rail, sleeper and gravel bedding started to come down again, and I was prostrate once more.

The next time I got to my feet all was well. I began to ascend the embankment again. Almost at once I ran straight into a stout barbed-wire fence. I am not entirely sure how I came to pass through it on the way down. I can only imagine I simply roared through in a sort of power-dive.

On top of the embankment I passed through the clouds of powder-smoke. I could see the fishplates wrenched apart and the lines badly bent on the near track, while a great stretch of the further track had altogether disappeared.

On the other side of the embankment, I found Jean-Paul and Grady where I had left them. A plan was beginning to form in my mind.

'I'll stay here,' I whispered, 'and make as much noise as I can. You two creep away to the left and see if you can get across the canal.'

'I cannot swim,' announced Jean-Paul distinctly.

'I'm hit,' said Grady, and for the first time I realised that the first burst had not been wasted on the empty air. This explained why Grady had not at once replied with the Tommy-gun. Now we were in a fix.

Not a sound had come from the enemy, so short a distance from us across the sunflowers, but sporadic firing on the other side of the canal showed that Jemson was still in action and diverting the attention of the enemy.

'Why do you not go to the help of Jemson?' asked Jean-Paul, and the advice seemed good.

'OK,' I said. 'I'll make as much noise as I can when I move away so that they think that we have all left. Then I will cross the canal, join Jemson and clear the bridge. As soon as it's all clear I shall whistle, and you can come across.' It was an ambitious programme. I didn't know if it would work.

I picked up Grady's Tommy-gun and pocketed a couple of magazines; then, slinging it on my back, I set off with my carbine in my hands. As soon as I was screened from the enemy by the trees, I began to make as much noise as I could, scuffling my feet and breaking branches as I went. I wanted to draw as much attention as possible to my movements, so I cocked my carbine and pressed the trigger. There was a faint click. I recocked, hearing the ejected shell tumble to the ground. I squeezed the trigger once more: another click. The firing pin was broken.

I unslung the Tommy-gun and tried again. This time the safety catch was on. There are three small levers on the body of a Tommy-gun. One is the single shot-automatic fire switch, one changes the magazines and one is the safety catch. I pressed a lever and the magazine fell out. It was not my lucky night.

After I had stumbled along about fifty yards, I came to a culvert beneath the embankment. A deep stream was surging through it and I saw a good chance to get down through the trees to the canal without being seen or heard. I left my now useless carbine well-hidden beside the culvert. Shoving a new magazine into the Tommy-gun, I lowered myself into the water.

It was waist-deep and after a few paces I came to a small regulating lock, where I had to submerge completely to get past. Now, step by step, as noiselessly as the movement of the water itself, I followed the stream towards the bank of the canal. I was soon vastly disappointed. Guttural voices and a sudden rattle of rifle fire showed an enemy position astride the mouth of the stream. They were firing away from me across the canal, but almost immobilised as I was in the water, I did not feel like trying conclusions with them.

Carefully, I retraced my steps to the culvert. Bending double, I pushed on under the embankment and gingerly emerged on the other side. No one was about. Here at last was an ideal way of evacuating the wounded man. I returned through the culvert and went back to the spot where I had left Grady. No one was in sight. I called softly. There was no answer. Where had they gone? Had they been captured? I didn't know.

All I could do was to continue with the original plan, but it was evident that I must take a wider sweep if I was to avoid the enemy positions.

Back I went through the culvert. Westward I headed, parallel with the railway, until I came to a place where the embankment had dropped until the line was running level with the ground. Here I nipped swiftly back across the lines on to the canal side.

Somewhere I remembered reading about people swimming in their clothes who carried their boots tied round their neck; so I took off my boots, and making my cautious way through the undergrowth, came out on the bank of the canal.

It was useless, I knew, to look for boats or crossing places. Jean-Paul and I had exhausted those possibilities last night. The canal looked very wide and sinister in the light of the pale moon, which was now beginning to illuminate the scene. I am not a good swimmer and I knew that fully clothed and weighed down as I was, I would not be able to cross unaided. I scarcely knew what to try next.

All along the banks of the canal, tall saplings grew in regimented rows. I took out my SOE knife with its small hacksaw blade to cut one down. It was like tackling iron bars with a nailfile. In a few moments I realised that it was a hopeless task. In despair I rested against another tree. It gave beneath my weight. I turned and seized it. Sure enough, it rocked to my push. It was dead. Hope rose anew, and I began to work the sapling backward and forward feverishly. In a matter of moments I had uprooted it. Now I felt that I had a chance.

I remembered that as a Boy Scout, one of the uses for the scout-stave was to help when swimming. With the rough diagram from the old scout notebook in the back of my mind, I dragged the sapling into the water, slung the Tommy-gun about my neck and lowered myself into the canal.

Even at the edge, the water came to my waist and within two paces I was out of my depth. At first, I expected momentarily to hear the crack of a rifle close behind me and to see little fountains of water fly up around me, but soon I was in such real danger from drowning that I had no time to torment myself with mere fancies.

I clasped the tree between my hands. It could not bear my weight but by moving it with a circular motion through the water, and kicking hard with my legs, I found that I got some measure of support and made fair progress. Soon, however, my clothes became thoroughly waterlogged and started to drag me down. Around the middle, I knew that it was either me or the Tommy-gun, and with a tremendous effort I forced it off my neck and let it go.

This struggle left me feeling very weak and with a good mouthful of water, but my log bore me up and I carried on. The bank seemed as far off as ever and my dead sapling was itself rapidly becoming soggy. I kept thinking, 'I'm damned if I'm going to escape being shot by the Boche, just to go and drown myself.' Then I started to pray. They weren't very long prayers but they were mighty fervent. I could feel myself getting weaker and the log was now more of a hindrance than a help. The bank was about ten feet away. I let go of the tree. I struck out with all my strength and felt myself sinking. Then my feet touched muddy bottom. I kicked out hard and found myself clutching the grass of the bank. I stumbled across the towpath, flopped through the bushes that lined it, fell down the steep, grassy causeway into the marshland below the canal and passed out.

Just how long I remained unconscious, I don't know. Probably a short while, for I was not chilled when I awoke. As soon as I had come fully to my senses, I emptied my boots and put them on. The bright person who had written about tying the boots around his neck can never have tried it. It had worked well enough for the first half of the journey but as soon as I began to make heavy weather of it, the boots filled and nearly had me under.

As soon as I was ready, I began to make my way gingerly through the water-meadows to where I had left Jemson. I had no weapons now except my .22 automatic and one grenade. Neither of these were likely to have been improved by their recent immersion. When I reached the corner of the marsh, where embankments rose steeply to the towpath and to the road by which we had come, I scrambled up and looked for Jemson in the ditch where I had left him. He was gone.

I walked forward as near the bridge as I could, still keeping in the shadows, and whistled. I heard someone moving about on the far bank, and whistled again. I whistled a third time very loudly and nothing answered me. In an awful instant, it dawned on me that the men across the bridge must be the enemy. It seemed that the moment had come to break off the engagement.

Behind me I heard noises on the Bourbince bridge and seeing no reason why Jemson should be there, I concluded that it was the enemy and quickly dropped down off the causeway into the friendly marsh. I had had enough of skylines for one night.

I made a wide detour, avoiding the bridge, and waded the Bourbince which was almost shoulder-deep in the middle, before setting off across country, guided by the stars.

Not long after I left the Bourbince, I was reminded that I was not the only human abroad that night by the unmistakable crashings of a man in a fence away to my right. I hit the road up to Vigny close by an important fork. The dew was beginning to drip off the trees and I thought that I heard a German patrol on the fork itself. I was too tired, however, to make any more detours and decided that capture was preferable to more violent exertion. Fortunately the patrol turned out to be a cow and I carried on, tramping straight up the Vigny road.

Back at the rendezvous, where the explosive was dumped, I hoped to find Grady or Jemson, but there was no sign of either, so I collected the wine and continued my march up to the Bois de Clessy. As I walked, I could not help feeling that there had been treachery somewhere. How was it that a patrol should have been waiting for us at just the right place and the right time? I began to suspect our erstwhile guide.

When at last, just as dawn was breaking, I got back to our rendezvous, I was distressed to find no one there. There was nothing that I could do about it so I prepared to go to bed. In case we had been betrayed, or on the off-chance that some of the boys had been caught and tortured, I collected my bedding, a few biscuits and some chocolate, and moved with them deeper into the wood.

By the time I had finished it was quite light. I stripped off my soaking clothes, wrung them out and hung them up to dry. I crept naked into my sleeping-bag and nibbled my meagre repast. My thoughts as I fell asleep were not very happy ones. This was my first operation and I had lost my entire patrol. There were still two days before the jeep would come to fetch us. The outlook was murky.

CHAPTER XVI

Reunited

When I awoke, I thought that a battalion of tanks was passing along the track. The whole world seemed to be shaking. As I pulled myself together I realised there was no noise, yet the ground on which I lay appeared to be trembling violently. At last, fully awake, I concluded that it was neither earth nor elements that were shivering, only me. It was 9 o'clock and I was bitterly cold.

I got up to find the sun shining brightly and about to climb above the surrounding trees. My clothes were still soaking, however, so I ran about to get warm. After a time I brewed some tea, ate a bit more chocolate and biscuits and bathed in the stream. I found to my annoyance that the level of the water was much lower than when we arrived, and little rivulets were barely trickling from pool to pool.

I had scarcely finished my toilet and was still stark naked, when a noise from the old campsite attracted my attention. I picked up my .22 and grenade before moving cautiously towards the sound. There, coming through the trees towards me, was a smart figure in an aged macintosh. It was Jean-Paul. I could have kissed him.

After shaking hands frenziedly, we pieced our stories together. His was not a long one. Soon after I had left, he had taken advantage of a moment when the enemy's attention appeared to be somewhat distracted, presumably by Jemson's efforts around the bridge, to slip back into the undergrowth near the level-crossing. That was why I was unable to find him when I returned from the culvert. Shortly afterwards he had taken another chance and nipped smartly over the railway line and into the open fields beyond. He had found it difficult helping Grady, who had taken one heavy bullet through the arm, breaking the bone, and another so close to his shoulder that it cut the lanyard he was wearing. After all our exertions, coupled to the shock of being wounded, Grady was just about all in, while noises on the *route nationale* and shots to the south made them realise that although they had evaded their immediate enemies, they were still surrounded.

After a time, it was evident that Grady could go no further and so, making him as comfortable as he could, Jean-Paul had made his way to a farm close to the *route nationale*, woken the farmer, explained the situation and been promised help. Having shown the farmer where Grady was lying, Jean-Paul had spent the rest of the night in a barn, and as soon as it was light had made his way down the *route nationale* as far as Digoin, where he had donned his civilian clothes to cross that bridge, quite openly. However, to avoid suspicion, he had to leave his carbine behind. He had taken the opportunity, as he trudged down the highway of getting a good look at one of the new airstrips close by. It was all more useful data for our report.

Scarcely had we finished comparing notes, before a further crashing in the undergrowth heralded the return of Swag. It was difficult to follow his story, as he had no great gift for expressing himself, but bit by bit we pieced it together.

In accordance with his orders, he had remained lying quietly in his ditch, until all of a sudden he was startled by a dark shadow flitting across the road in front of him. Soon he saw more shadows and heard low, gruff whispers from close at hand. He was convinced that these troops had been first-class men and we thought that they were probably good front-line troops passing through on their way back to Germany and providing their own protection along the route. Anyway, two things were certain, they were wearing felt-soled stalking boots, and unlike most German troops who fought noisily, these men worked in complete silence.

Swag knew his orders well enough and while a whole German platoon took up their positions around him, he lay still and never uttered a sound. The German officer placed one of his Spandaus in the other ditch just opposite Jemson and a second Spandau on the towpath just to his right. More troops took up their position on the Bourbince bridge and, as we already know, there were patrols on the other bank of the canal and along the *route nationale*.

For a few moments all had been quiet and then, as Grady came over the embankment, all hell was let loose. Immediately the first shot was fired, Jemson had risen out of his ditch and, firing his Bren from the shoulder, had sprayed the Spandau team across the road. That gun had not fired again and the gun to his right could not be brought to bear on him, so unexpected was the direction of this new attack. However, as Jemson seized his Bren and a couple of magazines to roll down into the low ground between the canal and the Bourbince, two grenades were flung at him. The first hit him in the back, but fortunately failed to explode, the second burst in the bank just above his head, but without touching him.

Now for an hour and a half, with the advantage of the low ground to silhouette his enemies, Jemson fought alone. He used all the ammunition from his Bren, firing in short bursts, and single-shot. He fired the magazine of his Colt. He so frightened and confused Jerry that for most of the time they were fighting among themselves. It was undoubtedly this brilliant diversion of Jemson's which allowed us to get away unfollowed and almost unscathed. How many casualties the enemy suffered we never learned, but from the volume of fire that he put up, he must have been badly shaken, and certainly two or three men were hit, though Jemson reckoned it was probably more.

When he had exhausted all his ammunition, Jemson thought that the time had come to call it a day. Knowing that the Bourbince bridge was held, he had the gravest doubts of his ability to get away, so, determined that his escape money should not fall as loot into the hands of any Germans, he buried it. He stripped his Bren-gun and threw the pieces away as far as he could in all directions. Then, wading the river, he made his way back towards the rendezvous. I must have only just missed him in the low ground by the Bourbince, for almost certainly it was he that I had heard crashing through the fences as I got away.

I must have made much faster time up the road than he did, for by the time that he reached the rendezvous I was asleep in my new location and he did not see me. Unable to find anyone in the Bois de Clessy, Swag had gone back to our dump near Vigny. Finding nobody there, he had slept a while in a ditch and now, carrying the rucksack, with the remnants of our explosive, he returned to the camp.

Our rejoicings were unbounded. We opened some of our precious tins of compo food for a really hearty breakfast and slept throughout the day. That evening, after another meal — for we did not want to risk approaching farms that night — Jean-Paul and I went down to the crossroads in the village where we had agreed to meet our erstwhile guide. I suspected some trickery and we did not approach the rendezvous but lay up in the fields, watching. At the stroke of 11.00, by which time the lad ought to have arrived, we left and returned to the camp for a good night's sleep.

Next morning, though running very short of food, we did not dare to light fires in case our smoke gave us away. Our solid methylated spirits for brewing tea was by now used up and we found that our only cooking material consisted of small pieces of judiciously applied Lewis bomb. Water, too, was now presenting a problem. There had been no rain since we arrived in the area and the sun was extraordinarily hot. Our stream had dried up completely and nothing remained except stagnant pools. We carried small sterilising tablets but when by the end of the day the only pool left was the one in which we normally washed, nothing could disguise the taste of soap.

During the morning Jean-Paul, convinced that the young Frenchman was not after all a traitor, went down towards Digoin to contact him. They returned about mid-day, bringing a little bread and cheese. The lad had not known anything about our night battle and had only been five minutes late at the rendezvous, but by that time we had gone. He brought his bicycle with him and in the afternoon he went down to the scene of the fight to survey the damage and try to bring back Swag's Bren-gun.

We were very badly off for weapons, having only two Colts, two grenades and my .22 automatic between us. Swag and I manufactured four makeshift grenades out of empty food tins, stones, Lewis bombs and miners' igniters.

In the early afternoon we heard a horse and trap going up the lane past our camp. It stopped. We heard voices and someone whistling 'Sur le Pont d'Avignon'. We went along to investigate. Driving the trap was a most attractive little French girl, very pretty in a green jumper and rough peasant's skirt. With her was one of the most villainous looking Frenchmen I have ever seen. He was dark and sinister, with a drooping black moustache and two days' growth of beard. He was dressed in filthy torn trousers, which had once been striped, and a loose black blouse. On his head he wore an oily black cap and his arm was in a rough sling. As he came nearer, he grinned broadly. It was Grady.

His story was as exciting as any. He had been left in the fields the entire day after the fight, carefully concealed in a ditch and fed as regularly as was safe by the peasants. After nightfall he had been brought into the farm buildings, made as comfortable as possible, and when it was quite dark, taken to the local *curé*, who had set the broken bone, bound up the wound and lent Grady some of the civilian clothes that he was now wearing. Grady spent the rest of the night at the farm, where the peasants turned out to be Communists and Resistance members of long standing. They had been very active in the RAF organisation for getting escaping airmen over the Vichy frontier and were very pleased to give us any assistance that they could.

That morning they had harnessed the pony trap, driven Grady as far as the approach to the Bourbince and canal bridges, and had then dropped him. The girl then drove across and waited out of sight on the other side. As Grady crossed the railway, he had a good view of the workmen repairing the line and a troop-train of German soldiers had clanked slowly past as he stood at the level-crossings. He was so close that he could pick out the insignia on their tunics. He had spat expressively in the dust and scowled at them as they rumbled through. When they had gone, he walked on, rejoining his fair assistant a few hundred yards down the road, and being brought by her right up to our camp.

Grady gave us a very accurate description of the disruption that we had caused. Throughout the night of the blowing no trains had passed, and he had heard the hootings and clankings as they piled up behind one another and then shunted away. It was not until 8 o'clock in the morning that the breakdown train arrived. At once a temporary track had been thrown across the 30-foot gap in the near line, without even replacing the shattered sleepers, and by mid-day the trains were able to creep very slowly but regularly across. For the next two days all traffic used the temporary rails, while gangs worked on repairing the wrecked fishplates and broken tie-rods of the other track. Up to the time that Grady crossed over, only the emergency line was in use. It must have been a week before the situation was normal again.

Grady's return had not materially eased our weapons' situation, as neither Grady nor the peasant lass had felt justified in taking the risk of passing the workmen, or encountering a German patrol while carrying arms. So both Grady's Colt and Jean-Paul's carbine had to be left behind. However, that afternoon we made a determined effort to find Jemson's Bren, sending our guide (whom I will call Gustaf, as I cannot remember his proper name) to see if he could find it – but he had no success.

That day was a bad one. The sun was very hot, and our camp, now set among low bushes, received little shade. Water was terribly short and Grady was suffering considerably from his wound. Also, we were in constant fear of pursuit. Every jingle of horses along the road, every breath of wind through the silent trees, led us to expect a merciless enemy tracking us to our lair. We knew that the Germans had dogs and we knew that there was plenty of our kit left at the scene of the ambush with which they could give the brutes the scent. We felt hunted. We were hungry. We sweltered in the sun. The loss of Grady and the shortage of arms forced us to abandon the idea of destroying the tramway. There was nothing to do but sit and think, and our thoughts were not pleasant. We dared not even console ourselves with the wireless in case its small sound might cover movements of the enemy and betray our position.

At last the sun sank and the air began to cool. At dusk we struck camp and as darkness fell we moved our kit out on to the track. In two journeys we carted all our stuff half a mile back along the road towards Clessy where, at a small fork in the track, we found a convenient shelter among the trees. Here we were close to a large stagnant lake which could provide us with brackish water. At about 11.30 Jemson and I set out for the cross-roads at Clessy to make sure of contacting the jeep and guiding it to our new RV. Jean-Paul and Gustaf stayed with Grady and the kit.

As Swag and I left the Bois de Clessy, we came across a small group of cottages. From the windows of the first of these came long fingers of light. Both of us had vivid memories of the light that had silhouetted us on our way to the bridges on that fateful evening of 14 July, and we had wondered afterwards if it had somehow been connected with our ambush. Now the same fears assailed us. Was this light left burning deliberately to show up any movement out of the Bois de Clessy along this little track? We crouched in the ditch, listening, watching, wondering.

I began to creep slowly forward along the ditch, but stopped suddenly as I felt Swag's hand grip my legs. Behind us I heard the soft patter of feet. I sank into the depths of the ditch. What could this be? Then it came. A man in white gym vest and running shorts. A large man wearing training shoes which padded stealthily on the dust of the track. A man moving with the light step and easy stride of an athlete, not the noisy flat-foot rush of fear.

We crouched in silence. The man loped past. Whether or not he saw us in the dim light of the fading afterglow, I do not know. He stopped at the hut of the lighted window and lithely vaulted the little wooden gate. He opened the big door without knocking. Was he an innocent athlete? Was he a spy? Was this a trap? We did not stay to see. Quickly and quietly, we retraced our steps to the edge of the Bois and making a wide detour by the edge of the wood and the open fields we at last came out on the more important road just short of the Clessy crossroads.

The crossroads, which we reached about 12.30, were set about with houses but to the left of the small road up which we had come there was a clump of tall trees, while in the angle between our road and the second-class road towards Paray there was a wide verge of grass running up to a thick-set hedge. Against the background of this hedge and sheltered in some small measure by a clump of nettles, we sat down to await the jeep.

For protection we had Swag's Colt, my automatic, two home-made bombs and one Mills' grenade. For signalling we had neither torch nor matches. We would have to make do with our voices.

It was 1 o'clock and Swag was sleeping while I watched, when suddenly, with a swish of wheels and a murmur of low voices, a bicycle patrol came whirring up the road from the direction of Gueugnon and turned down the road towards our rendezvous. So close to us did they pass that I could clearly see the outline of the rifles slung across their backs, silhouetted against the sky. It was a night black as pitch, relieved only by the light of the misted stars. As swiftly as they had come, the cyclists were gone and only the sudden barking of the dogs at the cottages behind me remained to show us that it was not all a fantastic dream. Swag was awake beside me in an instant and scarcely were we both alert behind our nettles before a second patrol swept down on the crossroads. Some of the men appeared to dismount and take up position covering the road but it was too dark to see clearly. A third patrol whirled through. Swag gripped a home-made bomb and, swearing vindictively, prepared to sling it at the passing patrol. I grabbed his hand and restrained him, fiercely whispering that our best chance lay in staying still.

Now there was a lull. The silence was broken only by the creaking of the trees, the drip of dew, the sound of stealthy movements on the road and the staccato barks from the dogs of every farm around. Then in the distance to the north came the rumble of a car's engine. We held our breath. If this was the jeep, something had got to be done and done quickly, or we would lose our only means of retreat to the fastnesses of the Morvan.

Nearer it came and nearer. I could see the headlights illuminating the trees and hedges. The note of the engine was unfamiliar. Urgently I whispered to Swag, 'Is that a jeep?'

'I don't think so, sir,' came the reassuring reply.

A pause as the car drew nearer and the engine began to labour on the last little incline up the crossroads.

'No,' he repeated with certainty. 'No, that's not a jeep!'

I drew a sigh of relief. But not for long. As the car came into view, the headlights fell full upon us. I held my breath and we cowered into the hedge, trying as far as possible to conceal the glistening whiteness of our hands and faces.

As the car reached the crossroad, the lights swerved away and shone straight down the road. But the vehicle was halted within a few yards of us. There was a muffled consultation. The car backed down the road towards Paray, so that the headlights illuminated the whole crossroad. Then the lights were switched off. This looked as though a deliberate trap was being set for the jeep. I began once more to fear that Gustaf had betrayed us. Only he could have known that the jeep must pass this way tonight. The ambush was being carefully and accurately prepared.

In the next short lull, I took the opportunity to tell Swag to black his hands with the mud of the hedgerow and keep his face hidden. I blacked my own hands and hung my camouflaged veil across my face. In a few moments a car came along the road from the direction of Gueugnon. It drew level with the crossroads before the headlights of the other car flicked on suddenly. That seemed to be a signal. The second car stopped and turned straight towards us. We found ourselves squarely in the beam of the headlights, and as the car ran its front wheels into the verge, it stopped. I scarcely dared to breathe. Full in the glare of the lamps, I felt as conspicuous as a nude in Piccadilly on a wet Saturday. My hand restrained the impetuous Jemson, and I found myself praying again.

Then men alighted from the first car, dim figures moving along in a vale of darkness that my eyes could not penetrate. The two parties talked in undertones, so low that I could not pick up the tongue they spoke. The second car appeared to be stuck in the soft earth of the verge, where its front wheels rested. Men appeared suddenly in the bright silhouette of the headlamps, and there was much grunting and heaving as the car was pushed out. My sigh of relief, as the lights turned away from us and down the road towards our camp, must have been almost audible.

First one car, and then the other following closely behind, glided smoothly away from the crossroads. We were left with the uncertain second bicycle patrol and the dripping trees.

How long we lay in our meagre cover, I do not know. The soft splash and creak of the trees might hide the stealthy stirrings of the sentinels. Across the road, in vague relief against a ragged hedge, I was convinced I could see a man whose bayonet glistened in the starlight. Once the door of the house opposite us across the main road opened, and the sounds of sabots, as a man made his way along the village street, echoed oddly in the stillness. After a few moments the clip-clop of the sabots returned and the figure of the man showed dimly in a glimmer of candlelight, as he re-entered his cottage. Then everything was quiet again, except for tiny unidentified sounds and the distant gurgle of a stream.

After a half-hour, I determined to have a showdown. It was useless for us to remain here until the jeep came, uncertain right up to the last moment whether the patrol was still there. Also, I was very doubtful as to whether these nocturnal prowlers were really Germans. I thought it much more likely that they were Maquisards. However, it was known that the Maquis of this area were a wild undisciplined lot; and they had not been informed that British were operating in the vicinity. Thus, in a surprise encounter, we were always likely to be taken as enemy by both Germans and French, and both patrols tended to shoot first and make enquiries afterwards.

Nevertheless, something must be done. So I told Jemson that I would go on to the crossroads, apparently unarmed, with only my automatic well hidden in my clothing. I would keep my hands in the air and see whether or not the road was manned: and if so, by whom. Jemson was to observe what happened to me, to determine the nationality of the patrol and to decide how best to warn the jeep. It was an unsatisfactory procedure but it seemed to be the surest way of learning the truth.

Stealthily I rose from our hiding place. Quietly I crept along the hedgeside away from Jemson. Then, rising to my full height and raising my hands, I walked out on to the road. There was absolute silence. I walked noisily along the road to a figure lying by the kerb. It was a pile of gravel. I walked towards my bayonet-shouldering sentry. It was a petrol pump. I made a complete circuit of the crossroads. It was completely deserted. I began to call out quietly in French. No one answered. I stamped about in the centre of the road. There was no reaction.

'OK,' I said. 'We appear to be alone.'

Jemson loomed out of the shadows. Together we crossed the road. For a short distance we went along the verge in the direction from which we expected the jeep to come. We took up our position in a little courtyard where we were able to see the road and where we had much better cover from view, as well as reasonable cover from fire. I tried to find a rear way out of the yard, while Swag watched the road, but I found the doors into the house behind were locked and the wall was topped by a high wire fence backed by a hedge. There was no rear way out, but now at least we stood a better chance of not being spotted.

After a while we heard noises back on the crossroads. There was the unmistakable clacking of sabots and mumbling voices. Later some more cyclists came past us down the road. It was useless trying to pick out their uniform, but there could be no doubt from their outline that they were armed men.

Noises in the field opposite began to disturb us. There was a rustling there and a movement, impossible to identify. We listened fascinated and began to wonder if we were being watched and followed. In a country occupied by the enemy, where treachery is always a possibility, it is very easy to feed on groundless fears. Every now and then they prove not to be so groundless after all, and this reinforces those fears. In the field opposite, there could be no doubt that there were strange things going on. Suddenly, a big white horse poked its head over the hedge and then, wheeling quickly, it galloped off. Perhaps this explained the sounds that we heard, but what accounted for a frightened horse, galloping round a field at 4 o'clock in the morning? We began to be afraid.

At last the sky began to lighten in the east and I knew that we must get away from the crossroads before the dawn caught us in the unfriendly open. Taking our courage in both hands and half expecting a rain of bullets to greet our emergence, we stepped out on to the road. There was not a sound. The horse was far away across the field. The roads were deserted. We turned north and skirted the village to the east, before turning southward again and heading for our camp. We crossed the second-class road as the half-light brightened into dawn and headed back across country all the way.

I did not know what to expect at our camp. I was aware that the patrols had entered the woods and that they had not re-emerged. I knew that our camp was well hidden and that there was little likelihood of the enemy stumbling upon it in the dark, but I still had no idea where the enemy would be or whether Jean-Paul might not have found it expedient to shift the camp. However, all my fears proved groundless. The camp was where I had left it and they had seen no signs of the enemy all night. But where had the patrols gone? And where was the jeep?

We ate the meagre remnants of our food for breakfast and brewed our last drop of tea. The sun was rising again and its broad light was beating down on that drying mud puddle of a lake. We would be in desperate straits if the jeep did not arrive by nightfall.

Then, on the warming air, the unmistakable note of a jeep engine broke the stillness. It was now 9 o'clock. We ran out of the wood and peered along the leafy avenue to the north. There it was. There, in a smother of brown dust, the jeep bounced towards us. There, grinning behind his goggles, his face caked with dust, was Middleton. There, smiling, his eyes red-rimmed with exposure to the wind and the dirt, was Tom Rennie. There in the back was our relief, Silvo, with Collison, Bass and Edwards. Here was reunion at last.

CHAPTER XVII

Return to Montsauche

The arrival of the jeep eased our food problems a little, but at the same time, we did not like to impose on the new arrivals who presumably would have similar problems of their own before their party was over. I was not very happy, however, about the composition of Corporal Sylvester's patrol. In the first place not one of them spoke a word of French. Moreover, Collison and Bass, who did not like each other, spent the whole time arguing at the top of their voices. We believed that enemy were in the area, which made them a real menace. Also, none of them seemed to have much idea of how to look after themselves in a place where enemy patrols were liable to be encountered. On several occasions we only just stopped the more foolish members of the party from wandering off alone down the main paths in search of water, or amusement. I doubted whether they would last a week.

Rennie had had a bad journey down with them. They had been squabbling all the way and had made an awful hash of the map-reading. They had tended to panic a bit when they were lost and had been thoroughly unsatisfactory passengers. Jean-Paul and I decided that it was imperative at least to get them a guide who could speak a little English. I would have chosen Gustaf, whom Jean-Paul still vouched for completely, in spite of my suspicions. But Jean-Paul pointed out that it was hardly fair on the lad to promise to get him into a Maquis and then leave him to his fate with these incompetents. Accordingly, we set out through the fields to the château east of Clessy, where we hoped to find an influential man to help us.

As we approached the château, we stopped at some outlying cottages and asked the tenants to give us some idea of the character and political leanings of their landlord. It turned out that he was the Baron de Something-or-other and a good man who sympathised with the Resistance, though not actively assisting it. So we crossed the secondary road again and approached the château where we found the baron in his garden. As usual, he was at first mistrustful, but after we had produced Koenig's letter, he said, 'Messieurs, je suis à votre disposition', and gave us what help he could. He was unable to put us in direct contact with any of the Maquis, but promised to lend us one of his men, whom he said was thoroughly reliable, spoke a little English and had been engaged in the task of smuggling British aviators across the frontier.

He also told us that he would get a small quantity of food for us and agreed to contact us at a rendezvous in the Bois de Clessy during the afternoon. We then returned to the new camp.

During the morning, Gustaf made another unsuccessful attempt to find Swag's Bren; but over lunch, with the aid of diagrams, he got a clearer idea of its location and throughout the afternoon tried again.

At about 3 o'clock, an hour late for his appointment, the baron turned up, with only a very little bread, although this was better than nothing. He also brought along the new guide – a tall blonde youth with a long, easy stride and athletic bearing. He was a woodsman, who carried with him as weapons a small hand-axe and a long hunting knife. I took an instinctive liking to him and felt that he should be able to give the Silvo outfit all the help they needed. He knew the whole area very well and he brought us news that a German petrol train, held up by the bottleneck we had created, was spending the night in the goods' yard at Digoin.

This made me think deeply. I still had a good quantity of unused explosive which I wanted to employ as usefully as possible. Dare I try an attack on the petrol train? I studied the map carefully and consulted with the two local men. The limiting factors were the time it would take and the risks involved. It was essential that the jeep return to Montsauche that night. It was already a day overdue and there were other parties to be brought in. If I was to do the job and get back to Montsauche tonight, it meant running the jeep very close in to the target so as not to waste any time, and even then the twin obstacles of river and canal still barred our path to the railway. Above all else, I must not lose the jeep – the only one that Alex had – for if it was lost, not only would it be impossible to send out any more parties, but those already in the field would be hopelessly marooned. Reluctantly, I abandoned the idea of attacking the petrol train and began thinking up an alternative. I suggested to Silvo that an assault on foot might prove profitable.

On the journey down I had noticed that we passed beneath some high-tension electric cables slung on tall pylons. I asked about them and looked at them on the map. They were part of the French grid system, linking the two important industrial towns of Moulins and Montceau-les-Mines. I decided that this was a suitable target and hoped to include a transformer house on the Gueugnon–Digoin road. From the map, I picked out what appeared to be a likely spot and, aided by Jean-Paul's engineering knowledge, we prepared our charges to demolish two pylons, using four two-hour time-pencils. Enough plastic was also primed to wreck the transformer house, using a ten-minute fuse. All we needed now was an accurate reconnaissance and the job could be done on our way home.

It was at this psychological moment that Gustaf returned from his third attempt to find the Bren. This time, wrapped in a dirty rag, strapped beneath the cross-bar of his bike, was a bulky bundle. With tender care he opened it. It was the long-lost Bren. Swag was called for. The gun was returned to him with all due ceremony. He fondled it lovingly. 'Chroist, it's filthy!' was all that he said, and getting out his gun kit, he sat down to clean it.

This great success gave me a new idea, and explaining carefully to Gustaf exactly what I wanted, I dispatched him to make the necessary recce of the pylons, the transformer house and a plausible line of retreat, which I picked from the map.

The rest of the afternoon we tried to sleep but the arguments of the other party and their inanities contrived effectively to keep us awake. At about 7 o'clock, Gustaf returned. He gave me a full description of the position of the pylons, and the setting of the transformer house. Also he pronounced my escape track as entirely suitable. I called the boys together, explained what I had in mind and issued my orders. We had a last small meal before the sun set. We wished the other party goodbye, and good luck, and in the grey twilight we bumped off up the track and away through the silent village of Clessy. No sign nor sound did we see of patrols, either Maquis or German.

It was pitch dark and beginning to rain as we reached the site of the first pylon. This was just beside the road at a spot where the wires ran over a long stretch of wood. The next pylon to the north-east had already been destroyed by the Maquis some time before and replaced by three wooden poles. It was my hope that the fall of this pylon would tear down the makeshift wooden one and my choice of pylons running through the trees should, I felt, make it difficult to replace them temporarily. Only a proper pylon could clear the branches.

I left Rennie and Gustaf to attend to this pylon, while Grady was left on the road to keep watch. With Middleton driving, we turned down the track to the spot where the next pylon ought, according to Gustaf, to have been. It was not there. I dived into the thick wet undergrowth looking for it. I couldn't find it. I struggled about in one direction, Jean-Paul in another. Not a sign of it. We returned to the jeep. Back we went to the pylon where we had left Rennie.

'You all right sir?' he shouted as we drew up. 'I've set off my time-pencil.'

'No,' I replied. 'We can't find the pylon this way. I'm going to follow down the wires!'

'Then for God's sake, be quick sir,' came back his answer. 'My time-pencil is making a most peculiar smell. I think it's faulty!'

Jumping out of the jeep and yelling to Middleton to take the jeep well clear in case the pylons came down prematurely, I blundered into the woods again, followed by Jean-Paul. The rain was now lashing down and it was not very easy to follow those slim lines of wire traced against a murky sky. All the time we knew that behind us a faulty time-pencil might go off at any moment, but somehow we did not think of this.

Suddenly we came upon our missing pylon and set to work laying the charges. We laid 1 lb charges against each of the legs and cross-supports, at an angle to the ground, in such a way that as soon as the supports were cut the whole huge structure would topple sideways. We ran the Cordtex swiftly from charge to charge until all were connected up.

'OK!' said Jean-Paul, doubling back up the track.

'OK!' I replied, biting the ends of the pencil till I heard the phial crack and felt the sting of acid on my tongue. Back I doubled, stumbling out on to the road, hard on Jean-Paul's heels. As we passed Tom Rennie's pylon, we could smell the queer acrid odour of his faulty time-pencil. We shouted for Grady as we ran and were glad to find the whole party assembled around the jeep. In a matter of moments we leapt aboard and began to drive back towards the get-away track that I had picked. In view of the inaccuracy of Gustaf's recce of the pylons, and the possibility of the faulty pencil giving our game away prematurely, I decided to forgo the assault on the transformer house, and we fled with all speed.

The get-away track proved to have been as badly studied as the second pylon. The surface was poor and the heavy rain did not improve it. The night was so dark that it was hopeless to try to follow the track without headlights, but running as it was across open fields, our lights could be seen for miles. On the narrow track we would have had no chance to turn. To add to our difficulties, there were dozens of gates, and on the slippery hills the wheels skidded so hard that we all had to get off the jeep and push. The worst moments came when we had to pass again under the high-tension wires close beside the wooden poles that we were hoping so confidently to drag down with the explosion: and again later, when we found ourselves in the open above the Toulon–Gueugnon road and saw a car pass along beneath us. At length we ran out on to the main road and the worst of the operation was over. Nevertheless, the nightmare of the return journey lay before us.

We found a good place to cross the Arroux at Vendenesse-sur-Arroux, which proved much safer than Toulon, though we had some bad moments when we saw headlights passing and repassing along the main road and feared that some inquisitive motorised patrol might come along to investigate our own lights.

The return journey was very like the outward run. We were even more heavily loaded, with the extra man and Gustaf's bicycle, while we had the additional problem of looking after Grady and making him as comfortable as we could.

I have four very distinct recollections of that final stage of the operation. The first was when we passed slowly through a sleepy village and were attacked by a big white dog. It seemed enormous as it bounded, barking, out of a farmer's yard and with extraordinary ferocity tore after the car, leaping up and snapping viciously at our dangling legs. I damned near shot the brute but decided against the noise. Luckily it grew tired before it had done us any harm.

The second memory is of a halt we made on a rocky mountain road that was slowly winding its way up into the Haute Morvan. It was a wild scene, with the wind whipping the scudding clouds along the horizon and the rain dying away to a dull drizzle. Below us, the ground fell sheer to a forest of pine. Behind us the shoulders of gaunt rock jutted out to the very edge of the road. Jean-Paul in the front pored over the map, and sitting on the back I admired the stern beauty of the dim scenery. Then suddenly, far below and behind, a ruddy glow lit up the skyline and immediately afterwards a great blue flash reflected to the very clouds. I looked at my watch. It was just two hours after Tom Rennie had set his pencil. It couldn't have been so very faulty after all.

We all watched and waited, looking for another flash. The dull rumble of Rennie's explosion echoed dimly across the distance. Then, in another burst of ruddy splendour, a second mushroom of light brightened the sky. It would be quite some time before they passed power again from Moulins to Montceau.

My third memory is of the awful feeling of trepidation as we approached the level-crossings. It was the fourth time that we had done it. Surely the railway guards must be wise to us by now; yet we passed it without incident. We were lucky, for unknown to us Sergeant Noble had been operating against this very stretch of line in our absence.

Finally, I remember passing through the Maquis Socrate, as the first pink streaks of a rosy dawn began to flush the sky. There we saw Socrate himself, tired and dirty from a night's *parachutage*, just coming in with his men. He told us that three of our boys had stopped in to his camp the night before, footsore and somewhat lost. He had fed them, and now they were sleeping. It turned out to be Nobby Noble's party, so, promising to send a jeep back to collect them, I declined Socrate's offer of a breakfast, and pushed on.

Dawn had fully broken as we bounced up the Maquis track towards the camp. Poor Gustaf nearly burst into tears when, in the last hundred yards, an unpredictable buck of the jeep cannoned us against a tree and irremediably buckled the wheel of his treasured bike. At the spot along the track where our guard watched, we found Alex himself doing his turn. He jumped on the back and I gave him my verbal report.

'I'm afraid we didn't get any aircraft,' I said. 'Grady has been wounded and I have lost one Tommy-gun, one Colt and two carbines!' I waited for his explosion, but I think that from the look on my face he knew that this was not the whole story. Then, over an early breakfast, I prepared a full report and wrote out the salient details for Bill to send back to England. At last I crept into my parachute tent and slept and slept and slept. It was 18 July.

While we had been away, there had been many minor adventures and some major ones. On 10 July, Alex, with Johnny Cooper, Sergeant Campbell and his mortar crew, had taken the 3-inch mortar by jeep to Autun. At extreme range, in bright moonlight, they had pumped forty HE and incendiary bombs into the synthetic oil factory and made a successful get-away. This had not materially damaged the factory but a petrol train hit in a siding burned for two days.

The next night, the jeep went out and brought in Dickie Grayson's party, leaving Sergeant Sturmey, with Lance-Corporals Cave and Dray in his place. In the La Charité area, Dickie had fallen in with a good Maquis who had given him plenty of work to do. His most exciting encounter was when the party drove across the important German-held Loire bridge at Nevers, in full view of the German guards, shooting their way through, without casualties.

On the 13th, Johnny Cooper had left the troop for Squadron HQ. On the 17th he went out to Dijon, where he joined Johnny Wiseman's troop.

On the 14th the jeep had taken Nobby Noble out, as already related. On the 18th it was sent to fetch in Sergeant Sturmey, who had blown the Nevers–Paris line, and who reported heavy German attacks in the Nevers area.

A gypsy, in the pay of the Gestapo, had been caught in this period by the Maquis Bernard. He had been given a very summary trial by the Maquisards, and a neat little note had arrived at the British camp offering us the 'honour of shooting the spy'. We politely declined, but Sergeant Zellic did in fact attend the ceremony at which the man was shot in the back after he had been made to dig his own grave.

Meanwhile, the strength of One Troop in the Dijon area had steadily been built up. They now had their own wireless set and were actively operating against the various railways running into Dijon. They were somewhat handicapped by being so close to the Germans, even getting their milk and eggs from the same farms, though managing to stagger their hours for collection.

Back at Squadron HQ, a party under Corporal Corbett had gone out on the 9th and returned on the 12th, having blown the lines again. On the 11th there had been a big *parachutage*, five fitters and another jeep. Unfortunately the jeep had parted from its parachute and landed as so much scrap-iron.

On the 12th, Bill moved Squadron HQ to another camp in the valley of the Chalaux river, just below the village of Le Meix Chalaux. He left Three Troop under Roy Bradford at the Mazignien camp. That night there was another *parachutage*, and Paddy Mayne came over in the plane intending to speak to Bill on the S-phones, a sort of ground-to-air wireless telephone. It did not work at all well, as Bill was unable to hear a sound. So furious was he that he started swearing viciously into the machine, and it was not until weeks later that we learned that every word he had said was clearly audible in the plane.

The next night brought the first disaster of a most tragic week. Two planes, one British and one American, had collided in the dark over the Mazignien camp. One had crashed on the road close to the village, the other had blown to bits all around the Three Troop tents. It was a miracle that none of the troops were hurt. As it was, not a man survived from either plane.

The next morning, the Germans demanded of the mayor of Marigny-l'Eglise, the commune in which the planes had fallen, an explanation of the noise. The mayor professed ignorance and asked Bill for instructions. Not wishing the American plane in Roy's camp to be found, Bill told the mayor to say that only one plane had crashed and this was done. This story has a sequel.

I myself spent the 19th doing little but eat, sleep and recuperate. On the following day I ran over to Bill's new camp and gave him a full personal report of my operation. He made me prepare a citation for Jemson, who subsequently received the DCM, and we returned safely to Montsauche.

It was about this time that we became useful in another way. Many refugees from Paris were beginning to filter down through our area, and with them they brought reports of German ruses and dispositions which, after carefully sifting, we duly wirelessed back to England. In this way we were able to give information about new flying-bomb sites and dumps, location of factories, position of German submerged bridges across the Seine, which were only used by night, and the latest details of Field-Marshal Rommel's HQ. Much of this news, no doubt, was already known in London but anything that came from a reliable source we sent back in the hope of its being of some use. Good RAF targets in our own vicinity were also given.

The case of Rommel's HQ was an amusing one, as it turned out to be in the château of a friend of Le Four's in Normandy. Le Four had a château of his own near at hand, and it was from one of his tenants that we had received the intelligence.

It was with much pleasure, therefore, that we learned of the château's blitzing; but it was a somewhat forced rejoicing on Le Four's part, for he had just discovered that all the furniture therein had been requisitioned from *his* château.

We have never known the absolute truth about Rommel's death, but I believe the Mosquitoes that had bombed this HQ caught Rommel in his car as they were leaving and riddled him with their bullets.

Thus, by all the means we could, we did our best to bring confusion to the enemy.

CHAPTER XVIII

Three Troop Tragedy

While at the Chalaux camp, on 20 July, I learned that Three Troop was now moving out into the Forêt des Dames area. The advance party of Ooly Ball, Jeff Duvivier and five men had set off on airborne bicycles on the evening of the 17th. Captain Bradford, with Sergeant Chalky White as front-gunner, Sergeant 'Maggie' McGinn as driver and Trooper Devine, the fitter, as rear-gunner, set out to join them by jeep on the evening of the 19th. As interpreter they took Jacques Morvillier of the Maquis Jean.

Chalky, who was a very fine soldier, having won the DCM and the MM in previous operations with the SAS, had been a peculiar jinx to his officers. His platoon commander had been killed on every operation in which he had engaged, and until now six officers had lost their lives in his company on patrols or skirmishes. This time, it was intended to outwit the jinx by giving Chalky his own section to command alone.

The next news that I heard of the movements of the troop was on the 21st. Towards dusk a message came from the Maquis via the station guardroom telephone to say that a British soldier had been brought in by a Maquis patrol, and wished to see us. The jeep was sent down to fetch him up and as he was helped out, he was a sorry sight. His shirt was torn, his face was white and drawn, and as he spoke he quivered with nervous tension and the strain of his experience. It was Maggie McGinn, and his tale was a sad one. After setting out from Chalaux in the late evening, the jeep had moved all night in a north-westerly direction, travelling by the side roads, and taking all the usual precautions. It was about 8 o'clock in the morning and the sun was just beginning to bathe the whole land in its warming glow, when in the little village of Lucy-sur-Yonne, they found themselves face to face with a German officer and his sergeant.

At first the officer had not realised that the car was British and had waved them down as though it was one of his own vehicles. Chalky had replied with a quick burst from the twin-Vickers and the Boche had dived for cover. Almost immediately, the jeep had come upon a German lorry parked at the roadside and behind it they could see another. Jerry troops on both sides of the road were lazing in the fields and in a matter of moments the crew of the little jeep realised that they had chanced upon a whole German troop-convoy preparing their breakfast. It was too late to turn back. Already the enemy were sprinting for their guns. There was only one thing to do and they did it. On Roy's orders,

Maggie put his foot hard down, and as Chalky sprayed the road ahead with burning lead, the jeep charged along the line of stationary trucks. There were seven lorries, each of which must have contained at least twenty Boche. Five men in an overloaded jeep against 150; no protection and a load of explosives under them; they were lucky to survive a minute.

As they began their deadly charge, a burst of Spandau fire from behind struck the jeep. Devine slumped over the rear-guns, his dead hands gripping the triggers. Roy Bradford reeled as he sat, a bullet through the arm. The jeep engine coughed harshly but carried on. Chalky fought his guns like a devil incarnate. Three times he paused to change magazines, as he poured 800 rounds into the swarming enemy at point-blank range. Everything was blurred confusion. The jeep gave a sickening lurch as the front wheels ran a screaming German down. Men in field-grey, with panic-struck faces, dived for the ditch as death roared by. But it could not last. Jacques and Roy passed the magazines to the gunner as quickly as he used them, but it was the dead man at the rear-guns who caused the final disaster.

As the jeep passed the last truck, and no gun could fire back, a long, accurate burst of Spandau fire caught the jeep and held it. Roy Bradford coughed and fell back, cut almost in half by the bullets. The Frenchman cried out sharply as a shot shattered his elbow. The gallant Chalky, badly hit, with bullets in one leg, his left hand shattered and his shoulder torn, whipped round in his seat. With a despairing grunt, the engine of the jeep gave up the ghost.

As the loaded vehicle coasted to a standstill, just out of sight of the enemy, Maggie leapt out. Pausing only long enough to be sure that Roy and Devine were both quite dead, he dragged his wounded companions out of the jeep and pushed them through the hedge.

Behind them they heard the Germans pounding down the road, but to their relief they dived safely into the shelter of the wood before the enemy came in sight. As always, the woods proved friendly and the Boche dared not follow; but the road areas were well patrolled, and the wounded, who were in a very bad condition, had to lie up among the trees, with Germans sometimes so close that they could hear their breathing.

When night fell, Maggie helped the others to move out of the area. He gave them what support he could, scouted ahead for signs of the enemy, and finally, when the wounded were too weak to move any further, he built a shelter for them from the corn sheaves and made them as comfortable as he could until dawn.

As soon as it was light, they moved on again, and after swimming the Yonne and bringing back a boat for the others, he got them across. They found a lock-keeper's cottage and Jacques, who had been complaining bitterly, now pulled himself together, and went forward to contact the civilians. He learned that there were still a lot of enemy in the region, and the whole party had to lie low most of that day in an orchard where they were brought a little food. In the evening the Maquis came for them and after various other adventures they at last were brought back, the wounded to the Maquis hospital, and Maggie to us. Maggie was given fresh clothes by the boys and we offered him a tent for the night, but he preferred to get back to his own camp, so we conveyed him there in the jeep.

That night Bill sent a wireless message back to England for retransmission, ordering the rest of Three Troop to rally back on to Squadron HQ. It was 25 July before they returned and they had very little but misery to recount when at last they did get back.

The collapsible airborne cycles proved hardly sturdy enough for the heavy going of the Morvan. The steep hills and rough tracks made it necessary to walk almost as much as they rode. The heavy rucksacks on the men's backs unbalanced them, making cycling difficult; and because these bikes had no racks, parcels had to be tied to the frames with string. This was a useless makeshift, for the vibration of the mountain roads continually dislodged the packs and the little cortège was forever stopping to tie on packages or readjust rucksacks. Consequently they were only able to do about eight to ten miles a day, whereas on foot they would have been able to carry almost as much twice the distance.

So Lieutenant Ball's party, weary and dispirited, arrived at their rendezvous one day late and very exhausted. On the evening of the arrival in the Forêt des Dames, an unusual explosion was heard from the direction of the town of Entrains-sur-Nohain, about three miles from the camp. The next morning Jeff Duvivier with his two companions in crime, the Australian Lance-Corporal 'Digger' Weller MM and Trooper 'Homer' Marshall, set out on reconnaissance. This was strongly opposed by Ball, who was in favour of lying doggo until Roy arrived, but Duvivier persuaded him to allow them to go.

At Entrains, they contacted the Maquis through an old fisherman whom they encountered working in the river, and discovered that the explosion of the previous evening had been the Maquis blowing a small culvert on the railway to delay the movement of a number of enemy munition trains. French workmen were repairing the culvert, so Jeff, guided by the Maquis, laid a very heavy charge of explosive on the line just beyond the culvert. They used a pressel switch instead of a fog-signal, dug all their charges in under the rails and carefully camouflaged their work. The whole job took more than two hours and the journey to the site was nine miles, which included passing through two enemy-occupied towns.

By the time that Jeff returned to the Forêt des Dames, the signal had come through telling them of Roy's death, and Ball took them back at once to the Chalaux camp, where they all arrived safely on the 25th.

The story of the blowing of the line and the wreck of the train near Entrains only filtered through later. It was the one bright spot in a tragic operation. Apparently the Frenchmen ordered to repair the culvert had adopted their usual go-slow policy and stated that it would take three days to repair it. Throughout the first day they had wielded pick and shovel slowly and cannily. When on the second day the rumour that a really lovely charge had been laid on the other side of the culvert got through to the French workmen, they started to put their backs into the job. Within three hours the culvert was as good as new. Then the train, with two engines, flak-trucks, forty big wagons and twenty-five German guards, steamed through. In a few hundred yards, just as it was nicely getting up speed, the train ran on to Jeff's charge. There had been a thoroughly satisfactory bang. The two engines had been completely wrecked, thrown off the track and on to their sides. With them had gone a 40-foot flak-truck. The next ten wagons were derailed and lay all over the tracks. The only unfortunate thing was that the guards had been in the last truck of all and were undamaged, but eyewitness accounts stated that they were more than a little shaken.

So began and ended the first operation of Three Troop. For almost the rest of the campaign, its remnants formed a part of the Squadron HQ, until in the last few weeks, with the new reinforcements still to come, it was resurrected; but that is another story.

On 23 July, between the return of Maggie McGinn and the return of the bicycle party, I almost had a tragedy myself. I was taking the jeep across to Bill's camp to bring back some rations and return Dr Mike McReady, who had been visiting us. I had intended to set out very sharp at 9.00, but in his usual dilatory manner, the doc was late. Nothing would speed up his slow, methodical preparations and it was not until twenty-past that I finally got away. We took one of the three normal routes between the two camps, passing through Savelot, Savault and Bonin. We crossed the important Lormes–Saulieu road at Brassy, for now that we were well known in the Morvan, we found safety in inhabited places, where we would be stopped and warned if there were any Boche about.

From Brassy, we climbed up the winding road through the pine-forested hills around Vermot, and dropped down again towards the valley of the Chalaux. Then, as we approached Mazignien, I sensed that something was wrong. The streets were deserted, not a cow, not an ox, not a villager could be seen. The peasants were not working in their fields, even the few chickens that pecked in the dust had an air of wishing they were elsewhere.

'I don't like it,' I said, clicking off the safety catch on the twin-Vickers that I held. 'It's too quiet!'

We passed through the silent, empty village without mishap. We ran on along the road to Le Meix Chalaux and took the turn down through the houses, over the boulder-strewn track to the bed of the valley. We ran the jeep through the deep ford of the Chalaux at the bottom of the track and debouched into the open fields along the edge of which lay the parachute tents and camouflaged 'Arctic' shelters of Bill's camp. Bill came down to greet us.

'How did you get here?' he enquired.

We looked at him surprised.

'Mazignien was full of Germans a few minutes ago,' he told us, and then we heard the whole story.

Having at last been informed by the mayor of Marigny that one British aircraft had crashed at Mazignien, the Boche had sent out a patrol to investigate it. The patrol had consisted of a lorry-load of frightened Germans from Avallon. So scared had they been that Spandaus had been mounted fore and aft on the truck, and the sides had been lined with riflemen, their guns pointing outward. When they dismounted, they had been trembling with fear as they tried to question the villagers.

A lad from Mazignien had run down the track to warn the camp and Bill had sent off two of his men to take a detour round the village and intercept my jeep. They had almost walked on to the German Spandau positions which were covering the village and had been forced to make an even wider detour than they expected. So it had been with deep mortification that they heard us pass them down the road before they could reach it. They had expected any moment to hear the sudden burst of firing, as we, all unsuspecting, ran into the Spandaus, but luck was with us.

The Shleuh had finished their questioning, examined the wreck, remounted their lorry and finally pulled out just five minutes before we came driving through.

The villagers of Marigny-l'Eglise were charged with the task of burying the British dead, which they did with all honours; and later a beautiful memorial of granite and marble was raised over their tomb. Throughout the occupation a bead and wire wreath inscribed 'A nos Alliés' was kept openly upon the grave.

The Americans had to be buried by our Padre in the woods, where they had fallen, but the good villagers remembered them in the inscription upon the tomb, and more than a year later they were bringing flowers to these lonely and pathetic graves in the heart of the wood.

Roy Bradford and Devine were also buried by villagers. Their graves lie side by side and well tended in the cemetery of Grain, close to where they fought their last action. On the bare, flower-strewn ground between the two crosses, a plaque has been laid. It is thus inscribed: 'Hommage affecteux et reconnaissant aux Vaillants, qui loin de leur Patrie, meurent bravement pour reconquérir notre Liberté'.

CHAPTER XIX

Hans

It was just about this time that we had another near tragedy in Ouroux. We had started to requisition and repair French civilian vehicles for use either independently, or in conjunction with the jeeps, for increasing our scope of action. One afternoon in late July, a party under Nobby Noble set out with a jeep to escort a civilian car into Ouroux for overhaul. We did not expect them back until teatime, so we were surprised in the middle of the afternoon to hear the racing of a jeep engine and see Middleton driving up the track like Jehu. Nobby was sitting in the gunner's seat and as they drew nearer we could see a trickle of blood coursing down his cheek and that the shoulder of his smock was caked with blood.

The story that they told and which we pieced together afterwards was almost a tragedy of errors.

Middleton, Nobby and Roger, the French Maquis mechanic, had been in the jeep. Roger was acting as front-gunner but only had the most hazy idea of how to work the guns, for they were deep in our own territory and never expected for a moment to meet an enemy. Lance-Corporal Bromfield and Lofty Langridge were in the private car. They had their personal arms with them but had not bothered to mount a Bren.

As they approached Ouroux, they were stopped by some women who warned them that a German car had just passed through the town. They helped to hide the car and went forward to find out if there were any more Boche about, but as no more appeared and the suspicious car had been gone some time, Nobby thought no more about it and carried on. Meanwhile, far away at a big petrol storage depot near Dijon, the German Officer Commanding had been worried about a petrol train from Nevers which had failed to reach him and had sent off a requisitioned French car to find it. So short of petrol was the depot that the car could not be allowed to follow the comparatively safe *routes nationales*, but had to take the shortest route, straight through the Morvan. Not unnaturally, on the tricky, winding hill roads, the Germans had got lost. Passing through the town of Ouroux, they found that they had taken the wrong road once again. They came back through Ouroux. All of a sudden, in the narrow streets between untidy gardens, they encountered a small military vehicle. It looked like a Volkswagen and it mounted machine-guns. The occupants were wearing a camouflaged uniform and wore some sort of red headgear – probably, they thought, Grey Cossacks from Château-Chinon.*

155

The jeep crew, seeing a small red saloon approaching them, never for a moment imagined it to contain Germans. It was the most natural thing to encounter a Maquis car hereabouts. The two vehicles closed. Just who first realised that the others were their enemies it was hard to say. All at once, with the two cars lying literally side by side in the roadway, pandemonium broke loose.

There were four Germans in the saloon, a regimental sergeant major, a corporal, a lance-corporal-driver and a civilian technician. As the car drew up, they leapt out with Schmeissers blazing. For some moments Roger had been struggling with the Vickers, but he was quite unable to get it to work. Nobby fired with his Colt and Langridge and Bromfield, jumping from their car, ran up to join the fray.

A homeric struggle now ensued in the middle of the road. A burst from the RSM's Schmeisser shattered Bromfield's ankle. A bullet through the German driver's thigh sent him cowering into the ditch. One of the Huns trying to escape across a garden was shot dead. A burst of Schmeisser fire ripped into the outside petrol tanks of the jeep and set it alight, so that Middleton had to concentrate on fighting the flames rather than pursuing the battle. Lofty, his Tommy-gun jammed, attacked the RSM, whose magazine was now empty. A fierce battle swayed across the street as the two big men tried to strike each other down with the butts of their weapons. Nobby, his eyebrow hit by a glancing blow and a bullet through his shoulder, managed to shoot down the technician before he could put a burst into Langridge's back. Langridge kicked his adversary shrewdly in the belly, but it appeared to be ineffective in the mêlée. Nobby emptied his automatic into the RSM's side but the fight reeled on. Middleton, having extinguished the blaze with his driving gloves, now turned his attention to the twin-Vickers and at point-blank range he put half a magazine into the big German's body. That was the end of the fight.

Not waiting to clear up the mess, Nobby bundled Bromfield into the jeep and Middleton drove them back to the Maquis guardroom as fast as he could. Roger explained the situation to the guard who phoned the Maquis Bernard to request that a party be sent down straight away to obliterate the evidence.

As soon as Nobby had told his story, I went down in the jeep with Tom Rennie to supervise. As we reached the bottom of the track by the guardroom, I came across the first results of the skirmish; a long string of Maquisards carrying stretchers up to the camp. They had with them three wounded Germans and Bromfield. I told them that the prisoners were ours and should be taken up to our camp without being molested. I talked to Bromfield, who was quite cheerful, although he must have been in great pain. The RSM was still conscious and was asking for water. He was offering all his money to buy it and seemed rather surprised that he had not yet been ill-treated. I ordered the Maquisards to fetch him a drink, telling him as best I could that he was a prisoner of the British army, then carried on to the scene of the fight. It was in the outskirts of Ouroux, close by its small lake. The Maquis, under Meurice, were sweeping the last specks of glass off the road. They had towed away the German car, only slightly damaged, and collected all prisoners. I checked with the eyewitnesses that no Germans had escaped and was assured that all had been safely picked up. Before I left the town, there was not a sign to show that there had ever been a fight there.

The German prisoners were interrogated by Alex. The RSM was in fact an anti-Nazi, but being a regular soldier, he had nevertheless fought loyally. We could not get much sense out of the civilian technician, and the driver was Hans.

Both of the badly wounded Germans were too far gone for there to be any hope of their recovery, and anyway the civilian had had no right to bear arms without a uniform. We handed them over to the Maquis and both were shot. They seemed to expect it and were quite resigned. It was a pity that we could not have saved the RSM, but with sixteen bullets through his body it was a miracle that he had lived so long.

Hans we kept. Hans it was, who with a bullet through the fleshy part of his thigh, took a dive into the ditch at the beginning of the action and stayed there to the very end.

After Nobby had left and while for a moment the streets of Ouroux were deserted, he had tried to escape. He had limped across the road and entered a little *estaminet* just off the main road. By now he was almost petrified with fear.

'Where is the nearest *route nationale*?' he had demanded.

'Far away,' replied the lady of the *estaminet*. 'Rest a while. I will hide you and attend to your wounds.'

'Mais ces terroristes?' quavered Hans.

'Il n'y a pas des terroristes ici,' answered Madame.

And feeling somewhat reassured, Hans had allowed himself to be guided to the back parlour and locked in. A few minutes later the Maquisards, hastily summoned by Madame, arrived to collect him.

Hans was an inoffensive little bank clerk from the Czech border. He was interested neither in politics nor war. As soon as he realised he was not going to be shot, he was the happiest German in all France, for he had been warned for a draft to the Normandy front and now he was safely out of it all. The only thing that worried him was whether his wife would be told that he was a deserter, but we put his mind at rest over this by wirelessing his number, rank and name to England for passing through to Geneva.

The reason that we kept Hans and treated him with such consideration was tied up with the problem of the wounded. Already we had more wounded men than we could hope to move safely in an emergency and there was always the danger that a large-scale enemy attack might develop in our woods. So we determined in the last resort to abandon our wounded, leaving Hans to look after them, hoping that the good treatment he had received might induce the enemy to treat our own wounded decently.

In the long run, Hans proved an asset as well as an insurance policy. At first he did not need guarding as he could not walk far with his damaged leg; but as this healed, his fear of the Maquis and the fact that he did not know the tracks through the woods made it equally unnecessary to watch him. He always appreciated that by keeping him from the Maquis we had saved his life, and was pathetically grateful. As soon as he could walk about he started to help Mickey Flynn to cook for us and eventually he and Mickey became joint cooks. Hans spoke no English when he arrived and his French was poor, with a dreadful accent. But very soon we reached common ground in a sort of mongrel Anglo-French and when we left France, Hans was understanding us very well.

As he became more one of the family he was allowed down to our car-park occasionally and helped to work on the cars. Eventually, with all insignia stripped from his tunic and wearing a gas-cape, he would go down with Flynn, or even alone, to the Maquis to collect the food. In fact, after a time the Maquisards thought that he was one of the SAS.

There were many funny stories concerning Hans. One day at the Maquis, a new Maquisard, seeing his trousers and boots, pointed to them and enquired, with a raise of his eyebrows, 'Shleuh?'

Hans nodded.

'Shleuh kaput?' asked the Maquisard, drawing his fingers expressively across his throat.

Hans shook his head.

'Pourquoi Shleuh non kaput?', obviously puzzled.

'Moi Shleuh,' replied the honest Hans, and the Maquisard nearly threw a fit.

Later, when a Gestapo car was ambushed by the Maquis and nobody knew enough German to translate the documents found in it, they were sent down to our troop and Hans was given the task of picking out the valuable stuff. It was very amusing to watch him pulling forth a 'most secret' document and with a 'Here's a good one for you' air, proceed to translate it. Out of this bag of mail, we retrieved all Roy Bradford's papers, which were being sent to Dijon for information. We also learned many facts about train movements and the latest German orders, which we wirelessed to London.

On 27 July three new developments began to shape the things to come. The first was the arrival of two airmen, one a Canadian and the other an American, at Bill's camp. The events which were now beginning to sweep the Boche out of Normandy were disrupting the normal RAF escape channels, and from now on, in ones and twos, airmen began to gather in our camps. They were of considerable technical assistance in repairing cars and maintaining the wireless sets, but none of them joined our operational patrols. In the end we brought them safely out with us.

The other new factors turned up at a big *parachutage* that we had on the Montsauche Lake DZ. Bill Fraser came over specially to see it and three jeeps and two 6-pounders were dropped to us, as well as six men of the Second SAS, an advance party to their Squadrons, soon to be coming through the enemy's lines.

As the first plane swooped over the DZ, I heard a swishing whistle and a heavy crump. For a moment I thought that it was a Jerry plane trying to bomb the lights and then the truth dawned. It was a 'candled' jeep. The second plane had better luck and we saw the amazing sight of four huge 60-foot chutes softly lowering a complete jeep. It was truly the most extraordinary sight.

'Never,' said a Maquisard standing beside me, 'did I think that I would live to see such a thing. A car descending from the clouds!'

The men of the Second SAS were, I think, a little shaken by their reception. They had imagined that they were dropping into hostile territory and quite expected to find themselves fighting on the DZ. So when they saw our jeeps touring the area with lights blazing to pick up containers and the search-parties working by bright torchlight, they assumed we were Boche. It was some time before some of them came in to report.

The two 6-pounders were a great boon. They descended perfectly, though one of them did a lot of damage to standing crops before it could be retrieved. They were our third new factor.

Bill Fraser and the Second SAS party stopped with us overnight. They had brought along far more kit than they could possibly carry on their jeeps and gave us many spare parts which were most welcome. Unfortunately, however, they made the mistake of rather pointedly mounting a guard over the rest of their kit; and the boys, taking this as a combined insult and challenge, helped themselves to some of their luxuries.

The next morning, Bill took his 6-pounder across to Chalaux and the other one was left with us. The two surviving jeeps were the property of the Second SAS, who also departed that day.

We set up our 6-pounder on the edge of the woods near our garage at the Poirot entrance to the Bois de Montsauche. Here we left Corporal Sylvester, who had returned safely from Clessy after blowing the Paray–Autun line. With him were Edwards and four other men. They formed a little camp of their own, which we came to call the Maquis Silvo. At first they lived in a deserted barn on the very fringe of the wood but later a better position was found higher up among the trees and further from the road.

On the 29th, Major Bob Melot arrived on the Chalaux DZ, but the two jeeps that he brought with him both 'pranged', which was a bitter disappointment. Bob Melot, who was to be tragically killed six months later in a jeep crash at

Brussels, was a legend of the SAS. He was a Belgian who had been a fighter ace of the last war. He had been doing liaison work with the Bedouin tribes in the Libyan desert when he first came in contact with the SAS. When the war had swept through North Africa, he had tagged along with the Regiment. In the desert his expert knowledge had been invaluable. In Italy his courage was exemplary. He won the MC and was wounded. During our preparations for the invasion of Europe he had been our intelligence officer and now, although well over forty, he had jumped into France.

On the 30th, with rather better luck, two jeeps were dropped undamaged, but the first was for the Second SAS and the other for Bob Melot.

All this time we were requisitioning more cars in our camps, and the war in the Morvan was beginning to take on a new guise.

The Germans' chance to catch us unprepared was gone.

CHAPTER XX

Alarms and Excursions

On 30 July I took explosives and trip-wires down to the Maquis Silvo and prepared booby-traps all around the area. As at our own camp, I set up only the detonators, but left plenty of plastic near at hand. I also warned Silvo to set the trip-wires every night. In addition to this, I prepared a nice little surprise in case of an enemy attack, whereby Silvo could break a time-pencil, so that ten minutes later the old farmhouse would reverberate to the rattle of machine-gun fire, climaxed by a grenade being lobbed out into the road. Thus up to ten minutes of Silvo abandoning his position, the Boche would believe that he still occupied it. I also left a stiff explosive charge and some more home-made dummy Bren-fire attached to a one-hour time-pencil, so that if the enemy ever entered the woods this would suddenly go off in his rear and demoralise him a bit.

It was shortly after 6 o'clock next morning that I was suddenly woken. At first I did not know what had disturbed my slumbers, then clear on the morning air I heard the rattle of automatic fire. I sat up in bed, listening carefully. Then it came again, two long bursts followed by a double explosion. This was the sound that my first little surprise ought to have made. I leapt out of bed, pulled on my shoes, trousers and Dennison smock, and hastened to rouse the camp. Alex told me to tell the boys to get their boots on and rest prepared. He ordered me down to see what was happening at the Maquis Silvo.

With Swag and Middleton we set off down the track in the jeep and as we approached the Poirot entrance we dismounted and went forward on foot. I was using the Schmeisser that I had collected from the German car on the day that we took Hans. It replaced the carbine that I had lost by the Bourbince and I continued to use it to the end of my stay in France. With this trusty weapon, firmly gripped, I edged down the last fifty yards of track towards the barn. First I saw the 6-pounder. It was still camouflaged in behind a low wall and no one was with it. Then I saw the courtyard of the barn. It, too, was deserted. I moved down towards the barn and as I approached it the savoury smell of frying bacon assailed my nostrils. There was Silvo cooking the breakfast, there were his men dozing in their sleeping bags and there, completely intact, was my booby-trap.

'What the hell was that noise about half an hour ago?' I demanded.

Silvo looked up. 'I don't know,' he replied. 'We heard the firing and Edwards, who was on guard, saw a big column of smoke over there!'

I followed his pointing finger to the south-west, where a smudge of oily smoke still discoloured the sky.

'OK,' I said. 'Keep your eyes open', and returned to report to Alex. Later we heard the full reports of the tragedy at Chaumard.

*   *   *

Not far from the town of Château-Chinon, the new Maquis of Chaumard had been formed. Neither well-armed nor well-disciplined, it had chosen a site rather close to a good road, and it paid the penalty.

A Gestapo spy managed to get accepted into the Maquis. He learned the strength, location and guard arrangements of the camp. He was caught out by the Maquisards, however, and locked up in a hut awaiting his trial, and the inevitable shooting party. This did not suit the plan of the spy and he escaped from the Maquis on one of its motorcycles.

The foolish Maquis chief did not appear at all perturbed by his prisoner's escape and neither changed the site of his camp nor took any further precautions. The reckoning was swift and merciless. Two mornings later a small German bicycle patrol approached the camp under cover of darkness. The only Maquis sentinel was asleep at his post. By an unguarded track, the enemy entered the dormant camp, then with sudden, brutal efficiency they flung incendiary bombs into the wooden huts and mowed down the Maquisards as they stumbled blindly out. It was a brilliant success. Twenty-seven Maquisards were killed, many more wounded escaping. All their arms and munitions were captured and the camp completely destroyed.

For several days after this the stragglers of the Maquis Chaumard trickled into the Bois de Montsauche and the group was reconstituted in the woods between us and Maquis Silvo.

Another arrival in our corner of the woods was the Maquis André, formed out of the finest fighting elements of the Maquis Bernard. This contained most of Georges' old Parisians, some young bloods from the country around Le Tour, and, among many others, our lady doctor and Gustaf. They shared and enlarged our water supply and took turns with our guards.

A strong wooden hospital was built in the wood between the Maquis André and the Maquis Bernard, where the Martells carried out their good work. No more operating on bare tables in peasants' huts. They could now use their own little surgery, separated from the patients in their rough wooden beds by a ragged partition of parachute silk.

Up on the high ground of the wood between the Maquis Bernard and the farm of La Verrerie was the Poste de Commandement, where Colonel Hastings and hosts of aged political colonels of the Maquis wrangled indefinitely. Colonel Hastings did much good work, but the politics of the French higher-ups were a constant source of difficulty to him, until the arrival of his French colleague, Colonel Diagram, who had to be flown out from England and landed by Lysander.

This PC achieved a good deal of power in the Morvan when Lemniscate, their powerful rival, came to grief on a visit to Paris. With more guts than good sense, this important commander had been visiting Paris with his wife, to negotiate more arms for the Maquis, and had been picked up by the Gestapo. Fortunately they thought that they had caught a black marketeer and he was not too closely questioned, but, while being shipped off by train to a concentration camp, he was recognised by a member of the *Milice* – a French Fascist para-military organisation. At once he was hauled out and shot without the semblance of a trial. However, his summary execution no doubt prevented the Germans learning the secrets that their torture might have extracted. Nevertheless it was a sad end to a brave man and, in his own way, a dedicated patriot.

After Diagram's arrival, the central control of the Morvan became vested in his perambulating PC, so that the power of the Montsauche PC once more waned. But around the beginning of August it was at the height of its power. The long and unintelligible conferences that took place day after day did much to interfere with the fighting and, as far as I could see, nothing to encourage it.

On 31 July, Dickie Grayson set out with Langridge and two other men in a big French Ford to operate in the south. He returned on 4 August, having blown the lines in two places and destroyed every point in the marshalling yards at the little town of Semelay. Forced to contend with continual punctures in the rotten tyres of his car, he had been delayed a day on his return journey by encountering the tail-end of determined German attacks on the Maquis Socrate.

In two days of heavy fighting, and virtually unsupported by the other Maquis, Socrate beat off the enemy attack. A big *parachutage* at our DZ did much to discourage the Germans who were led to believe that strong airborne reinforcements were being dropped to the Maquis.

It was about two days after this that we had another alarm. A neat little intelligence note from the PC informed Alex that a big attack on the Maquis was imminent. Enemy lorries had been heard passing northward through Ouroux during the night and Cossack cavalry were already stationed at the south of the wood. For some reason Alex distrusted this message, probably because not a sound of these warlike preparations had come to us over the still air. To make sure, however, he sent Dickie off to make a recce on his own.

Within a few hours he was back, cursing the incompetence of the Maquis and explaining the results of his investigations.

The 'hostile' lorries, moving northward, had apparently been Socrate's garage changing its location, while his interview with the scout who reported the cavalry went something like this.

'How many of these Cossacks did you see?'

'Well, I didn't actually see them. It would have been dangerous as close to the road as that.'

'How many did you hear, then?'

'Well, I couldn't rightly say, but it must have been quite a lot.'

'About how many? Twenty? Fifty? A hundred?'

'I couldn't rightly say, I didn't see them.'

'What makes you think that they were Cossacks, then?'

'I heard the jingling of their equipment and the clicking of their horses' hooves. They must have been Cossacks.'

'Did you speak to anyone who had seen them?'

'Well, no.'

'Then let's go and speak to someone now.'

And of course as soon as Dickie had spoken to the old lady at the nearest farm, he learned the truth. At 8 o'clock that morning, a funeral cortège had passed. So much for our Cossacks!

Another day, there were more rumours of impending attacks that did not materialise. I went down with one of André's patrols along the Poirot road and was surprised at the new keenness and efficiency that I saw. They were no longer the rabble that I had known in the early days, but real soldiers now. They worked in sections, each man with his rifle and grenades and an automatic weapon or two to each section. They used camouflage and concealment properly, and it seemed strangely incongruous that these soldiers of France wore the battledresses of the British, the boots of their foes, and the shirts, trousers and berets of their civilian life. Indeed, many of them were not even as uniformed as this.

One day, with a big Citroën car, and with Swag and Bass as my companions, I worked eastward, past the Lac des Settons, beyond the villages of Moux and Aligny-en-Morvan, and crossed the main Paris–Autun *route nationale* at the village of Pierre-Ecrite. We skirted the town of Liernais and recced right up to the Paris–Chalon *route nationale*. Here, close to the village of Nailly, we found an ideal spot for an ambush, with a good fast cross-country get-away. All afternoon we lay on road-watch and awaited a suitable target. None came, and as evening approached we had to return to camp. At that time it was the most easterly penetration that we had attempted.

During this period we were loaned Major Melot's jeep and with two jeeps to play about with, Alex took us down to the Paris–Autun road for a joint strafe. However, we had not made a recce of the area and could not find really suitable sites. Once in position we found the lack of control and the difficulty of telling the difference between German and French civilian cars almost insurmountable. We came home feeling frustrated.

Meanwhile, at Bill's camp, there had been a real pitched battle, against a very genuine enemy threat. On 1 August, the 6-pounder at Bill's camp, under the command of Sergeant 'Bunker' Burgess, had been attached to the Maquis Camille, an offshoot of the Maquis Jean. [In fact, Camille was by this time the chief of the 'Maquis Jean', which therefore was strictly the 'Maquis Camille' itself. However, the author did not learn this until some thirty years later.} It had been dragged into a good position by four oxen, whence it commanded all the roads approaching the area from the north-west. The Maquisards had prepared entrenched positions around it and it was intended that Burgess should, as far as language difficulties permitted, work under the orders of the Maquis officer commanding in that sector.

On 3 August an attack was launched against the Maquis Camille by a battalion of Luftwaffe potential pilots who had just completed their basic training. The battle opened at about 9 o'clock and Bill's camp was in considerable danger of being cut off. All jeeps were therefore evacuated to Montsauche. The camp was never discovered.

The brunt of the battle, however, was borne by the 6-pounder and its protecting Bren, in close co-operation with the Maquis. Engaging the enemy with high explosive and armour-piercing ammunition at ranges from 1000 to 700 yards, it knocked out three machine-gun positions, demolished a wall behind which the enemy were hiding and destroyed a mortar that was foolish enough to take up its position in the open. Three successive attacks were beaten off, but at 7.30 in the evening a final effort evicted the Maquisards from their trenches; and Burgess, after camouflaging the gun and removing the breech-block, had to retire with them. The enemy failed to find the gun in the heavy undergrowth and soon withdrew. By 8.30 Burgess had brought up two oxen and retrieved the gun. When darkness fell, the enemy retired and made no attempt to renew the attack the following day. The allied losses in this sector were two Maquisards killed and one wounded. The most pessimistic reports of German losses were nineteen killed and many others wounded.

In another sector one wounded German fell into our hands and was taken over by the doc, primarily as a patient but later as a batman.

After the fight, Paul, the Red Russian, appeared somewhat anxious and eager to explain something: but as everyone was pretty busy, not much notice was taken of him. Eventually he shrugged his shoulders and gave up. Some days later, when the wind changed, they found out what he had been getting at. Half-a-dozen dead Germans whom he had killed single-handed in the wood were in dire need of burial.

There was an unfortunate incident on the 5th, when the 6-pounder, which had been dragged back by the bullocks into a new position the previous day, opened fire on a Maquis column. After an enquiry, however, the fault was attributed to the column commander who had failed to give the proper recognition signal. Unhappily, there were three Maquis casualties.

On 1 August SQMS McLennon set off with Trooper Babbington on bicycles from Bill's camp. They carried a small quantity of explosive and snipers' rifles. They were away until the 17th of the month but did not have very good hunting, though they were successful in derailing a train on the Nevers–Paris line.

Johnny Wiseman came back to Squadron HQ on 9 August for a short visit. From him we learned that he was forming, arming and training three strong Maquis. He had destroyed a gasogene factory at Malain and blown the lines and mined the roads on numerous occasions. He had a couple of good tales concerning these exploits.

The young Maquisard sent to report on one of the blown lines asked a railway worker the extent of the damage.

'Are you really interested?' enquired the railwayman.

'Yes.'

'Rotten, then,' came the reply. 'Next time, if you lay it just up the line by that bend there you will get much better results.'

Next time it was laid on the bend.

Johnny told us, too, of another Maquis lad who, having been caught and tortured by the Gestapo, had been forced to disclose the presence of the camp. Some *milice*, expecting only a few unarmed Maquis to deal with, got the shock of their lives when they encountered British with Brens. They returned, those that did return, sadder and wiser men. Later a grand attack was launched against the camp at dawn. The *milice* swept the wood, while the Germans waited in ambush on the other side to catch Johnny's men as they came out. Warned just in time, the British skipped out the night before, so that the first people to emerge from the woods in the misty light of the dawn were the *milice* themselves. They were duly, though inadvertently, mown down by the Boche.

Alex's troop, too, made liaison with the Maquis of the Côte d'Or, and 'Mees', the beautiful red-haired mistress of Captain Robert, used to visit us often, trying to 'borrow' ammunition and bringing us wine. The captain commanded the Maquis Robert which lay close to Saulieu. He was a very fine organiser and a brave man, having been a pilot in the French air force before the war. His dependent Maquis were spread all along the *routes nationales*, running south from Dijon.

'Mees', so called by the French on account of her English education and her English mother, spoke perfect English and was always a welcome visitor. Alex's variation of 'Come up and see my etchings' was 'Come down and see my ammunition dump', but I don't think that it proved particularly efficacious.

I had a couple of narrow escapes in quick succession. On one visit that I made to the Maquis Robert, I passed through the village of Alligny-en-Morvan at about 1.30 in the afternoon. That evening I learned that a Maquis car had been ambushed and the occupants killed by a German patrol in that very village around midday. The other episode was rather more eventful.

At this time there was a grave shortage of tobacco in the camp, so that when, one afternoon, André came along and proposed a joint raid on a tobacco convoy, it was universally acclaimed. The tobacco had been requisitioned by the Germans and would be travelling in unescorted lorries to Château-Chinon. The general idea was that the British should provide one jeep and some high explosives, and the Maquis three sections each of ten well-armed men, all in one enormous gasogene truck. The jeep would act as escort to the vulnerable truck as far as the little town of Tamnay, on the *route nationale*, from Nevers to Château-Chinon. Here the men would debus and form a picket around the bridge, incidentally seizing the tobacco trucks if they showed up. We would lay our charges preparatory to blowing the bridge, wait until the convoy had been taken, explode our charges and escort the tobacco and the Maquis truck safely back to camp. An important bridge would have been destroyed and the tobacco captured, all very conveniently and in broad daylight.

Alex gave me the task of escorting the Maquis truck. In my jeep I took Middleton as driver, Worn as rear-gunner, Swag Jemson to help with the explosives and a young French gendarme, Pierre Demongeot, from the Maquis André, to act as guide. We took with us about 100 lb of plastic explosive primed and prepared, in metal containers. We made sure that it was completely ready for use before we set out.

At 3 o'clock, we rendezvoused with the Maquis truck in the outskirts of Ouroux and moved off towards Tamnay. We travelled by little-used roads through the hills, speeding from road junction to road junction and from feature to feature, ahead of the huge, slow lorry.

In the valley of the Yonne, we crossed the good second-class road from Château-Chinon to Lormes and began to climb the steep hill to the little village of Montigny-en-Morvan. The road out of the valley winds up between two spurs, zig-zagging back and forth. In low gear the jeep had little difficulty in pulling to the top but the Maquis lorry was very slow indeed on the steep gradients.

As we approached the forked road, just below the village, Middleton, pointing to some shirt-sleeved figures in the field above us, said, 'Those look like Jerries to me!'

The gendarme vaguely indicated some other men standing on the balcony of a house, but the distance was great and no one was seriously perturbed. Having had many false alarms before, I uttered some 'famous last words'.

'There aren't any Germans here!' I said.

We stopped at the road junctions and I stepped out of my front-gunner's seat to point my twin-Vickers across the bonnet, up the road towards the centre of the village. From the position in which we had halted, Worn was just able to cover down the other road fork with the rear-guns.

All of a sudden I saw three figures walking down the road from the village. They were wearing peaked caps and jack-boots. They carried weapons slung across their shoulders. As they came nearer I could see the brilliant polish on their boots and the silver braid sparkling in the sun. They were dressed in field-grey.

'Good God!' I said. 'Germans!'

In our camouflaged smocks with our red berets and our military-looking little vehicle, I can only assume that we had once more been taken for motorised Grey Cossacks and that these two officers and their sergeant were coming to warn us of their ambush. Be that as it may, the range was a hundred yards when I pressed the triggers and I aimed low. With a cheerful chatter, red tracer and brilliant white incendiary bullets leaped from the guns. They flashed down on to the road and went ricocheting up again, whining viciously. One officer, throwing up his hands, fell back, writhing. The other clutched both hands to his stomach and pitched forward on his face. The sergeant leapt for the cover of the ditch. In an instant, all hell was loose about us. We were right in the middle of an ambush without knowing it. Spandaus opened up with their vicious brrrrup. The crack of passing bullets was unpleasantly close.

At this vital juncture, the rear-guns jammed, the jeep stalled, and my magazines were empty. Thank God I did not have time to think. Never have I changed drums so fast. Middleton was kicking frantically at the foot-starter and trying to turn the jeep in the narrow road at the same time. Worn, Jemson and the gendarme abandoned their useless gun and jumped for the ditch. There was a small footpath through the trees, cutting straight down the hillside. The last glimpse I had of my crew, as Middleton finally got the jeep started, was their bent figures doubling down this little track.

The next instant I saw a German with a Schmeisser to his shoulder taking a bead on us from the corner of the road not 50 feet away. I swung the front-guns around and blazed off at him over the back of the jeep, and at the same moment he opened fire. I heard Middleton gasp and thought he had been hit. The German's head disappeared. I think that he, too, had been given something to think about.

The jeep's nose was now pointing downhill and beginning to gather speed as we raced away. With no gunner on the rear-guns we were likely to suffer Roy Bradford's fate, so, stretching myself across the bonnet, I kept up the firing of my front-guns over the back of the jeep till they also jammed. I couldn't see at what I was shooting but I sprayed the hedges along the crest of the hill and the houses of the village that overlooked the road. I don't think that I did any damage but at least I put the Boche off sufficiently to spoil their aim. Middleton, driving like a maniac, was taking the hairpin bends on two wheels. Hardly able to see the road for the bulk of my body across the bonnet, he drove by instinct and blind good luck.

Meanwhile, with the sudden outbreak of fire from the top of the hill, the Maquis truck had stopped and the men had taken up positions to cover our withdrawal. For an instant we had to run the gauntlet of their inaccurate supporting fire and then we were at last safely behind the protecting line of Maquisards.

Seeing André crouched in the ditch, I drew up and did my best, in bad French, to explain the position to him. I told him that the enemy appeared to be in ambush and that the best thing we could do was to get out quickly in case there was a further enemy force waiting to cut off our retreat to the mountain fastnesses. He agreed and I told him that I would try to collect my missing men and drop back to the second-class road in the valley to cover his own disengagement. Luck was with me once more and I had hardly left André and found the bottom end of the footpath than I heard a heavy clumping in the undergrowth.

'Ahoy! SAS!' I cried.

A voice close at hand answered my hail and Swag, very much out of breath, but still carrying his beloved Bren, appeared on the track. The others were close behind him.

Dropping back to the crossroads, we took up an all-round defensive position and having cleared the stoppages on the guns, we fired a few shots at extreme range towards Montigny, to discourage any enemy ideas about pursuit.

Drifting back in some semblance of order, but hardly in the approved battle-school formations, came the men of the Maquis. As they arrived, I asked them to take up other positions on either side of us along the road. I was much obsessed with the danger of an enemy, already warned of our projected movements by treachery, having prepared a mobile force to isolate us from our base.

The lorry proved a grave disadvantage. It was much too large to be manoeuvred on these narrow roads and slowly, foot by foot, it had to be guided backwards down the twisting track. At last the lorry, too, reached the crossroads, was able to turn round and point its head for home.

André came up.

'Are all your men here?' I asked.

He shook his head; one section complete was unaccounted for. 'This jeep is very valuable,' I told him. 'It is the only one that the troop has in its own right and without it we cannot operate. The time is now 4 o'clock. I am prepared to wait for your men until half past. Then, I dare risk my jeep no longer. I will have to leave.'

André quite understood, and calling up two of his best men, a wiry little man of the Morvan, and a coal-black negro of the French Colonial Army, he sent them off to try to find the missing section.

After a quarter of an hour they returned without success. He sent them off again. At 4.30 there was still no sign of them and I gave them a few more minutes' grace, but it seemed probable to me that they would have made their own way across country back towards the Maquis, for they knew the ground well.

At last I could risk it no longer. I promised to see that some of the men of the Maquis Bernard would come out and cover the final stages of the withdrawal by providing holding forces on the road junctions that they must pass, and I duly departed. Before I had gone a couple of hundred yards the jeep broke down again and while we were repairing it, I was surprised and startled by a fresh outburst of firing from the village of Montigny. I ran back along the road to where I had left André. It was his lost section, he declared. He would return and collect it: I should carry on.

By the time that I returned to the jeep, Middleton had got it going again and we drove back to the Maquis as fast as we could. I reported straight in to the Maquis Colonel Dubois. I requested that the covering parties be sent out. He hesitated, then talked at length and said that he had not the men to do it. I went up the rough Maquis track to our own camp and saw Alex. In a few minutes he was getting his own jeep stripped for action and preparing his men. I returned to Ouroux to give cover there at least and waited for Alex.

At about 6 o'clock, and practically simultaneously, Alex arrived from the camp and the lorry returned from Montigny. André thanked us for our efforts and we all rejoiced together. The missing section, far from retiring, had crept up on the German-held village and attacked it. They had caused further casualties and had been successfully extricated, without even having a man wounded.

Later we discovered that there had been ambushes out on all the roads leading south that day. Using the tobacco convoy as a bait, the enemy had hoped to make a good killing of Maquis raiders. It was only our good luck that he did not succeed. Back in the camp, we examined our jeep and had a nasty shock. The shot from the Schmeisser-man at close range had ripped through the back of the vehicle, struck the back of Middleton's seat a glancing blow and buried itself in our prepared explosives. This was what had caused Middleton to gasp, and no wonder, for it bruised his skin. In spite of the shock, the plastic had not gone up, which was fortunate for me and a fine testimony to the reliability of the explosive.

CHAPTER XXI

With Bombs and Bullets to Autun

The night after the abortive raid on the tobacco convoy there was an important *parachutage* at the Montsauche DZ. Major Fraser and Major Melot came over for it. It was a good night and Paddy Mayne, Captain Mike Sadler, Intelligence Sergeant Ridler and a couple of other men were dropped.

Up in our camp there was a pleasant reunion. The whisky was produced and passed round. I learned that I had now been promoted captain in Roy's place, and we sat up drinking half the night.

Next morning, we got a rude shock. The crashing of bombs awoke us and we were startled to hear the roar of aircraft engines as five hostile planes wheeled overhead. Middleton, with long experience of aerial bombardment, was out of the tent so quickly that he was still in his sleeping-bag, performing a sort of quadruped sack-race from a flying start. In an instant, the whole camp was a hive of buzzing activity as the food containers were whisked out of their trenches and our boys dived for shelter. There was nothing that we could do against the planes, as the foliage was too thick for a clear shot, which would anyway have given away our position. I did take a Bren-gun out on to an open patch of hillside about quarter of a mile from the camp, but nothing came within range.

Later we learned that the target for the raid had been the Maquis car-park on the edge of our DZ. This was quite unconcealed from the air and it was surprising perhaps that it had not been attacked sooner. The planes, however, were aged trainers, and the pilots must have been students. Only the first bomb, presumably dropped by the instructor, landed squarely in the middle of the park, leaving a large crater, blowing down a couple of trees and damaging three cars, none of which were much good anyway. All the other bombs landed very wide and did no harm, except for one which landed with great perversity on a brand-new, first-rate car that Georges had just requisitioned and carefully hidden well away from the obvious target of the car-park.

The planes then strafed the Maquis guard, but since their gunning was as inaccurate as their bombing, no casualties resulted.

Following this warm welcome, Paddy, Bill and the rest of the visitors returned in the morning to squadron HQ. Paddy wanted to confer with Colonel Isaac, who was supposed to be at the Maquis Socrate. So that afternoon I set off in the jeep with Middleton and went to find him.

Lavault we found peculiarly quiet. In the Forêt d'Anost there were no signs of the usual Maquis guards. The deeper I pushed into the woods the more worried I became. The place was unnaturally silent and none of the normal Maquis noises broke the stillness. At Socrate's car-park I found nothing except a few broken-down lorries and junk scattered in all directions. The quiet was uncanny.

'Let's get out of here,' I said, and we returned quicker than we had come. At Lavault we made enquiries. Most of the villagers either could not or would not help us, but we did learn that a German patrol had been prowling around the previous day and the Maquis had decided to pull out.

One old man told us that the *curé* of Planchez – the Abbé de Chabanne – might know where the Maquis had gone. So back we went and eventually, among the deserted and burnt-out streets of his little parish, we found the *curé*. He was happy to give us the information we needed. The Maquis was at the village of L'Huis Prunelle on the road to Anost.

We followed up this clue and in due course fell in with some of Socrate's guards, who led us to their chief. Broad back bared and glistening with sweat, he was helping his men to install their new headquarters in a farmhouse. Colonel Isaac, however, had left the previous day and returned to the Maquis Bernard.

On our way back to the Bois de Montsauche, we had a puncture and stopped to change wheels. While we were working at the roadside, the planes came back. Low, they swooped over the road, heading for the Maquis car-park, and we had a fine view of them diving in to the attack. Some of the Maquisards appeared to be replying with Bren-fire but we had little time to wait and watch. I have never seen a wheel changed so quickly with fingers that trembled so hard. Both my companions had been heavily strafed previously. Indeed Worn, on Malta, had been entombed in his gun-pit by an aerial bomb. Before the planes came round for a second time we were well under the cover of a farm building and there we jacked up the jeep once more, secured the wheels, and made another dash for the woods. On the outskirts I stopped and we took up a good position in a piece of open ground, awaiting a chance for a pot-shot as the aircraft came round again.

It was then that Worn's nerve went. He began yelling at me not to fire. Panic-stricken, almost gibbering, he grabbed the gun, desperate to escape the attention of the enemy planes. They passed overhead to conclude another ineffectual attack on the car-park, causing no damage. I was furious with Worn and we returned to camp. Later that night I spoke to Alex about him, demanding he be sent to Squadron HQ, and not employed again. Alex, however, with his longer battle experience, told me to leave him in the camp for a day or two and then give him another chance. Sound advice, as his subsequent conduct at Tamnay was to prove.

The night of 10/11 August, with the advantage of a full moon, saw the most spectacular attack that Two Troop launched while it was in France. As we had only the one jeep in the troop, we borrowed Bill's jeep as well as that of Major Melot, which Alex adapted to carry the 3-inch mortar. The other two vehicles, in addition to their normal complement of four Vickers' guns, carried a number of Lewis bombs.

Our target, for the second time, was to be the synthetic oil plant, and from the aerial photograph of it in our possession we very carefully worked out a plan of action.

I was to command the leading jeep, with Georges, who had already done the trip twice, as navigator. I carried Jemson as my rear-gunner and had Bass on board as an additional man for Alex's mortar team. We were to recce ahead of the others as far as the fork road at Millery, about 1000 yards from the factory. Then, leaving Bass to join the mortar jeep, we would scout on foot as far as another building that we could see about 500 yards nearer the target.

The mortar jeep would then enter a field on the right of the road and the mortar would be erected to fire into the plant at a range of 700 yards. The mortar jeep now consisted of Sergeant Campbell, Roger, Troopers Close and Docherty, and Alex himself. The third jeep, commanded by Dickie Grayson and driven by Lofty Langridge, carried Corporal Sylvester, Sergeant Rennie and Sergeant Ridler, who spoke French and German perfectly. Silvo was to be dropped to guard the fork road that covered our rear and then the rear jeep, joining up with my own, would close to the shortest feasible range and strafe the plant with the Vickers-K's.

The night was perfect. There was not a cloud in the sky, nor a breath of wind, and at about 10.30 the little column set off into the twilight along the route that Georges had so carefully selected. The Lac des Settons looked beautiful as we passed its southern shore, a thin mist shimmering in the light of the rising moon. By Cussy and Tavernay we went, the gaunt empty squares echoing to the roar of our exhausts.

At midnight we halted on the fern-clad shoulder of a hill hanging over the River Ternin. There we checked our ammunition and explosives, making sure that everything was ready for the attack and waiting for the moon to climb to its zenith. About 1 o'clock we moved forward once more and as we reached Millery farm, I felt almost overpowered by excitement. Georges and I confirmed that the farm was clear and examined a small defensive position near by that we had picked out from the aerial photos. Jemson, now manning the front guns, kept us covered, while Middleton drove behind us. Having made sure that Alex had come up and there were no enemy about, we climbed on to the front of the jeep and were carried down to our next objective. As we reached the brow of the hill I could see the whole factory clearly outlined in the moonlight. The huge slag heap lay like an enormous ant-hill, overshadowing the entire scene, its dull glitter contrasting strangely with the bright reflections from the cluster of roofs which huddled around its broad base.

The second building we reached proved to be a new shale mining shaft, which must have been producing the raw material for the plant. I gave it a very peremptory examination and then, leaving Georges with his Bren-gun to cover it, I went back for a quick conference with Dickie. Alex was already hard at work setting his mortar into position and making all the necessary adjustments.

'How long will you be?' I asked.

'Oh, quite some time,' he replied; and supposing this meant about twenty minutes, I conferred with Dickie.

It would obviously be a good thing to blow up the wheel-house above the shaft, and I gave him the option of doing the strafing or the blowing. He chose the strafe, so, gathering all the explosives from both jeeps, I got a lift back to the wheel-house and jumped off.

With Georges covering me, I squeezed in through the narrow slit used by the hawsers for pulling up the truck-loads of shale. I dragged in my Lewis bombs and pressed them firmly into position around the spokes of both the huge wheels that stood within. As I started this operation, I was startled to hear the plop-whee-bang of the first mortar bomb; and in a moment, having got the range, Alex started pumping them into the factory area as fast as he could cram them into the muzzle. I heard the two jeeps moving swiftly down the road towards the factory, and could hardly suppress a chuckle as the shrill whine of the air-raid siren broke out. Almost immediately came the staccato rattle of eight Vickers-K's firing off their hundred-round magazines in long, smooth bursts.

Time was very short. I connected up my charges with Cordtex-detonating fuse and searched for my time-pencils. Luck was against me. By wriggling through the small aperture into the wheel-house, I had crushed and broken almost all the pencils. I searched frantically for an undamaged one and found two. Unfortunately, they were both two-hour delays. I connected them up, however, and pulled out the pins. As I crawled out of the wheel-house, I heard the jeeps coming back up the road at top speed. I waited just long enough to crush the acid phials of the pencils and, running out into the road, leapt on to the leading jeep. I had a momentary vision of Georges rising from the ditch and shouting 'Wait for me!' as the second jeep breasted the rise and took him on board.

Back at Millery, we found the mortar jeep ready loaded and as we approached it accelerated away. We picked up Bass and Sylvester, then raced after it.

Back we went, high-tailing it for the hills as fast as the loaded jeeps would take us. On the corners we swung dangerously. Sometimes the leading jeep missed a corner in the maze of little roads that we were trying to follow. Then the other jeeps, hooting derisively, swept past and the flight continued.

Half an hour later, on the slope overlooking the Ternin, we halted and compared notes. There was quite a lot of leg-pulling at my expense, as I was still carrying the broken pencils in my pocket, and if the pin had come out, some of them were about due to go off. I threw them away rather quickly.

Alex was unsure of the damage he had done, but his bombs had plumped very satisfactorily into the target area and he had been rewarded by the sight of clouds of steam rising from a broken pipe.

Dickie had had difficulty in positioning his jeeps, as the spot we had picked from the photographs had proved impracticable, but he had closed to 200 yards and strafed the whole area from the road. Again there was no certainty of the damage, but a great electrical spark had shown that at least he had cut the power lines.

Georges, meanwhile, had seen ten dim figures bolt out of the back of the wheel-house, as I climbed in by the hawser-slit. He had not fired as he did not want to give his position away and was uncertain whether they were civilians or Boche, though he could almost swear that he had heard the click of a rifle bolt. Later he was furious to learn that these men had been *milice* – French Fascist soldiers – whom he would happily have shot down. Worse still, having watched me laying the charges, they had routed civilians out of bed and forced them to pull my explosives off the wheels.

Roger, like me, also came in for some ridicule. Having helped load the mortar back on to the jeep immediately after the strafe, he had jumped in and straddled the barrel. It was nearly red hot!

In the end it transpired that we had not done nearly as much damage as we had hoped. Although highly spectacular, it was not in fact very useful. But as a model of a nice little operation going according to plan, it was delightful. The whole attack, from the moment I dismounted at Millery to the moment that Silvo remounted at the same spot, had taken exactly twenty-five minutes. Before the sun had even begun to lighten the sky we were all safely back in camp and sleeping peacefully in our parachute tents.

The next day Bob Melot's and Bill's jeeps had to be handed over to Paddy Mayne and his intelligence officer. The following evening they left us, making their way back through the lines to bring in C Squadron. Our jeep situation was worse than ever before. Only mine and Johnny Wiseman's remained. On the 13th, one more jeep was dropped on the Mazignien DZ for Bill himself. But the next day Johnny departed with his own, Dijon bound once more.

CHAPTER XXII

Tamnay Again

On 9 August, Robert McReady, the doc's brother, was dropped to us. His task was to discover an airfield from which the wounded could be flown out. He borrowed a civilian car from us and with one companion began to search the area for a suitable landing zone.

He did at least manage to discover the mobile headquarters set up by Isaac and Diagram who, with a flair for the obscure that amounted to genius, had hidden this base so effectively that not even their allies, let alone the enemy, could find it. Consequently they were seldom available to give decisions, and policies requiring their approval tended to stagnate. In theory they had *agents de liaison* and rendezvous by some indeterminate milestone, passwords and all the rest, but in practice it was usually quicker and simpler to follow tyre tracks. Nevertheless, this PC did much to unify the Morvan and during August a network of Maquis ambushes sprang up along all the important roads so that small enemy forces could be repulsed and large detachments delayed.

These ambushes affected us in two ways. First, we needed to be aware of them so as to give the correct signal at the appropriate place; second, they afforded us far greater freedom of movement close to our own areas.

On two occasions I fell into Maquis ambushes. The only intimation I had of the existence of the first one was when I saw a stream of tracer play across my bonnet. I was driving a private car at the time and stopped so suddenly that my gunner inadvertently pulled his own trigger and there was nearly an international incident. Fortunately, no one was hurt. The second was my own fault, for I forgot a well-known ambush and drove straight through it. If I had kept going all would have been well, but catching a glimpse of a Maquisard face staring at me through the bushes, I pulled up to apologise. As I stepped out of the car, the guard emerged from the trees with a Sten-gun in his hand and let fly. The dust kicked up about my boots and my driver ducked for cover. Having just run through their ambush, I could hardly blame them for taking a pot-shot at me, so I relieved my feelings by balling them out for being such rotten shots. At that range they ought to have cut us in half.

With freer movement near at home we now began to visit the Lac des Settons and the exclusive resort of Les Settons. Sometimes we went with the Maquisards for meals at the Hôtel de la Plage, but more often we dropped in at the twin hotels of the Morvandelle and the Beau Rivage. The latter was owned by a M. Lambert. He had been a collaborator with the Germans and at one time

Frau Goering had stopped there. Now he lived in daily dread of raids by the Maquis and couldn't do enough for the British, hoping to receive some measure of protection.

Lambert lived with the daughter of his wife by an earlier marriage. His proper wife, i.e. the mother of his mistress, called herself Madame Duru and ran the Morvandelle. Not unnaturally, the two ex-partners were now at daggers drawn. Madam Duru was a very pleasant and vivacious woman withal and she, too, often fed us, though there had never been any hint of her collaborating with the Boche.

Rich Parisians eager to escape the war were vacationing at these hotels and, though not packed to capacity, they had quite a holiday air about them. It was amusing to contrast a group of fat, sleek businessmen dining in one corner with a party of tough, travel-stained Maquisards, their rifles and grenades slung from the hat-racks, carousing in another. But there were many such incongruities, the strangest, according to hearsay, being at Nevers, where armed Maquisards and armed Germans found themselves drinking in the same bar. The Germans had come in first and left their rifles just out of reach. When the Maquisards entered, they dared not fire for fear of raising the alarm, or causing reprisals. Nothing remained for both parties but to keep their eyes skinned and get on with their drinking.

I well remember the glorious luxury of my first hot bath for almost three months in the Beau Rivage. I remember, too, the amusement we derived from talking to the evacuees from Paris. Some were quite attractive and we had many laughs at Alex's expense when a girl with whom he had been trying to get on closer terms for a fortnight went for a walk in the woods with Jock Christie the first day she met him — and Jock could not speak a word of French.

We had marvellous meals at these hotels: meats and salads beautifully prepared in the French style, good wines, even a little pre-war whisky, and one day some magnificent Cliquot Rose Champagne — all well worth the risk we took in dining out.

When the sun shone we were able occasionally to bathe or boat on the lake, and very nice it was, too, to laze on the sandy beach, idly surveying the pine-clad shore, the deep blue water and the misty Morvan hills in the background.

There was plenty of rain, too, accompanied by lightning and thunder. At night the effects could be supreme and rather terrifying — storm silhouetting storm, great mountains of clouds piling up beneath a waning moon and brilliant flashes of dazzling light sweeping over us from all points of the compass.

Sometimes we were able neatly to combine business with pleasure, as on the day when Alex, on the way to a dinner at Les Settons, saw a German Ju 52 fly low across the road in front of him. At once he engaged it with his two forward Vickers. The tracer bullets could be seen entering the fuselage and it was smoking as it dipped from view. Later we heard, though unable to confirm, that it had crashed near Lormes.

About the same time we had a rather less happy excursion. Our good friend Socrate was killed. One of his lorries ran into a German convoy. They shot their way through successfully but there were casualties. It was necessary to take up a Maquis nurse to attend to them. Socrate went with her in his car. Where his boys had gone he could go, and he, in his turn, deliberately shot his way through the convoy. This time the Germans were ready. The car got through, riddled with bullets. The driver was fortunate merely to be cut with flying glass. Socrate and the young nurse were mortally wounded. Before help could arrive, they were dead.

The girl was buried in the Bois de Montsauche, in the little cemetery of the Maquisards. Later her body was moved to the lovely old cemetery at Lavault-de-Fretoy, among those hilly woods where she had lived, saved lives and died. The dead chief was borne back to the camp that he had fought to guard so well, and on the sad 13th, at the stroke of midnight, he was buried close by at Cussy-en-Morvan.

Middleton, Tom Rennie, Nobby Noble and I attended the funeral. All the great men of the Maquis were there: Georges, Roger and the Martells, Dubois himself, Serge and many more. Some of them I was to meet the following year when I taxed my French to the utmost to make a funeral oration beside his grave.

We travelled in a very unreliable Maquis car which ran on wood alcohol, smelt foul and broke down repeatedly. We had difficulty, too, in finding the latest headquarters of his Maquis, where his body was lying in state. At one prolonged stop, while the Maquis driver was cleaning the carburettor without any great apparent success, the sound of screaming engines made us look up. There, silhouetted against the fading yellow of the sky, three aircraft were circling and plummeting down in the general direction of Ouroux. Only that day, confident in the strength of the surrounding Maquis, Ouroux had hung out the flags and declared itself liberated. Here was swift retribution. One after another the Stukas dive-bombed the town, finally subjecting it to a hail of cannon fire. At a distance it looked terrifying and dangerous. Later we were to learn that it had been entirely ineffective, most of the bombs landing in the fields and the worst havoc being the uprooting of one paving stone.

Predictably, we arrived at the Maquis HQ late, but not too late, and soon the cortège was forming up. It was dark before we moved off and the improvised hearse backfired viciously all the way down the hill out of the Maquis, so that one might have been excused for believing that a German attack was developing.

At the bottom of the hill the hearse stalled and the mourners had to get out of their cars to push. None of the batteries were much good after four years of disuse, so that as soon as the hearse was safely started, most of the mourners had to push their own cars to get them going. This for a moment produced the ludicrous situation of the mourners' cars having to tear along at full speed in an effort to catch the hearse, which could not slow down for fear of stalling again.

From the dry earth road a great column of dust towered into the air with the swift passing of the cortège, and as every car in the convoy had its lights full on, the general effect from a distance must have been that of the pillar of fire by night.

As we reached Cussy, the tempo slackened and the humour dried out of the situation. The great square was filled with silent cars. At every corner of the little town and all around the cemetery the Maquis Bren-posts stood on guard. Slowly and solemnly the body of the great leader was carried up the hill to his last resting place. Now everything was very silent except for the shuffling of feet and muffled sobs, and only the occasional flicker of a torch relieved the darkness which began to close in on us.

In the cemetery a great crowd stood bare-headed in the dark as the priest began the burial service in Latin. The service over, Dubois began to speak. The light of his torch reflecting off the papers he held shone upward on to his face, giving it a strangely mystical and disembodied look. I could not follow much of the tributes that he lauded on this fallen patriot, but I echoed them in my heart, and all around strong men were weeping audibly, not attempting to stifle their sobs. The oration made, the great congregation filed past the coffin, softly illuminated by a single lamp, crossing themselves or making the sign of the cross over the dead man as they moved slowly by. At length, I gathered the British contingent and we saluted the coffin, our faces made eerie by odd reflections of the lamp, and then, as the church bell mournfully pealed the hour of midnight, a very gallant Frenchman was lowered into his grave.

The night of the 14/15 August, too, brought its harvest of humour, near-tragedy and failure. This night I took an expedition to destroy the Tamnay bridge in a repeat of the venture that had so nearly ended fatally for me when we went after the tobacco convoy the week before.

My party consisted of three cars. The first was a small and somewhat ancient Fiat, driven by Christie, carrying Sergeant Ken Sturmey and Lance-Corporal Dolly Dray, their objective being the turntable at Tamnay station. The second was Dickie Grayson's Ford with Langridge driving. Their target was the mass of points north of the town where the railway from Nevers branched to Château-Chinon and Corbigny. They also carried Short and Collison, who were going to help me. I travelled in my jeep with Middleton driving as usual. Jemson had been over to Squadron HQ for the day and did not get back until too late to come with us. I took Fernand as my interpreter, and gave Worn his second chance. I asked Lance-Corporal Cave to accompany me, but he refused point-blank. I was not surprised as there was constant friction between us in camp, though I had hoped an operation together might cure this. My own objective was the Tamnay bridge itself.

We spent the afternoon of the 14th preparing our charges. I was told by the Maquis that the bridge in question was a low round-arched bridge of stone. Accordingly I employed the 100 lb charges that I had already prepared. I took with me some lengths of thin steel hawser, salvaged from the harness of a jeep chute, to pull the explosive up tight beneath the bridge. All that would then be necessary was to wedge it firmly against the bottom of the bridge with any old pole that came handy. The theory of this type of charge is that the first jar of the explosion shakes the structure, while the pressure waves recoiling from the ground beneath lift the bridge off its foundations and drop it into the stream.

Before setting out we all studied very carefully the maps and the aerial photo that we had of the area under attack. The final approach to Tamnay from the north was down the second-class road from Corbigny. Just before reaching the Nevers–Château-Chinon *route nationale*, which runs east and west through Tamnay, it is cut by an old disused single-track line running parallel to the highway. This old track crossed the River Trait and the new lines just north of Tamnay, and then swung south under the *route nationale*. This was the bridge that I intended to destroy. Beyond it the overgrown sleepers led on into the modern goods-yard of Tamnay and it was there that the turntable would be discovered.

The Germans were known to be patrolling pretty actively now and it was for this reason that we brought the three cars and were well armed. As it began to get dark, we set out.

Almost at once we were dogged by bad luck, for the Ford had one of its frequent punctures, and just as we got that repaired the Fiat started to cough and splutter again. We were well within friendly territory and so, putting Short on to my jeep and Sturmey and Dray into the Ford, we carried on, leaving Christie to make his way back as best he could.

I had another alarm a few moments later as I saw, in the half-light, a steel-helmeted figure in a loose tunic, with a rifle slung across his back, cycling round the corner ahead of me. The tail-end of a Jerry bicycle patrol, I thought to myself. I was wrong. At the next bend we caught him up. The tin hat revealed itself as a shiny bald pate, the rifle resolved into a stick, and it was an old peasant, cycling back from his hard day's toil.

The journey was much like any other run across the Morvan by night. It seemed interminable. At last we reached the second-class road at the village of Ougny, where we paused to prepare for the last stage of the assault and to enquire of the locals the habits of the hostile patrols.

After a brief rest we turned down our road to the south. Without difficulty we found the disused railway which had crossed this road at a level-crossing. Now we were able to drive straight along it.

For perhaps a quarter of a mile we bumped along the rough path over the sleepers, hemmed in close by bramble hedges, and quite trapped if we ran into any trouble. Then, little by little, the track began to rise on a small embankment until right behind Tamnay itself it cut across a raised track running down to a farm. I had hardly passed over this before I was brought up dead by the river. The bridge had long since rotted away and nothing but a couple of heavy wooden beams spanning the gap remained to show where the railway had formerly crossed. Now we had to back out of this awkward predicament. First the Ford and then the jeep began the slow return. The track was narrow and very tricky in the dark.

At last the Ford emerged safely at the track crossing behind Tamnay and began to turn round. Middleton drove the jeep past the Ford and began to make his own turn. The trees hung darkly over the spot and the moon had not yet begun to rise. The junction of railroad and track was hard to see. No lights were being used for the Germans might well be in the town. Middleton went a tiny bit too far. Next moment, it was too late. He was over the embankment, wheels well down, beyond hope of human extrication.

In the limited space at our disposal, it was hopeless to think of manoeuvring the Ford to give a tow, even if that game civilian vehicle had stood a chance of pulling up the well-wedged jeep. Besides, we would risk losing the Ford over the embankment as well. There was nothing for it but to try manhandling, but we might as well have tried shifting the Eiffel Tower. It was hopeless.

Imagine our position. We were in the outskirts of a town patrolled by the enemy, within 200 yards of a very important road in constant use. Of the only two jeeps in the Morvan mine was stuck over the edge of a railway embankment, not 500 yards from our target. There were ten of us and the only surviving transport at my disposal was a not-over-reliable Ford. The prospect was not cheering. It was at this moment that Fernand had an idea.

'I'll get some oxen from the farm,' he announced, and off he went to do it. Meanwhile I organised an all-round defence of our little crossing and set the boys to work to dig channels to help the jeep out.

It must have been half-an-hour before Fernand returned, but close on his heels came two old peasants, each with a yoke of oxen. In a matter of moments we had harnessed them to the jeep and with a grunt and a heave, and a little swearing from the French, out it came. I have seldom been so relieved in all my life.

As soon as we had turned the jeep round safely, we thanked our friends and got down to business. Fernand, Collison and Short, under the direction of Worn, lugged the heavy explosives along the track; and leaving Middleton to guard the vehicles, I took the rest ahead to the beams over the Trait. I went over first and they held our weight all right. Dickie and Lofty then dropped down the embankment and began their arduous task of putting bombs into every set of points in this big junction of double-track rails.

With Sturmey and Dray, I pushed on along the old track as far as the bridge, where I wished them good luck and watched them tramp on along the line until they disappeared around a bend.

For me the bridge was a nasty shock. It was fully 25 feet above the level of the track, so that I could not hope to attach the explosives firmly. Moreover, it was not of stone but a steel girder affair; and it was not arched but straight. A very different proposition from what I had been led to expect, requiring a very different type of charge. Anyway it was now too late. All I could do was to use what I had and hope for the best, but I was not particularly optimistic.

I went back along the track to where the rest of my party was struggling with the explosive. I gave them a hand. When we got to the bridge, Worn supervised the men working on the top and I remained below to see to the proper positioning of the charges. As they let down the hawsers from above, I fixed on the explosive and they hauled it up, one hawser on each side of the bridge, raising the charge towards the bottom centre part of the span. Owing to its size and shape they could not make a very good job of it but after climbing up to survey their handiwork, I decided that it was the best we could hope for and ordered them to return to the cars. I waited for Sturmey. It was not a long vigil. In a few moments they came back together, well pleased with themselves. They had fixed the turntable, good and proper, and had left the Lewis bombs with one-hour time-pencils in a string of stationary goods' wagons.

As soon as they were safely past the bridge I set off the hour time-pencils that we had attached to the bridge charge and hurried after the others. As I ran along the track I heard a sudden shot from the direction of Tamnay. I didn't know what it was but it didn't sound healthy. I crossed the new railway and saw that Dickie and Lofty were still working.

'OK?' I shouted.

'Just fixing the time-pencils,' he replied and I waited on the bridge until they scrambled up to me and we made our way across the beams.

Back at the cars everything was in order.

'What was that shot?' I demanded.

No one knew. I have no idea to this day but it certainly speeded our parting footsteps.

On the road back, on a nice desolate stretch of track, we pulled off underneath the trees to listen. The hour was almost up. The boys began to smoke. Flash – flick – flick – flash. Then from the distance the crash and rumble of the explosions. We counted them, guessing the significance of each alternate flash and bang. Of one, there could be no doubt. It was five minutes overdue by my watch but when it came, it lit the whole sky. With the roar of its explosion the ground seemed to tremble.

'Well, there's the bridge. I wonder what damage it has done?' asked Worn. I wondered too. Later I discovered that both the sides of the bridge had been blown away, but it had not fallen. The Germans were able to patch it up and continue using it. All the other bombs were successful.

More excitement occurred before we could turn in. This was caused by the planes that kept sweeping over on some mission or other. Only the other night a passing plane had directed a stream of tracer at Bill's torch, and there was always the danger that our airmen, mistaking our lights for Jerries, would take a pot at us. Thus, each time a plane came past there was a minor panic, until the lights were extinguished. After all, one would feel pretty silly being shot up by the RAF.

The final hallucination was when I woke suddenly from a doze and mistook a line of painted poles along the roadside for a German patrol. I shouted something silly, but was wide enough awake to spot my error before I pressed the triggers.

Back at camp we were happy to hear that Christie had got back safely and were asleep by 2 o'clock, after a not unsatisfactory night's work.

CHAPTER XXIII

Failures

The Germans were now becoming more active all around the fringes of the Morvan. Another attack had been launched against the Maquis Camille. It was easily beaten off and the gun did not have to be used but it was a symptom of what what was happening. Strong columns of enemy fleeing eastward were forcing their way, despite suffering casualties, through Maquis territory. Because of this it was decided to evacuate all wounded, both British and Maquis, to the greater safety of Montsauche and the comparative comfort of the new hospital.

Accordingly, on the 16th, a column consisting of the two jeeps, two lorry-loads of Maquis, an ambulance and a number of civilian cars assembled at Le Meix Chalaux. I acted as advance scout with my usual crew of Middleton, Jemson and Worn. Alex, with a crew of his own in the major's jeep, headed the convoy itself. The wounded were in the ambulance and the civvy cars, while the Maquisards brought up the rear. We moved very slowly through familiar country. A cameraman of the Maquis, who had come down specially from Paris, took moving pictures of the whole operation. The evacuation was completely successful. No enemy were encountered and the wounded were duly installed in the Bois de Montsauche.

Two days later we were on the move again with the ambulances. Robert McReady had at last found a suitable site for a Dakota to land, but it was in the Côte d'Or, beyond Saulieu. Nevertheless it was arranged that the plane should come and in the morning we set off in much the same order as before but with only our own wounded and no escort of Maquisards.

We were most fortunate in encountering no enemy, though I did have one bad moment when I came round a corner and found myself head-on to a lorry-load of armed men. They were men of the Maquis, however, and we all waved cheerfully as we passed.

We took the unusual step of passing straight through the big town of Saulieu itself. An *agent de liaison* from the PC met us on the outskirts and told us that there were no Germans staying there at present. He then bicycled through ahead of us, assuring himself that none had moved in or were passing through. In this way the town was safely negotiated among the cheers of those townsfolk who saw our little Union Jacks, or realised what was going on.

We rendezvoused with Bill Fraser and Robert McReady at one of the subsidiary Maquis controlled by Captain Robert. Arrangements had been made for the night and the wounded were all very excited at the prospect of going home.

At this time we had Adamson with his pelvis, Chalky and Grady with their arms and Bromfield and Burgess with their legs. Nobby Noble, the sergeant-major and our other minor wounded had all recovered. The terrible journey had been absolute torture for Adamson but he bore it all very bravely.

While at this Maquis we saw the chains of German prisoners they had captured by skilful attacks on isolated enemy observer posts. The Germans had retaliated in their usual way against the villages. So, approaching the German commander through the local *curé*, Robert had swapped his prisoners against the promise of immunity for the villages. Surprisingly, the enemy kept their word and Robert was quite satisfied, as he had entirely demolished the posts.

We also saw the Maquisards beating up some Frenchmen they had taken. These men were genuine brigands. They lacked political convictions and did not fight the Hun; but claiming to be Maquis, they had terrorised the local civilians. The bringing of the Maquis into disrepute by gangsters could not be tolerated and their punishment, now that they had been caught, was extremely severe. They were knocked about until all possible information about their associates had been extracted, and then shot. It was brutal but it discouraged brigandage.

It was a long evening waiting for the plane and praying for good weather. Alex and I went on a recce with Robert with a view to co-operating in an attack on one very big post which he had not been able to tackle alone. This fight never in fact materialised, but we had a very nice supper of biscuits, peaches and red wine in another of his subsidiary Maquis.

When we got back, however, bad news awaited us. The 7 o'clock broadcast had postponed indefinitely the arrival of the Dakota. The moon was on the wane now, so we knew that there was no hope for another fortnight. To the poor wounded it was bitterly disappointing. For us it was infuriating.

As soon as it was dark we drove straight back to the Bois de Montsauche. It was a nightmare journey in the dark and as there was no *agent de liaison* awaiting us at Saulieu, we had to take the long way round, avoiding the town. This meant crossing two busy *routes nationales*, and on one of these we only just missed a large German convoy coming up from the south, whose twinkling headlights seemed to stretch for miles.

I managed to lose the way in the darkness before the moon rose and the column moved on without its scout. They were lucky to find no enemy about. I searched for them for some time then pushed on with all speed. Somehow I missed them along the road and reached the wood ahead of them again. I was very worried for about a quarter of an hour until they turned up safely.

Adamson was in a truly dreadful state by this time and had been screaming deliriously most of the way back, which had been pretty terrible for the other wounded. Dr Martell was gravely worried about his condition and said that we ought to get the wounded out of the woods as soon as possible. Accordingly, Alex arranged with the 'old collab' at the Beau Rivage that the wounded be boarded there. M. Lambert was nothing loath, as the presence of our wounded saved him from the depredations of the Maquis.

In these more congenial surroundings and often visited by the pretty girls from the hotels around, the wounded soon began to pick up, but we were always worried in case a German column, while forcing its way through the Morvan, should stop at the Beau Rivage for a drink.

On 20 August there was a major engagement when the Germans attacked the Maquis at Vernay, close to Nevers. Support was sent from many of the Maquis around. André led his own group out in great force. The Maquis Camille, which now possessed an armoured car, stolen from a factory in Paris, did yeoman service. We, too, were asked to help, but with only the one jeep at his disposal, Alex felt that the effort was hardly worth the risk involved. Moreover, only recently he had received orders from Brigade to keep out of Maquis battles. The Maquis at Vernay was driven out, but the assistance received from the other Maquis enabled them to extricate themselves intact and reform in the woods near Ouroux.

André's men returned in very fine fettle, bringing two German parachutists whom they had taken prisoner.

On the 21st we had reason to suspect that something big was afoot. German planes were strafing the roads and villages around Ouroux and Montsauche. They were as ineffective as usual, though they did tend to restrict Maquis movements along the roads.

That day I went into Saulieu with Christie, Roger and Tom Rennie, to requisition some more cars. We posted sentries at each end of the street in which we were working and having overcome the usual difficulty with tyres, batteries and tools, managed to get a fine big Ford car on the road. It was about 4.30 when we left Saulieu. An hour later, Marshal Pétain, with a bodyguard of 600 *milice* and SS, moved into Saulieu. It was a narrow shave.

The presence in Saulieu of the head of the puppet French government at once threw the whole Maquis into a ferment. The PC started issuing orders in all directions. At the Maquis Bernard we were told the true strength of the enemy by a civilian who had cycled over with the news at about 8 o'clock, but half an hour later the 'official' figures given out by the PC was 6000 Germans with tank and air support. Not unnaturally, the Maquis thought twice about taking on so powerful a force without concentrating their troops and co-ordinating a plan.

As soon as it was light, strong ambushing forces were sent out to lie in wait along the roads out of Saulieu. It was too late. Before the ambushes were in position, the convoy had passed. The Maquis Bernard succeeded in capturing

Pétain's *chef de gendarmerie*, but that was all. A great opportunity had been missed. Or had it? I think that the false information may have been deliberately put out by the PC because they feared the political consequence of the death or capture of Pétain. Perhaps, in the long run, they were right. After all, his regime was already discredited; it would have been a mistake to martyrise him.

On the night of the 21st there was a big *parachutage* of arms on the Mazignien DZ, and Bill Fraser was able to arm the new Maquis Verneuil, which had sprung up in his area. Two nights later two more jeeps were dropped. One of them crashed but the other one survived.

During the following two days, there was considerable fighting all along the Château-Chinon road, with the Maquis ambushing enemy columns as they tried to push their way through.

On the night of 23/24 August I was ordered to cut the Château-Chinon road so effectively that the enemy would be forced to fight the Maquis in the hills, where they would be at an even greater disadvantage. With this in view, I picked out a culvert on the road between Château-Chinon and Autun, not far from the garrison town of Arleuf, which I decided to blow with one of my 100 lb charges.

I took Middleton, Worn and Jemson in the jeep and stopped at the town of Anost, which had now been completely taken over by the Maquis Socrate. There I explained to Dédé, the chief, what I wanted to do and he offered me the loan of four men and a civilian car.

With this reinforcement we made our way cautiously down the forest road close to Arleuf, finally halting in a small village as near as I dared approach the probable position of the culvert. It was my intention to manhandle the explosives up the hill to the culvert, lay the charge at leisure, lying doggo if patrols approached, and then return to the jeep on foot, leaving a half-hour time-pencil. So much for the plan. The practice was a very different matter. The hill up to the road seemed interminable. Up and up and up we toiled. I kept scouting ahead to look out for enemy patrols and occasionally we heard the engines of passing cars, but each false crest produced another crest beyond and the heavy, awkward charges were very difficult to carry. I got lost and found myself again. We had to cross and recross streams running down the hillside. Fences and hedges barred our way. For one long strip we had to pass in full view of the road, which towered over us as it ran along the summit. For three hours of heartbreaking labour we toiled upward. One of the Maquisards passed out from his exertions. Still the top seemed no nearer.

I was following up the stream which should have bubbled out from under the culvert; and so indeed it did, but the culvert was through a 30-foot high embankment. My poor charge would have no more effect against that than a peashooter against the Forth Bridge. After so much hard work it was a bitter disappointment. I could see again how very important was accurate reconnaissance. Nothing remained but for me to leave the explosive where it was, put a time-pencil to it so that it would not be found by the enemy, and sadly retrace our steps.

So far had we come that there was a roar and spurt of flame as the charge went up, long before we had returned to our parked vehicles. Back at the village a shock awaited us. There were no signs of either the jeep or the car. For an awful moment we thought that a patrol must have snaffled them, and that Middleton, their guard, was now a prisoner. But after much yelling he was found quietly asleep in a barn, having hidden the vehicles well against the possibility of a Boche patrol.

There was much ribaldry at our expense when we returned from this unsuccessful outing. The next morning, Alex took the jeep and with Dickie Grayson and two civilian car-loads of his boys, including Ken Sturmey and Nobby Noble, he determined to block the road himself.

He drove boldly on to the *route nationale*, posted pickets at each end of the stretch along which he intended to work, and proceeded to lay demolition charges against the tall trees that lined the road. He finished the task successfully and withdrew to watch the result. The laugh was on him. The charges exploded all right. Bark flew off the trees but they refused to fall, and they certainly did not block the road.

That night, the 24/25 August, determined to make a job of it, Tom Rennie, with Christie as driver, and one companion, went in the Fiat close up to the road. They had prepared their charges very carefully all afternoon. They were not interrupted in their work by any enemy, and they did finally succeed in blowing three large trees across the road. On the way back to camp they informed the Maquis Socrate of the location of the block, with the result that the next morning the Maquis sprang a very good ambush, inflicting thirty casualties on a big enemy column.

That same night we were warned to expect two jeeps on the Montsauche DZ. It was a filthy night, pouring with rain, and with quite a wind blowing. Alex was out of the camp at the time that the message came through, but I decided that it would be dangerous to man the DZ, tonight, as we would risk losing both jeeps. Accordingly I did not send out the Eureka, nor the lights.

Towards 1 o'clock it began to clear a little and as I expected Alex to be back soon I ran down the slippery muddy track to the Maquis Silvo to intercept him as soon as possible. It was still drizzling unpleasantly when I reached the Poirot entrance and I met Alex just as he got back. He confirmed my decision and we went to our tents to sleep.

Early next morning a messenger arrived from the Maquis to say that two jeeps had dropped mysteriously on the DZ the previous night. We rushed down to investigate. Apparently the Maquis Bernard made a habit of manning the DZ every night and flashing a torch hopefully at any aircraft that passed within range. That night, without Eureka, and to the wrong recognition letter, the RAF had dropped our two precious jeeps on the right DZ. One of them had been dragged by the wind, its automatic harness release having failed, and was upside down in a clump of trees. The other had lost two of its parachutes on the way down and would probably have been severely damaged but for the good luck of landing in some thick bushes. We really had been more fortunate than we deserved. After a hard morning's work, both were successfully retrieved.

On the 25th, the Maquis Silvo was dissolved and he and his 6-pounder were sent to a Maquis near Clamecy, where German tanks were reported to be active. He spent a week there before being brought back to Squadron, and never got a tank within range.

Another misfortune in this period of repeated failures was Bill's 'Jock Column', which set out to harry the Château-Chinon road. This consisted of two jeeps, one doing the scouting, the other pulling Sergeant Burgess's 6-pounder and three civilian cars carrying men and automatic weapons, mostly HQ Squadron personnel. It set out on the evening of the 26th and spent the night at the Bois de Montsauche, where Bill saw the *parachutage* of Feebury and the reinforcements, as recounted in the next chapter. He carried on to Anost the next day. The weather was pretty miserable as usual and a Maquis battle to the south held them up there. During the night, in consultation with the Maquis, an all-out assault on Château-Chinon was planned. Bill sent off urgent messages to Alex and me.

At this time, Alex had moved with an advance party of men from his troop to set up a new camp very close to Bill's in the valley of the Chalaux. I was left in charge of the remnants of Two Troop in the Bois de Montsauche. I set out at dawn with the two jeeps that I could muster, leaving a sergeant to clean up the campsite. Alex, who was supposed to bring the 3-inch mortar, did not materialise; he was too far away and did not get the message until too late. His absence, however, was of no consequence, as an urgent message had arrived from Colonels Isaac and Diagram, requesting that no attempt be made against Château-Chinon. Their reason was sound enough, for the Maquis was not sufficiently strong to have held the town against tanks and artillery if the Germans decided to fight to keep their supply lines clear. The killing of a Grey Russian garrison would hardly compensate for the razing of Château-Chinon, if the Germans recaptured it.

Bill had also realised that the dragging of a 6-pounder and its ammunition for any distance by jeep along these rotten roads was very tricky work. So, after considerable thought, he reluctantly abandoned the 'Jock Column' idea and returned to the valley of the Chalaux.

One further attempt to secure Château-Chinon, peacefully through the desertion of the garrison, was attempted. Denby, with Sergeant Zellic and one of the Grey Russians captured at Montsauche in June, were taken down by

Lofty Langridge in the Ford to the outskirts of Château-Chinon. They waited for an hour or two, during which time the Russian was supposed to bring out his friends to surrender. Eventually Denby's party began to get jittery, not without reason. The prisoner had no intention of returning and the British were lucky that they were not caught by a patrol sent out to trap them.

It was at the last *parachutage* that we had on the Montsauche DZ before the arrival of the reinforcements that I once more crossed verbal swords with Cave. There turned out to be a Maquis *parachutage* at the same time as our own, and while collecting the containers in the morning I caught Sturmey, Cave and some of the others taking the American-type waterproof jackets out of the Maquis containers. These jackets were shoved in as packing for the munitions, but could then be used by the Maquisards as uniforms. We certainly were in need of waterproofs ourselves, for the weather was seldom clement; and as the containers were dropped by British planes, the boys felt that they ought to get first pick of the contents.

The Maquis, however, as might well be imagined, were furious. As soon as I knew what was happening I demanded that all the coats be handed in to me. I had arranged with the Maquis that I should give them one of the spare battle-dresses, of which we had several in sizes that none of our men required, in exchange for the waterproofs. But I wanted to know how many had been taken and teach the men a temporary lesson in honesty.

I had no difficulty in collecting the coats from the others, but Cave was adamant. Finally I left him, stating that I would be forced to bring the whole matter up before Major Fraser on the next opportunity. However, before I had gone down to the Maquis with the coats, the other boys got to work on him, with the result that he brought me the coat himself.

'I'll get you for this,' he said, not melodramatically, but sincerely, through his teeth.'I don't care how long it takes but I'll get you for this!'

Certainly, our private feud was not over. In Norway, some months later, after a couple of drinks he became remarkably abusive to me in the presence of some of the men of my troop. I went with him to a lonely spot in a woody knoll on a rocky crag overlooking the sea; and there, with two sergeants to see fair play, we had a barefist brawl. I knocked him down three times, cut the skin between his eyebrows and made his nose bleed. Then he decided to call it a day. Whether he considered he was even with me, I don't know. But as far as personal relationships went, I regarded it as another of my failures.

During the heavy cross-country haul, while trying to block the Château-Chinon road, I had forced a splinter through my fingernail. This went septic, swelled up my whole hand and throbbed painfully. One afternoon I went down to the Maquis hospital and got Martell to operate on it. He used a local anaesthetic, for which I was thankful. Even so the cutting away of the nail was a nasty and uncomfortable process. After the wound had been dressed I started back up the track but was very white and groggy. Luckily I encountered André, who brought me into his Maquis 'office' and gave me a liberal dose of red wine, which revived me a bit. Even so, I very nearly fainted with pain as life began to come back to my numbed finger.

Le Four took me along to his tent and gave me a really good swig of some excellent Kümmel which he had been keeping under his bed, and I stayed on for dinner with André, though I did not eat very much.

I kept Martell's dressing on for the rest of the time I was in France. By the end it was smelling pretty horrid but it kept the cut clean and the finger never bothered me again. The only trouble it caused was a slight difficulty in getting my bandaged finger curled round the trigger of my Vickers-K's.

CHAPTER XXIV

Linking-up

During the fateful days between 20 and 25 August, the Resistance of Paris was fighting to free the city. All along the line the Germans were falling back as fast as they could, many of them in considerable confusion. Now was the time for us all to operate in real earnest against the lines of withdrawal. Now we were getting the jeeps which we could have done with so well before. Now we received reinforcements.

It was the night of 26/27 August that Captain Bridgeford, with six of his airborne Royal Engineers, attached SAS, and Squadron Sergeant Major Feebury of Headquarters Squadron, with twenty-one SAS recruits dropped to us on the Montsauche DZ.

Alex had already left with his advance party, and Bill came up to see the new troops arrive. I arranged for there to be plenty of Maquisards scattered around the DZ to help the men along with their kitbags and parachutes and to guide them to my collecting post in the Maquis car-park. Here I got big hay-boxes prepared, full of tea, and the arrival of the reinforcements was almost like a training drop, even down to an ambulance and a medical officer in attendance. Happily, neither were required. The reinforcements felt a little flat, I think. Expecting to be greeted like heroes and being given a cup of tea instead.

Nor were they much happier at having to sleep in the open that night, as it rained. Needless to say, the Two Troop remnants slept back in their old camp. Next morning we wished Bill's abortive Jock Column farewell and arranged for the loan of a very large Maquis lorry. Into this truck we piled the containers, on top of which we perched all twenty-nine men, with their kit. After lunch I convoyed this rather vulnerable target to the camp by the Chalaux in my trusty jeep.

Chalaux had now become three camps in one. There was the old Squadron HQ camp, which remained where it was strung along the edge of the woods, just opposite the ford. At the head of the little valley, where the river ran out through the trees, Alex was setting up his camp; and half-way between the two, but on the other side of the river, which here was crossed by a series of very precarious stepping-stones, stood Jeff Duvivier's tent. It was around this tent that the new Three Troop camp was to spring up.

The bestowal of Roy Bradford's captaincy entailed more than getting the girls of Ouroux to sew home-made pips of parachute silk on to my battledress. I was now to command a troop, consisting of Lieutenant Ball, Sergeant Duvivier and his two merry men of the original Three Troop, Lance-Corporal Robinson, Trooper Thornton from Squadron HQ, and Sergeant Tom Rennie, Middleton, Worn and Jemson from Two Troop. Sylvester, his gun and gun-crew, were theoretically a part of my force, but detached at Clamecy. SSM Feebury, with the nine best men that he could pick from the reinforcements, completed my command. Georges and Roger were attached as interpreters.

I gave Feebury the job of erecting as many parachute tents as he could manage in the little strip of wood along the edge of the river beside Duvivier's tent. I allocated another strip of wood about 300 yards away as the latrine area and managed to find a small spring on the edge of another wood just above our camp, where I told him to prepare a cookhouse. The fact that we took our water from this little spring instead of relying on the river, as did the other troops, spared us the tummy troubles from which they often suffered.

Feebury was also able to cut down several large trees and manhandle them into position across the river so that we had a bridge and did not have to use the tricky stepping-stones. Then, leaving my new command to prepare their camp, I returned to the Bois de Montsauche for just one more night. We were abandoning the camp there completely and there were several tasks still to be done. All the really important kit we put into our underground ammo dump, and Dickie Grayson very carefully connected the explosives to a series of trip-wires and booby-traps around the dump. We labelled it clearly with the word 'Mines!' and the even more expressive skull and crossbones. The rest of the stuff I laid out neatly and brought Bernard along to investigate. After much haggling we exchanged a very large barrel of wine for the surplus kit that we were leaving in the camp. The Maquis, however, got the best of the bargain, as Dickie's booby-traps failed to explode and they pinched all the stuff that we had left in the dump as well.

The next morning we made a quick trek to see Bill at Anost. When I returned I saw the last of the good kit loaded on to the jeep and taken down to the site of the Maquis Silvo. After lunch I set off with the last men of Two Troop for the Chalaux camp, leaving Tom Rennie and Middleton to repair one of our cars which was still off the road and join us later. As we passed through Ouroux we were surprised suddenly to see a patrol of four new jeeps. There was something strange about them and I knew that they were not ours. One of them had a high fishing-rod aerial sprouting from the back and I went forward to investigate. The crews wore the red beret and the flying sword badge of the SAS but they were speaking French. They turned out to be a patrol from one of the two Regiments of French SAS in our Brigade and had just passed through the lines. I wished them good luck and soon they went about their appointed business.

There had been a similar link-up at Bill's camp on the 25th, when an officer of the Second SAS arrived with five jeeps and a number of trailers. They were the sole survivors of twenty that had tried to break through the lines a few nights before. They had run into a German tank brigade in harbour and that had been that. A few days later they returned through the lines with their invaluable jeeps. They left us the trailers but we felt very bitter about watching them take away these precious vehicles again.

We were kept busy again on 28 August. A telephone line was installed connecting us up to the Chalaux exchange. Many of the Maquis were already on the telephone and this greatly simplified liaison. Now, to reach Bill from anywhere in the Nièvre, all I had to do was to ask for the Chalaux exchange and demand 'Le Camp Anglais', and I was put straight through. Our MO became the chief telephone orderly.

During the afternoon news came in that there had been an SAS fight in Semur. It was said that four of our men had been taken prisoner and shot in the cemetery, but we never heard the truth about this and they were definitely not First SAS.

As dusk was falling Paddy, Bob Melot and Major Marsh of C Squadron turned up at camp in three jeeps. Paddy had led them safely through the lines and the Squadron was now bedding down in the woods just outside Brassy. We had a minor party to celebrate.

All that day, Two and Three Troops were settling into their new camps and preparing to set out on their strafes the following morning.

That night two foot parties from Squadron HQ, approaching their objectives in civvy cars, blew the lines Nevers–Clamecy and Autun–Dijon. These were Bridgeford's RE's and Sergeant Burgess, tired of being tied to his gun.

On the 29th, Alex went out on a strafe with two jeeps. He also attempted to obtain the surrender of the Château-Chinon garrison. Unfortunately a further garrison of 200 Germans turned up at the last moment and the plan fell through. He did a certain amount of damage to German troops along the roads and returned to camp on 1 September.

There was one other worthwhile link-up at about this time. Denby, in a civilian car, made his way north-westward with a few Maquis companions and managed to contact the advance patrols of the swiftly advancing American army in the neighbourhood of Joigny, some fifty-five miles away. Next day he returned safely.

On the 28th, I took my own Ford, which I had collected the day that Pétain visited Saulieu, and went with one of my new men, a lad called Turner, to see the colonels at the PC. On the way we stopped in the ruined town of Mont-sauche itself. The day was hot and there were signs of life beginning to return to the fire-stained buildings. We stopped at the Hôtel de la Poste, where we had a few drinks. The white wine was good and it was strong. The people of the *estaminet* were pleased to see us and after we had talked a bit we continued on our way.

Between Moux and Alligny we turned away to the left and I stopped by the second kilometre stone. We hooted three times and almost at once two pretty girls emerged from the woods and asked us what we wanted. I told them that I wished to see Isaac. 'Tell him it is "Le Capitaine Gremlin",' I said. They asked me to send the car away and wait in the woods. I told Turner to go back to the last track junction and to stay there until he heard me whistle. While one of the girls walked up the road, the other led me back into the wood, where a third girl was sitting beside a picnic lunch basket. The girls were very pleasant, intelligent and well educated, and all spoke a little English. Many of them were working for the PC. They did much useful work carrying messages and watching troop movements. After a few minutes the first girl returned.

'Will you follow me?' she said. 'Colonel Isaac will see you.' I rose and she led me to another stretch of the woods where I saw Colonel Hastings sitting on the grass. I gave him the latest news of our movements and of my projected strafe. I asked for an *agent de liaison* to guide my column through Saulieu the following morning and for contacts with the Maquis of the Côte d'Or.

The *agent de liaison* was arranged without difficulty, but beyond Saulieu Hastings only knew the Maquis Robert and as I knew Robert well enough myself this was not much help. Anyway I thanked him and returned to the road.

I whistled up Turner and we returned to the Chalaux camp. Among the *agents de liaison* that we encountered, one is worth mentioning. An English girl, Peggy Knight, had been dropped to the Maquis around Auxerre as a radio operator before D-day. She had been promised only three months behind the lines but now that this period was more than up she was getting rather tired of the company of nobody but Frenchmen. One day, quite unheralded, she had turned up at the camp by the Chalaux.

Not unnaturally, we had been most suspicious and wirelessed London for confirmation. London told us that there was such a person and even told us of some rather intimate birthmarks to verify. They added that she ought to go back to Auxerre. We did not verify all the birthmarks, as the less intimate ones seemed pretty conclusive. We kept her with us for several days and she was a great help, going into Lormes and obtaining all the latest information about German movements. Then she went back to Auxerre, thankful for having had a few days of our company.

On the morning of the 29th I set off on my first independent command. My orders were very simple. 'Make a nuisance of yourself between Dijon and Autun,' Bill had said, and that was all. My force consisted of a brand-new jeep, which I handed over to Duvivier and which was manned by his two inseparables. I usually travelled on this jeep myself and it led the way.

Behind it came my old jeep, which I had assigned to Feebury. By now it was really on its last legs and I considered it too unreliable for road strafing, but we hitched a trailer on to it, borrowed from the 2nd SAS, and manned it with three troopers, one of whom, Francis, spoke a little French. In the trailer we carried our extra supplies of food, mortar bombs and Piat ammunition.

Besides this we had three civilian cars. The first was a handsome Citroën belonging to Georges. He carried Corporal McGinnis, one of my reinforcements, and two new troopers. They were armed with a Bren and a Piat. The second was my big Ford, carrying Lieutenant Ball, Turner, two other troopers and the 2-inch mortar. Last came Lance-Corporal Robinson, Thornton and Roger in a little open Peugeot. They had a rifle with telescopic sights.

We set out from the camp at about 9 am. We were due to meet our *agent de liaison* at noon, but the civilian cars proved as unreliable as usual and it was 2 pm before we were all safely assembled outside Saulieu.

The *agent de liaison* proved to be another pretty girl on a bicycle and we passed through without difficulty, driving into the Maquis Robert at about 3 o'clock. The Maquis was a strongly built series of barrack huts in the Bois de Villargoix and was well protected by outlying subsidiary Maquis and a network of ambushes.

As soon as we reached the Maquis we were given a meal and I learned the latest news. Saulieu was virtually liberated. There had been so many ambushes along the *routes nationales* leading into it that Jerry had for some days past stopped sending convoys this way. However, a German tank had broken down in the area of Vitteaux. I sent Feebury off in his jeep to see if he could deal with this. Robert did not know any of the other local Maquis very intimately but he had a truck that was going up to the PC of all the Maquis of the Côte d'Or that very afternoon. If I liked to go with my jeep as convoy to the truck, he could give me a letter to the Commandant Guy, who would surely be able to put me in touch with a good Maquis. Meanwhile, Robert very kindly loaned us his Maquis mechanics to put our wretched civilian vehicles right. The Citroën proved to be in such bad shape that it had to be taken into a civilian workshop in Saulieu.

The journey over to the PC of the Côte d'Or at Saussey, though quite a distance over rather tricky country, which included a second-class road and a railway, was uneventful.

While the Maquisards loaded a new supply of rifles into their truck, I explained my requirements to the commandant. He was of the opinion that the Maquis Valmy in the Bois de la Chaume, close to the city of Beaune, would be most suitable, gave me another letter to the district commander and told me where to find him. He informed me of next day's horn-signals for the Maquis ambushes of the Côte d'Or, and as the truck-load of arms was already loaded, I thanked him for his assistance and set off once more with my truck.

The return journey was again uneventful and as darkness was falling I got back to the Bois de Villargoix. Neither Feebury nor the mechanics had yet returned, so I went into Saulieu with Georges, Duvivier and Weller where we visited the convalescing Jacques Morvillier.

I prepared a message for Bill Fraser which in English read, 'I am going to a Maquis fifteen kilometres west of the place that a dog would gnaw. Request permission to remain there indefinitely. Wellsted.' In French, this was quite unintelligible if intercepted, and Jacques phoned it through for us to Bill's camp.

While we awaited an answer we had a fine dinner in one of the smartest restaurants in Saulieu, leaving the jeep parked out of sight in a courtyard behind. The fact that it was always possible for a German convoy to pass below the window added a certain spice to the meal.

After a time Jacques returned to say that Bill had been out, that he had left my message and I would get the reply by wireless. This was a nuisance, as provisionally I only had five days in which to work; and as it was evidently going to be at least another day before I could begin to operate, this rather restricted my activities.

Having rounded off our meal with a good liqueur, we returned to the Maquis. The civilian cars were now back from their garages and all fit for the road. The sergeant-major had returned somewhat depressed by a minor failure, for they had missed the stranded tank by just one hour.

The Maquis Robert gave us some wine, so we had a bit of a party before we went to bed in one of the barrack huts kindly lent us for the night. It was warm and protected us from the rain that fell that night, but I collected a colony of fleas in my sleeping-bag which I never again managed to lose until we had quit France.

The swift advance of the Allies had provided us with another kind of link, but one that was likely to be more of a hindrance than a help in the expedition to come. This was the arrival of British and American short-range fighters strafing the roads. When they first appeared we took it as a sure sign of our approaching deliverance and used to wave and cheer. As they grew more common, they became a greater menace, attacking almost everything in sight. On several occasions I had to order my jeep to halt under cover while the RAF passed overhead. Only a few days previously there had been a nasty accident when a loaded Maquis supply lorry had been set on fire and several of the occupants killed by a marauding Mosquito. In addition to avoiding German patrols and Maquis ambushes, we were going to have to beware Allied aircraft as well.

CHAPTER XXV

Away to Burgundy

Between Autun and Dijon there are two *routes nationales*. One runs due north to Saulieu, cuts across to Precy-sous-Thil and thence eastward to Dijon. The other goes first to the east by way of Nolay and Beaune before running north. There is one other *route nationale* in the area which cuts across at right-angles to the other two, from Saulieu, through Arnay-le-Duc to Nolay. In the Beaune region there is a network of these *routes*, a Nolay–Chagny–Beaune triangle, a trunk road running south by Chagny and Mâcon to Lyons and a road eastward by Seurre to the German border.

This Saulieu–Dijon–Beaune–Autun quadrilateral was like the mouth of a sack, the fabric of which was made up on the one side by the Americans pushing east from Brittany and on the other by the armies pressing north from the Riviera beach-head. Across the mouth of this sack our hunting should be good.

With these broad considerations in mind, I carefully studied the map of the Côte de Nuits and the Côte d'Or, dotted with places that in happier days had become familiar to me on bottles of liquid joy – Beaune itself, Meursault, Pommard, Aloxe-Corton, Volnay, Pernand, Nuits St Georges – what pleasure the very names could conjure up. This was the heart of the true Burgundy country. This was the area where the given business of harassing the enemy could still be combined with fleeting pleasure.

At 9 o'clock on the morning of 30 August, my little column set out, headed for new pastures. South we drove along the little tracks that we always used: past the little village of Varennes (not the Varennes where Marie-Antoinette ended her unhappy flight from France), a tiny cluster of thatched cottages about mud-covered cobbles; across the second-class road by Thoisy-la-Berchère; over river and railway close by Musigny; through woods and alongside lakes that shimmered in the sun, south to Burgundy.

We had to follow a *route nationale* for one short stretch. We drove over its smooth, swift surface with all possible speed. We raced along it with our loaded jeeps flat out. Then, as we turned a slight bend, we saw before us a complete block across the road. Duvivier stamped on the brakes. We drew to a screaming halt. From the thick foliage around, dark bearded faces glared at us evilly. Panic in the jeep. Everyone was trying to do everything at once. Some were reaching for their weapons. Jeff was trying to control his bucking jeep. I felt feverishly for the horn. It was all over in less time than it takes to describe. The jeep was stopped, the horn was hooting a frantic signal, and the bearded faces had broken into beaming smiles.

We stopped for a few minutes to exchange greetings with the Maquisards of the ambush, asked the best way to go round and soon were carrying on. Now we were running close along a railway, crossing and recrossing, passing sleepy villages deep in the woods. Twice the leading jeep ran over a slow-moving chicken, and the crew, leaning from the second jeep, picked it up without checking speed.

At last, about 11.30, we dipped down a grassy green hill, past the red-roofed houses of Molinot to where a sluggish stream meandered between rushy banks. There, idle and in disrepair, stood the mill of Molinot. At first we did not connect this dilapidated building with the rendezvous we sought; but having passed it twice and seen no other, we parked our cars in a spacious courtyard behind and I entered the house. Inside it was clean and cosy. Three Maquisards in neat suits and wearing the arm-bands of the FFI de Bourgogne came forward to wecome me. I introduced myself as 'Le Capitaine Gremlin', for even the commandant of the Côte d'Or had heard of me by that name, while my proper surname would have meant nothing to him. We discussed my requirements and they promised all assistance in their power, while the boys made use of the plentiful hot water in the house to brew some tea and get a shave. Our greatest need was maps. There was not a single issue-map of reasonable scale in our possession that covered the ground as far east as we had now travelled. The Maquis themselves were short of maps, however, and we were grateful when they lent us two.

They decided to take us along to the Maquis Valmy, so as soon as we had drunk our tea and had a small snack, we set off again. I had one of the Maquis officers sitting on my jeep guiding me and we cut back along the little back-tracks to the east. On our approach to one small village, a young peasant ran out waving for us to stop. As we pulled up he spoke swiftly to our guide, waving his hand expansively and jabbering in a patois too fast and too idiomatic for me to follow. The guide looked mildly surprised and explained the situation to me. There was an enemy patrol in the next village. I ran back to my stationary vehicles and told them to prepare for trouble and follow me closely. The guide turned us off the road we were following and we began to bypass the village along cart-tracks and over the edge of fields. At last, we re-emerged on to the road and carried on towards the Maquis.

At top speed we ran through the town of Ivry-en-Montagne, which lay on the Arnay-le-Duc *route nationale* and was known to have Germans stationed in it. They must have been lunching in their billets, for we passed through unmolested, and were soon running along the pretty little road which cut through the hills towards Beaune. On top of the cliffs that overlooked the valley of the Côte d'Or we turned off to the left along a track that jolted over the short rough turf. After a time the track dived into a maze of thick furze and soon we were brought up sharp by a rough barrier across the road. A Bren covered us from a gorse-bush. This was the guard to the Maquis Valmy.

Once past the guard, we ran out on to another open grassy field. Here we stopped and several Maquisards approached us from the wood. They were mostly young men and much less well-dressed than were the Maquisards of the Morvan. Indeed, they were too close to the *routes nationales* to have been able to organise themselves in scraps of uniform like those of the Nivernais, but they all wore the Burgundian arm-band and were a determined-looking crowd. A tall good-looking man with the three *galons* of a French captain was introduced to me as Eric, chief of the Maquis Valmy. He wore riding breeches and an American side-hat. His smooth dark hair and well-cut, clean-shaven face reminded me very much of the film star Stewart Granger. He turned out to be a very good leader and most popular with his men.

His Maquis, though new and not well armed, proved to be most pugnacious and very efficient, a marked contrast to the Maquis Bernard. Here we heard news of Johnny Wiseman's troop, with whom they had been in liaison and from whom they had obtained some invaluable incendiary ammunition in exchange for wine. The Maquis were very full of this success at barter, for they had shot down a German aeroplane with this very ammunition in the vicinity of Bligny only a few days before.

Eric arranged for some of his men to build new wooden huts for my boys close to the huts of his own Maquis. This was a kindly gesture and one which we were to appreciate greatly, as each night throughout our stay it rained continually.

I left most of the men to carry out maintenance and went with Georges and Duvivier in the jeep to interview a Maquis agent in the little town of Aloxe-Corton. It was a fine day and the evening's storm had not yet driven up to darken the sky. The scenery was indescribable. From the edge of the plateau great rocky cliffs fell sheer away for 50 feet or more before giving way to steeply sloping meadows of lush grass and terraced vineyards. The little villages hung precariously on the hillsides, or perched crazily on craggy outcrops, as though uncertain of how to get down to the valleys below.

The grapes were just beginning to ripen on the vines. The floor of the valley and the terraces which mounted one on the other to the very bottom of the cliffs were a mass of low vines in serried ranks, bent with the weight of fruit and green with succulence.

From the valley we wound steeply upward into Aloxe-Corton itself. There, among the higgledy-piggledy maze of houses which climbed over each other up the hillsides, we hid the jeep in a stable and went to find the *agent*.

Liberation already was in the air. The little Union Jack fluttering from our bonnet brought cheers from the inquisitive knots of people who had viewed our passage. Soon we were being offered more wine than it was good for us to drink, and our walk in search of the *agent* became a triumphal procession. The wine was strong and white and truly excellent. Aloxe-Corton, Corton and Corton Charlemagne are among the finest wines of all France.

We found the *agent* at last, in a little terrace cottage overlooking a sea of vines. He called himself Pavlov, in memory of some long dead benefactor of Aloxe-Corton. He took us into his neat little house, dark and cool inside, against the heat of the white courtyard. His wife was suckling their child at her breast. She looked up as we entered but continued unconcerned and it seemed very right and natural that she should.

Pavlov fetched some glasses and gave us Pernod, creamy green, sweetly strong and vilely aniseedy. Then he began to talk. I followed the gist of the conversation. He had not much news about the Boche, except that they were falling back faster and faster, blocking the roads in their haste to evade the oncoming Americans. However, in the woods near here were some ninety-five Poles who, having been conscripted into the German army against their will, had taken the opportunity to desert. He wanted the Maquis to take charge of them, as they were beginning to prey upon the neighbourhood. They were well armed and were a grave potential menace to the peaceful villagers.

Having learned all we could, and with a letter from Pavlov to Eric, we returned to our hidden jeep. It might have been concealed from the enemy but not from our friends of the village. When we came to take it out it had been loaded down with flowers, and as we mounted girls brought us great bunches of grapes. It was the first time that anyone had fêted us and we returned to the camp greatly elated and pretty full of good Burgundy.

Back at the Maquis Valmy, Georges, Ball and I had dinner washed down with fine wine. In this camp on the hilltop, water was very scarce, but with all the richest wine land in France spread out below us, drink was never lacking. After supper I went with Eric and Michaud, an Alsatian speaking both French and German fluently, to accept the surrender of some more Poles. We went in Eric's big open Peugeot. It was a powerful blue coupé and in it we drove swiftly down the steep escarpment, roared through the narrow winding streets, between the high red-roofed houses of St Romain, and out into the open country beyond.

Our rendezvous with the Poles was an old farm standing on the edge of a wood and well away from any other habitations. Some Maquisards had been watching the Poles all day, but I was not prepared for the reception that we received at the farmhouse. The strong headlights of the car, cutting the drizzling darkness like a knife, swung suddenly round a bend and fell full upon the courtyard of the farm. There, standing out bright and menacing in the beams, were half a dozen German soldiers. Their shining steel-helmets, their camouflaged ground-sheets, their arms and their bearing were unmistakable.

My hand leapt to the Schmeisser which was slung across my chest, but in an instant I let it drop. The NCO was falling in his men. As we swept up they presented arms. It was a contingent of surrendering Poles.

In the farmhouse, a long conversation followed, in which Polish, German, French and English were used impartially. The Poles, after being conscripted into the Russian army to fight the Germans, had after capture volunteered to join the enemy rather than starve. They did not want to fight for the Germans. They had not wanted to fight for the Russians. If they must, they wished to fight as Poles for Poland. Would we allow them to join us against the Germans to prove their sincerity? They had killed their German officers before deserting en masse, so there was little risk of treachery. Eric and I agreed, and the interview was over.

Eric took me back to the camp where, after a few more drinks, I went to bed and slept like a log. The rain had begun in real earnest. During the night a further fifteen Poles came in, making a total of about 120. An extraordinary situation for a Maquis which could not muster a hundred armed men.

I woke about 8 o'clock and called my men. I had found from experience that I could will myself to wake at the time I wanted to, so I habitually pulled out the boys.

The Maquisards gave us a small continental breakfast and I sent everyone off to do road watches. I wanted to be sure of the German movements before I committed myself to any definite plan. However, I told each party to do their best to spring an ambush before they left, but to avoid attacking in a place that I was likely to use as a trap the following day.

Robinson's party had the Nolay–Autun road, McGinnis the Nolay–Beaune, Ball the Beaune–Dijon. The more difficult roads I gave to the more experienced commanders. The Beaune–Seurre road, which entailed the crossing of the Beaune–Dijon road, I gave to Jeff Duvivier, and the Beaune–Chagny, with the crossing of the Nolay–Beaune, to Feebury. I told Ball and McGinnis to be sure not to carry out any ambush on their roads until they knew that Duvivier and Feebury were safely back, as I did not want my returning patrols to run into hornets' nests that the others had stirred up for them.

I myself went with Eric and Georges in the big coupé to have a look at all the suitable sites in the area for one really first-rate ambush the next day. I also took a little explosive to blow down some telegraph lines that the enemy were known to be using between Dijon and Nevers. In fact, I never had the chance to blow them as Eric arranged for some of his Maquisards to cut them down with hand-saws. A cheaper and more silent process.

The first place we visited was a little hill near the village of Baubigny, not far from Nolay. Here we found McGinnis and his boys busily engaged in watching the road, and I examined the site very carefully, for it seemed absolutely ideal. I told McGinnis that this looked just what I wanted for the morrow, and dropping back into the hills, we swung round in a wide detour, crossed the *route nationale*, and ran down into the back streets of Meursault.

It was strange to pass along the narrow lanes behind the back-gardens of the imposing Burgundian houses, with their multi-coloured roof tiles and their high medieval façades, knowing that only a few streets away the enemy convoys were rumbling through. At last we emerged from Meursault into wide flat fields of vineyards and from the slightly raised track along which we were driving we could see clearly across to the *route nationale* not more than 700 yards away.

We stopped the car and examined the stream of hostile vehicles that was pouring along in never-ending flow. There was a big horse-drawn convoy, widely dispersed, wagon after wagon, half camouflaged with brushwood, plodding slowly by. There were shorter columns of buses and trucks running swiftly down the smooth, straight road; and now and then a staff-car, a few motorcyclists or a small patrol of armoured cars would go flying past.

While we were thus standing on the track and watching this passing parade, we were surprised to see the jeep bumping along the track towards us. It was Feebury. He had crossed the Nolay–Beaune road all right and had quartered the ground between in search of a reasonable spot for a strafe. He had decided, however, that the ground here was too flat and open for an attack to be successfully carried out. The vines gave fine cover from view but it was necessary to kneel up to fire over them and at the same time they did not stand high enough to give cover to the jeeps. So the only places where jeeps could be secreted were farmhouses, which would be exposed to the gravest reprisals as soon as we had left them. An additional disadvantage of this spot for an ambush was the fact that once the Germans had abandoned their vehicles, the vines gave them excellent cover as well as us. I concurred with the sergeant-major's appreciation and told him of the site that I had found on McGinnis's stretch of road.

While our two vehicles thus stood on the track in full view of the enemy, and we held our conference, two farmers from a nearby house spotted our nationality and came up with bottles of young Meursault, which they pressed upon us. The greeny-golden liquor was a little immature but we passed the bottles around and drank greedily, for the sun was out again and the day very hot. The fantastic aspect of standing in open vineyards, drinking wine in plain view of the passing enemy, occurred to us. It made us laugh.

Soon we rejoined our vehicles and, turning them round, went about our respective businesses: Feebury to rejoin McGinnis, the party in the blue Peugeot to continue their reconnaissance. Back through Meursault, and back to the hills. Round in another quick sweep and down to the *route nationale*, again close by Pommard. Here the two main roads into Beaune, from Nolay and from Chagny, were converging and there was only a strip of vineyard some 200 yards wide, backed by the brick walls of Pommard, between them. As we approached the first *route nationale*, down a narrow cart-track between the walled vineyards, an argument broke out in French as to whether it was better to leave the car on the track above the highway or to run down and park in the narrow strip of vineyards between the two roads. Eric, the driver, was all for going into the strip, and the argument reached its climax as the car rolled out on to the first *route nationale* and there stopped.

My French was neither fast nor fluent enough to enter into the discussion, but it seemed to me that the last place to have an argument was bang in the middle of a road down which the enemy might drive at any moment. At last Georges' argument prevailed. The car came round in a single well-executed turn and ran back up the hill under the cover of a vineyard wall. It had hardly come to rest before two large lorry-loads of Huns went past along the road we had scarcely quit.

With rather more care than on the previous occasions, we now crossed the road on foot and tried to work our way round to the bridge on the further *route nationale*, which Eric seemed to think would be well worth blowing. As we walked along this track we found ourselves less than fifty yards from the second road, along which the traffic was passing non-stop. A bus-load of the enemy had halted not far down the road and the troops had fallen out to relieve nature. They did not take the least notice of us, though even the least observant of them ought to have wondered why civilians and red-bereted Britons were bearing arms on the outskirts of Pommard.

It was not necessary to get a very close look at the bridge to realise that there were two strong arguments against blowing it. The first was the volume of traffic that was crossing it, which made it doubtful whether one would ever have a long enough period free from passing Boche to get the charges laid. The second was that it would not be a very difficult feat to divert the convoys through Pommard and to cross the stream by the other *route nationale*. Having seen what we had come to see, we returned regretfully to the car. We could not fire on the enemy from Pommard because of the inevitable reprisals, so, leaving the enemy unscathed, we went back to the camp.

After a late lunch with the Maquis officers I waited in camp for the return of my road-watching patrols. Robinson was the first back. He reported having had the fright of his life when re-entering the Maquis, for the guard was now being mounted by the Poles and the only thing to distinguish them from their German counterparts was a soft forage cap and a red-and-white FFI armband. However, seeing the British flag, the Poles had saluted smartly, just in time to prevent an international incident. Robinson's patrol had entered Nolay and reported the town full of troops. He had not, however, had a chance to use his Bren or his sniper's rifle, as there was either no cover or there were houses about. This was disappointing.

Next in were Feebury and McGinnis, displaying a mixture of elation and frustration. They had found that the enemy were using their road to run petrol up from Autun to Beaune. Convenient little convoys of fourteen or fifteen vehicles were passing every two or three hours and they had watched two convoys passing each other at a dead crawl right in front of where they were hiding. They had not fired, however, in spite of the temptation, because they knew that I hoped to be able to arrange an even bigger and better ambush the next day.

Duvivier was the next to arrive. He was very full of himself and was proudly displaying the Union Jack on his bonnet, almost shot to ribbons. At first his day had been uneventful. He had crossed the Beaune–Dijon road without difficulty. He had watched the Seurre road all day, but practically nothing had come along it. He had not been able to find any really good ambush sites and eventually he had decided at about 3 o'clock to return to camp. On the way back he had crossed the Beaune–Dijon railway line and as he had heard a train on it during the course of the afternoon, he had determined to blow it. He had laid his charge without difficulty, left a half-hour time-pencil and driven on, well content.

Half-way down the slope out of the woods towards the *route nationale*, he had suddenly seen to his horror that a convoy was moving along it. There were sentries posted at the crossroads and he had either to run the gauntlet or turn back. It was too late to turn back, so shouting to 'Digger' Weller to open fire, he had charged down on the crossing at top speed. The two sentries were mown down with the first burst, a passing truck was riddled, and the jeep was climbing up towards the woods on the other side before the startled enemy had a chance to reply to this unexpected fire. In the back, 'Homer' Marshall took up the battle with the rear-Vickers, and when the guns jammed he picked up his Bren and was able to get off three magazines before the jeep dived once more into the friendly safety of the woods. The British had suffered neither serious damage nor casualties. One heavy enemy lorry was definitely destroyed and a number of men killed and wounded.

Last to return to the Maquis were Ball and his men. He had taken Michau, the Alsatian, with him for liaison, because although Ball spoke no French, his German was fluent and he was able to talk to Michau in that language. They had found one or two quite fair ambush sites and had watched the road all day. It was almost constantly in use. However, they had not been able to do a strafe on their own, as they had had to wait for Duvivier to get safely across, and after Duvivier's battle nothing more came up the road that night.

After supper, at which the boys regaled themselves on red wine, I went down with Eric to the little subsidiary Maquis that he had set up for the Poles. They all seemed to be quite cheerful and contented. As we left I said, 'Dobranos!' ('Good-night!') At once I was besieged by about fifty Poles all talking Polish at the top of their voices, and it was some time before I was able to explain in slow French that it was the only word of Polish that I knew.

That night Georges went off with René Monnier, one of the officers of the Maquis, into Meursault, where they requisitioned a fine Hotchkiss car to take back with us to Montsauche. During the night the Maquis had a *parachutage*.

Over dinner we received the unwelcome news on the wireless: 'You will NOT, repeat NOT, remain more than five days away from base.' It was most disappointing, but it was imperative.

On 1 September I got the boys out at 8 o'clock as usual. It had rained all night and it was raining as we prepared to leave. The civilian cars proved more recalcitrant than usual and we could not get them to start. At last, leaving Ball to deal with them, and Feebury to instruct the Maquis in the use of the Bazooka, which had arrived at the *parachutage*, I went with Eric, Paul Bresson, his huge sergeant major, and several of his other officers to plan the ambush thoroughly.

We returned in time for an early lunch, at which I had to forbid the boys to drink any wine in case it made them sleepy, and we set out soon afterwards. Ill-luck dogged us all the way. First one car broke down and had to be abandoned, then another, and we had to send off for a mechanic. The jeep packed in and was only got going with difficulty. The certainty that I had to return to Montsauche the following day, whatever happened, irked me. I was commanding a large mixed force of British, French and Poles and the fact that it was the British cars that were holding up the show made me furious. I could do nothing but sit on on a grassy bank and wait, swearing loud and long in every language I could think of. It amused the French, it relieved my feelings, and it helped to pass the time.

At last, at about 3.30, we entered Baubigny and I began to get the ambush organised. A Polish patrol with a Maquis officer, a Bazooka and some anti-tank grenades covered the road up behind our position from Nolay. In Baubigny itself, guarded by this patrol, we left our transport. The rest of the troops comprised the ambush proper.

The position was absolutely ideal. The *route nationale*, lined with well-spaced trees, ran along the foot of a deep valley. On either side the fields rose steeply, bare of cover, so that once off the road the enemy were at our mercy. All along the crest of the hill on the Baubigny side of the valley were thick bushes, boulders and the remains of a broken-down wall, which gave good visibility and perfect cover. At one place a little re-entrant ran up from the valley between two small hills and a narrow walled road wound up it. Near the junction of this road and the *route nationale* there was a little scrub in the bottom of the valley, with a covered line of withdrawal to the walled road. Beyond this the ground rose again to another hill. On this second hill and covering our flanks from the Beaune direction was a strong force of Maquisards with several Bren-guns. The road was mined at the point where it left the *route nationale*. Half-way up the track, where the walls gave it complete cover except for the guns, and the more reliable jeep was in position to enfilade the whole of the valley with its fire. Covered by the jeep and concealed by the low scrub, McGinnis and Feebury, with Bazooka and Piat, were within 50 yards of the main road, ready to stop the leading vehicle dead in its tracks. Right along the crest of the hill I had sited Brens, so that every inch of the road was covered for more than a mile, and close beside me Ooly Ball was waiting with the 2-inch mortar, to blast out any enemy lucky enough to find cover in that shelterless valley. From a position of vantage, where I could see down the road almost into Nolay, I waited with a Very pistol. As soon as I judged the convoy to be in position, I would fire. Piat, Bazooka and Vickers-K could be relied upon to blast the head of the column. As soon as it was stationary, a merciless fire would mow down the enemy, vainly trying to escape our trap.

When all opposition had ceased, the infantry force of forty Poles, with Maquis officers, who were awaiting the signal behind the hill, would sweep round. While the Bren-gunners kept down the heads of the enemy, the Poles would move relentlessly forward down the length of the convoy, killing every German who still survived. The Maquisards would then have a chance to salvage any weapons, trucks or ammunition that had escaped the withering blasts of fire.

From the villagers we learned that the Germans had passed a convoy along the road at 8 o'clock that morning. Since then nothing had passed. A column ought to be along soon. Meanwhile we waited in silence.

CHAPTER XXVI

The Road Back

It was the perfect ambush. The position was ideal. The forces were the strongest possible in the space we intended to use. The convoys were just the right size to fit into the ground. There was only one flaw, and as the afternoon wore on and the shades of night began to gather chillily around us, it became more and more evident. The Germans were just not going to oblige.

Whether it was sheer bad luck, whether the good people of Baubigny or the Maquisards themselves had talked too much, or whether there had been treachery, we never knew. Suffice it to say, the perfect ambush never came off. The convoys never arrived.

At last, when it became too dark to shoot, we reluctantly withdrew our forces to their vehicles and as a final gesture of contempt we drove down on to the *route nationale* and back to the Maquis along this German-occupied highway. We encountered nothing.

There was one moment of excitement, when for an instant we mistook a huge tree stump by the roadside for a parked staff-car, but after a hasty examination we continued on our way to the Maquis, to dinner and to bed.

We had a further disappointment that night as well. With great care I had brought an enormous stone rum-jar all the way from Chalaux and as we were all a little damp and dispirited I took it out as a treat for the boys and Maquisards alike. Everyone waited eager-eyed and expectant while the cork was drawn. Then with due ceremony the bottle was tipped up. Up and up and up it was tipped. It was empty.

That night it rained and next morning it was raining. I woke the boys at 8.00 and reminded them that today we must go back to the Morvan. This was our last opportunity to retrieve our fortunes.

I had agreed to spend the morning giving the Maquisards lectures on the uses of the explosives that they had received in their *parachutages*. I also had to explain the operating and maintaining of the Vickers-K, which I had presented to Eric as a parting gift. Accordingly, I told Ball to take out as much of the force as he could and lay an ambush at one of the spots that he had picked out on the Dijon—Beaune road.

Once more the civilian cars let us down and Ball was unable to get his started, in spite of repeated pushes and tows. The swirling rain was getting into everything and turning the ground into a quagmire, which hardly assisted the maintenance. At last I ordered Feebury and Duvivier to take out the two jeeps and see what they could do. They were to be back by 1 o'clock by which time I would have lunch ready for them. They were not to do anything rash and they were to take Michau as their guide. Meanwhile Ball and a Maquis mechanic were detailed to get all the vehicles fit for the road by lunch-time as it was essential that we move off immediately afterwards.

Having lectured the Maquis and arranged all the details for the afternoon's move, I went down again to the Polish camp and took all the particulars of their regiments, the place from which they had deserted and the locations of other German troops in the area. At lunch-time we all rendezvoused.

Georges had been down into Meursault again with René Monnier, who presented us with four dozen bottles of fine wines, Meursault and Beaune. While Georges had been in the cellar collecting this delectable gift a German flak battery was being erected in the garden, but he was not spotted.

At 1.15, just when I was beginning to worry seriously about them, the two jeeps came racing back to camp. Even the rain could not damp the elation on their mud-besplattered faces. They had enjoyed a good strafe.

Finding a side road that ran more or less parallel to the *route nationale*, they had followed it until they came to a place where it overlooked the main road. There they had waited for the first convoy to come in sight. They had let loose with everything and when the enemy began to take a lively interest, they had driven on once more. Taking up another position above the *route nationale*, they had halted, waiting for their next victims to arrive. In this way they had strafed the enemy columns three times, estimating the damage at three heavy trucks, two 3-ton lorries, one small utility, a staff-car and some thirty-five men. No wonder they were pleased.

There had been one amusing moment when Michau was left behind after a strafe but with enormous strides overtook the accelerating jeep and leapt on in the nick of time.

We had a last heavy meal with the Maquis, took as much wine to drink as we dared considering the long drive ahead, and at 2.15 said a fond farewell to our friends. We promised to return if ever we had the chance and set off for Chalaux, little guessing how far we were to travel. One week later the Maquis Valmy was strong enough to liberate Beaune ahead of the advancing Americans. I wish that we had been permitted to stay to see that day.

Our own troubles, however, were not yet over. We had hardly gone five miles along the road before the Hotchkiss broke down. It was water in the carburettor, but uncertain whether this was due to rain or to water in the petrol tank, I could not risk being held up any longer. So, not wishing to leave Georges in this hostile country to make his own way back, I ordered him to abandon the car. Having transferred all its load to the others, we left it by the roadside with a note to the effect that we bequeathed it to the Maquis Valmy. Later we heard that they had picked it up intact.

We still had trouble with the cars. At a swollen ford all the vehicles crossed safely except the Citroën and Robinson's little Peugeot. The former was so low-slung that it got water into the distributor and stalled in the middle. The lane was too narrow for us to get either of the jeeps back to help and we had no tow-rope for the Ford to pull the Citroën out. After a moment of despair, we decided to give the Peugeot a chance to push it through, and were pleasantly surprised when it duly obliged. After we had cleaned and dried the points, the Citroën carried on happily.

In Ivry-en-Montagne we were held up by a big block of trees across the road and when we got back into the Morvan we found that these road-blocks had sprung up everywhere. Some were manned by the Maquis. Many others were not manned at all, but we were in constant dread of being attacked before we could identify ourselves. We also had a chance meeting with a convoy of three Maquis cars in the unknown country south of Saulieu. There was momentary distrust on their part, for they had never met any SAS before, but I found that they had heard of the Captain Gremlin and we parted friends.

At last, as dusk was settling over Les Settons, and the still surface of the lake was reflecting in all its clarity the last rosy glow in the summer's sky, we drew the whole column up in the yard of the Morvandelle and ordered a celebratory dinner for the party.

To my astonishment I found Paddy and Bob Melot also at the hotel; so I took the opportunity of making a report and presented him with a dozen bottles of our Burgundy.

We sat down to a marvellous dinner. Our physical weariness and the sense of a task accomplished to the best of our ability gave us a deep feeling of well-being which the good wine and excellent food did much to enhance.

Learning that there had been a convoy of Germans through Montsauche during the day, we drove with circumspection as we returned through its war-scarred streets, but the only vehicle we met on the way was the other Citroën of my troop, with Tom Rennie at the wheel.

Tom was astonished to see us. There had been a rumour from a more than usually reliable Maquis source that the whole column had been ambushed and that I had been killed. When we got back to the camp we found everyone firmly convinced that we had met with some fearful disaster and our friends were mourning my somewhat premature demise.

Just after passing Brassy we almost had a nasty accident when the heavily laden jeep-trailer lurched out of control and began to whip Feebury's jeep viciously from side to side. By superb driving he managed to regain control and no one was hurt.

Throughout the trip and particularly on the journey home, I had been worried about petrol and I was very thankful to get my vehicles safely back to Chalaux. So close had we run it that all the gauges were registering empty and the Citroën actually ran out at Mazignien, but was able to coast in along the steep slope to Le Meix Chalaux and down the track into the valley.

When all the vehicles were safely in, I went over and reported to Alex. From him I learned the latest news. Returning on the 1st, he had taken over the camp, while Bill and a Two Troop column under Dickie Grayson had gone off operating in the St Saulge area, near Nevers. Dickie got back just before I did after a fine ambush at Billy where, more or less aided by the Maquis, he had destroyed six enemy trucks and taken five prisoners.

Johnny Wiseman's party had been recalled from Dijon and Tony Trower had come over to Chalaux to collect the transport to bring them all back. C Squadron had now arrived in the Morvan in force and was taking over from us. We had to be concentrated and ready to move as soon as possible. Most of the reinforcements in my troop and all the jeeps were to be left behind to strengthen C Squadron. The rest of us were to go back through the lines. Paddy himself, with Bob Melot, were leaving that night.

Back in Three Troop camp I heard the amusing tale of poor Middleton. I had left Middleton, Worn, Jemson and Rennie behind to look after my camp and to give them a rest, as they had been operating much harder than Duvivier, Ball or my reinforcements. Not content with sitting in their tents, however, Middleton and Rennie had gone with Doc Martell to look at a Maquis battle at the village of Corancy, close to Château-Chinon. They had walked down the road with a Maquis officer, who said quite cheerfully, 'We hold the village. The fighting is going on beyond.' At this crucial moment a burst of Spandau fire from the church proved him a liar and heavy rifle and machine-gun fire pinned the party in the ditches. Suddenly there had been a cry from Middleton, 'I'm hit,' and Rennie, who knew that they should never have been near the battle in the first place, feared the worst.

He was greatly relieved, therefore, to see Middleton bounding like a gazelle for the nearest strip of woods and clutching the seat of his pants. For the third time in this war Middleton had been shot through the cheeks of his backside. Yet just what happened to the bullet remained a mystery. There were two holes through Mid's flesh, there were two holes in his underpants, yet search as he might, he could only find one hole in the battledress trousers!

That night, as I lay down to sleep, a problem confronted me. I knew that most of the men who had just served under me would now be going to C Squadron. Ought I not to volunteer to remain with them? For a long time I debated the choice in my mind. Three months of this hunter-hunted existence had worn down my nerves quite a lot, but it was obvious that the end of the French campaign was very near. I had taken these lads off on their first taste of active servicing. With Feebury to help me, could we not form a troop on our own attached to C Squadron? If I made the request, I was sure that Bill would listen to it. Then I thought of Margot and how much I wanted to get home to see her. I felt she would never forgive me if I turned down a chance of getting home. This finally decided me. No one ever suggested that I should stay; indeed I had been in France longer than any of them. So I let the matter rest and dropped off to sleep, lulled by the babbling of the river close beside my tent.

The next day, I rested with my troop. We cleaned our weapons, did our maintenance and in the evening, having scrounged rum and our share of the cheap red wine from Montsauche, we had a party, eating a huge meal and then singing around the campfire until it came on to rain again.

That evening Bill and Fraser McLuskey got back from St Saulge. The Padre had inadvertently driven a jeep through a road-strafe and Bill had carried out a very neat little ambush near Nevers, where he killed a car loaded with seven German officers. He had lost Cave and Dray and was somewhat worried about them. When we left two days later they still hadn't turned up and Bill had to wait behind for them. We learned afterwards that they, too, had done some ambushing on their own, and the mines that they laid on the *route nationale* had blown up a staff car carrying German General Deinherdt, who had been killed.

All this time the Maquisards were gathering their strength and striking increasingly heavy blows against the passing columns. The Maquis Camille destroyed a German 88-mm gun with its tractor and crew, burned out some half-tracks and blew up a tank. All the other Maquis with whom we had worked were hitting out harder and harder in all directions. No longer did they need our help. They could fend for themselves and were fighting magnificently. C Squadron, almost fresh from England, well equipped with armoured jeeps, self-sealing petrol tanks and ample supplies, were road-strafing on a scale that we had never been able to attempt. Our work was over now. We must return and rest.

On 4 September, Johnny Wiseman arrived with the whole of his troop and encamped a little further down the Chalaux. In the squadron garage behind Le Meix Chalaux, our fitters, the Maquis mechanics, and everyone with any engineering knowledge were working from dawn to dusk to get all the requisitioned cars into reasonable shape. The moment for our departure drew near.

On the 5th, Bill gave me my last independent mission to perform. The wounded were still at the Lac des Settons. I was to bring them up to Chalaux. The force of the enemy's withdrawal was driving him by sheer pressure of necessity across the Morvan. The roads Lormes–Brassy–Dun les Places–Saulieu, and Corbigny–Montsauche–Alligny, were alive with the enemy. Only that morning one of our fitters, out testing a car, had run into an enemy party near Bonin and had been lucky to get away unscathed.

Soon the weight of traffic on these narrow ambushed roads would become so great and – thanks to the brilliant sweep of the French SAS to seize the Loire bridges – so dangerous, that the bulk of the enemy forces remaining in the trap, some 24,000 of them, would surrender to the nearest American patrol. But that time was not yet and the second-class roads traversing the Morvan were teeming with enemy troops.

In order to convoy the wounded through this dangerous area I took the good jeep, with McGinnis and his men as crew, Georges in a big open Mercedes, the Peugeot, and two small saloon cars, one driven by the MO and the other by a Frenchman. These had both been adapted to carry a stretcher and were to act as ambulances.

Our outward journey was without mishap. Passing through Savault, now occupied by the Maquis André, and Ouroux, now firmly held by Bernard, we skirted Planchez, where the Maquis Serge had come into the open, to approach Les Settons from the south and avoid the Montsauche road.

We found that the wounded were thoroughly enjoying themselves. Beautiful girls were visiting them. They had English books to read, a lovely view from their windows, their food was excellent and the fact that the Germans were moving just across the lake from them seemed to worry them not at all.

We had a last hearty meal at the Beau Rivage and I gave the 'old collab' a chit, saying that he had looked after our wounded, and asking that he be paid for his generosity. Apparently this note failed to save him, for the last I heard of him he was languishing in jail at Nevers; and his hotel, empty and abandoned, had been lent to the Americans.

After lunch we loaded the wounded into their uncomfortable makeshift ambulances and set off to retrace our steps. At Ouroux there was some sort of hold-up and we had to wait for Georges who had some business there. At Bonin we learned that the enemy were moving through Brassy in force. Between Bonin and Brassy we came suddenly round a corner to find ourselves confronted with a huge diesel truck of unmistakably German design. McGinnis, who was acting as gunner at the time, believed in acting first and asking questions afterwards. Before I could move he had loosed a quick burst through the window of the cab, and it was only when a startled French face bobbed up out of the ditch that I managed to persuade him that it was a harmless civilian and not the head of a convoy.

The burst of fire, very rightly, had brought the other vehicles to a halt. When we turned back to fetch them, we found them all half off the road in the process of turning round, and nearly got shot by Roger who was covering the road in case of accidents.

The most dangerous moment of all was at the Brassy–Dun-les-Places road. This we crossed by Vermot, where there was a straight run-over. I took Georges and his Bren-gun on to my jeep and we nosed down to the road. There was not a truck in sight, so leaving Georges at the crossroads to cover the crossing, I waved the vehicles on and continued up the hill.

One by one the cars sped across the road behind me, the Peugeot in the rear stopping just long enough to pick up Georges. As the Peugeot began to gather way up the hill, the head of the next German convoy hove in sight, but we were all safe across.

I left the wounded with the doc at Mazignien and reached the Chalaux camp just as the light was fading. Bill was very pleased to see me, as he had not expected us until nearly midnight and wanted us to get away as early as possible the following morning. That night I listened to the plans for our attempt to recross the lines, and slept the sleep of the weary.

It was 6 September, three months to the very day since I had taken off from England and flown over the embattled beaches that had been the coast of France. The convoy that was drawn up to break back through the lines was a strange one: twenty-one requisitioned civilian cars of all shapes, sorts and sizes, two enormous German diesel lorries captured by the Maquis and loaned to us, and an escort of six jeeps, half from C Squadron and half from our own reinforcements who were staying behind.

Carried in this fleet of vehicles were upward of 120 men, almost the whole strength of the Squadron with the addition of the rescued RAF and USAAF personnel whom we had picked up. Only Bill, the reinforcements and half a dozen men still to come in, remained behind.

Before moving off we telephoned to Quarré-les-Tombes to check that there were no enemy around, and then we started. Jeeps in front, jeeps behind, the odd jeep patrolling the length of the column, the whole long snake wound slowly up the twisty road out of the Chalaux valley and into the Bas Morvan.

At Quarré-les-Tombes we had our first halt, where Johnny checked the column, while Captain Tim Iredale of C Squadron, in charge of the escort, phoned on to Avallon.

Then, along meandering second-class roads, past the pretty lakes at Marrault, where an aged château reflected its mature beauty from the placid pools, to Avallon.

Avallon, where terrace climbs on terrace above the winding road, and old French houses with round towers and spired roofs smile down over a tumbling riot of tiny gardens. Avallon, so long a German garrison town, now held by the FFI. Here Tim phoned ahead to the city of Auxerre.

Now we pushed rapidly along the *route nationale*; broad and flat and fast. Here at any moment it was possible to meet a German convoy flying east that had run in upon the road between us and Auxerre. But nowhere did we encounter the foe. From almost every house flew the Tricolour and the Cross of Lorraine. Here and there along the route we met Maquisards holding roadblocks, or watching their well-laid mines. They waved as we passed, puzzled at the direction in which we were travelling, but recognising the jeeps and the red berets.

From Givry we looked back up the valley of the Cure and saw in the distance the fortress-crowned crag of Vézelay, with its exquisite old church — as fine an example of pure Roman architecture as can be found anywhere — and, from its parapets, one of the loveliest views in all France.

At one point the road suddenly dived through a tunnel in the hillsides. A thought flashed through our minds. What a place for an ambush! But there were no enemy about, and we carried on to Auxerre.

Auxerre too was in the hands of the FFI, already visited by an American patrol but still in no man's land. The Americans had not yet occupied it and it was always possible for the Germans, if they wished, to seize it back.

In the big square of the city railway station we had another halt and some of the boys brewed tea. Here we left MO Mike McReady and the wounded. From the big modern airfield just outside the city it was possible to fly the wounded back to England by Dakota and the arrangements for this had already been put in hand.

From Auxerre we rang Joigny, not far to the north. The Americans were there all right. We pushed on, entering Joigny from the south and driving down long boulevards lined with trees. We came to the River Yonne, here flowing broad and deep. Across the river there was a long, wide bridge. We drove across it. Beyond the bridge was a lamp-post. Against the lamp-post, chewing gum and idly swinging his white baton, was a military policeman; an American military policeman. We had recrossed the lines.

CHAPTER XXVII

The Hunter Home from the Hills

The great adventure was over. Two days later Bill crossed with the rest of the Squadron. The C Squadron escort returned to the Morvan and my reinforcements remained with them, fighting and strafing all the way up through France and Belgium to the frontiers of Holland, where the winter bogged them down. But of all the British SAS operations, that of A Squadron was the most successful. Everything went as nearly as possible according to plan. The total casualties were extremely light and the damage we did was incalculable.

A summary of the destruction we wrought takes no account of the moral strain we imposed on the enemy, or of the numbers of guards he had to set looking for us, whom we never even saw. This is what we are known to have achieved:

Blown railway lines	— Dijon—Beaune	Seven times
	Nevers—Autun	Four times
	Dijon—Paris	Twice
	Nevers—Paris	Twice
	Nevers—Clamecy	Twice
	Nevers—Château-Chinon	Once
	Digoin—Paray le Monial	Once
	Autun—Paray le Monial	Once
	Autun—Dijon	Once
	Pont d'Oche, branch lines	Once

In all twenty-two lines blown.

Power lines blown	— Moulins—Montceau les Mines	Once
Roads blocked effectively	— Autun—Château-Chinon Dijon—Langres	
Telephonic communications interrupted	— Nevers—Dijon in three places	

German vehicles destroyed	– Lorries, trucks or cars	25
	Railway engines	3
	Railway trucks	40
German vehicles captured	– Motorcycles	1
	Cars	2
German vehicles damaged	– Many of all types	
Trains derailed	–	At least 6
Aircraft shot down	–	Probable 1
	Certainly (by the Maquis, using our ammunition)	1

Autun synthetic oil refinery mortared twice.

Semelay goods-yard entirely destroyed.

Tamnay points and turntable blown.

Malain gasogene factory demolished.

Sixteen men from Allied air crews rescued, and brought safely through the lines.

Maquis troops (2000–3000) armed.

Training of Maquisards, and boosting their morale.

Depression of German morale.

About a dozen airfields reconnoitred and the results wirelessed to England.

About thirty civilian cars and one motorcycle requisitioned, which prevented them from falling into the hands of the enemy.

Valuable information including troop movements, location of dumps and bridges, flying bomb assembly and factory areas, and Rommel's HQ wirelessed to the RAF.

Estimated German casualties in killed and wounded (including General Deinherdt)		220
Prisoners taken (including one officer)		12
Deserters accepted		120

Own casualties (out of an absolute maximum of about 150)

Killed	Officers	1
	OR's	1
Wounded severely	OR's	3
slightly	OR's	3
Injured severely	OR's	2
Missing	Officers	1
	OR's	15
	Total	26

*   *   *

At Joigny, free at last from all hint of fear, we really let ourselves go. The *estaminets* and less reputable haunts of the town were filled with the boys having their first real fling for three months.

Even Hans was paid out and let loose with the British, much to everyone's delight, the best part of the jest being when he completely 'wiped the eye' of Sergeant Sturmey, our No. 1 Romeo, by taking his girl away from him.

The Americans could not understand us at all and refused to believe that we had just come through the lines. I think they just got the impression that we were a lost English convoy that had somehow wandered down from the north.

I heard one of the boys getting a bit of his own back on a particularly loud-mouthed American.

'This is a mighty tough division. Yes, sir!' said the Yank. 'Fought its way into St Lô last June.'

'Last June,' said our lad, 'that would be about the time we crossed the Loire at Nevers!'

We slept the night, those of us that did any sleeping, billeted in hotels around Joigny and the following morning we set off at about 10 o'clock on the next stage of our drive home. All day we drove westward in our strange convoy, passing all manner of American vehicles moving forward towards the battle front. On every side, as we went, was the evidence that the hand of war had recently passed by. Here we would see a shattered house, here a tank knocked out by the roadside, here a string of derelict lorries that not so many days ago had been burning in the ditch.

About midday we halted in the great square of Montargis and some of the boys took the chance to brew up. Here we met Paddy, who had come through the lines unscathed and carried out the business that had attended him on this side. Now he was on his way back to join C Squadron. He was clearly glad to see that we had got through safely and Johnny Wiseman told him that we were making for Orléans to see if we could get a lift back to England from there.

From Montargis we drove on along the lovely wide valley of the Loire, where beautiful châteaux stood back amid forests of young green trees on smoothly sloping hills.

At Orléans we found evidence of more destruction, but we pressed through and came out on to the aerodrome several miles beyond the city. Here we found a makeshift American ground staff in operation, and although flying was finished for the day they expressed themselves willing to fly us over the next morning. Meanwhile they gave us an enormous meal at their canteen. I remember that I made a thorough pig of myself, had two helpings of everything and had to sleep it off.

A number of people went into Orléans to see the sights, but there was not much doing and so I stayed at the aerodrome talking to the boys. We amused ourselves by exploding captured German incendiary bombs and I had some target practice with my Schmeisser. After supper, we went down beyond the airfield to have a look at a German flying-bomb site and afterwards we drank a rosy wine from the Loire vineyards at a little *estaminet*. At 10.30 we went to beds that the Americans had lent us in one of the hangars and slept despite the noise of drunks returning in dribs and drabs from Orléans.

Hans was in for one more adventure, for Alex felt that the time had come to turn him over to the Military Police. However, this proved to be easier said than done. All the prisoners' cages in the region were either full, unable even to take one more, or empty, refusing to mount a guard for a single man. In the end, Alex had either to take Hans all the way to Fontainebleau, or keep him, so we decided to keep him and he slept the night with the boys in the hangar.

Next morning we were up at dawn. There was a thin drizzle dampening the sky and we were half afraid that the aircraft would not come after all. But scarcely had we been given an extraordinarily large American breakfast than a heavy droning overhead began to beat about our ears, and one by one, in endless stream, the American Liberators that carried food for Paris came swooping in.

We paraded on the tarmac. We were numbered and allotted to planes. Hans caused a great deal of amusement as he was the first live German soldier that most of the Americans had seen, and everyone was busy taking his photograph.

Civilian workmen were unloading the aircraft and as they emptied we climbed aboard. I forget which plane I was in but I do remember that one of my fellow passengers was Nobby Noble who felt pretty ill most of the way, and another was Hans. I felt fine. The Liberator, though not equipped with seats, had large perspex windows and we were able to watch the countryside slipping away beneath us. The rain had stopped now and the sun was jumping in and out between fast-racing clouds which dappled the green fields below.

As we crossed those appalling battlefields around Falaise, we were shocked by the utter devastation. Some villages had been so destroyed that nothing remained around a ruined spire but a vast garden of rubble in which nothing could live.

Here and there, as we approached the coast, in twos and threes and half-dozens, lay the skeletons of crashed aircraft. A deep brown cruciform stain was branded into the meadows where they had fallen and burnt out upon the grass. Somehow I was irresistibly reminded of moths that had singed their wings at the candle's flame.

Now we were beginning to head out over the blue Channel and, tucked in against the French coast, near the base of the Cherbourg Peninsula, I could pick out the mass of shipping lying in the artificial harbour of Arromanches. On the other side I could soon pick out through a thin haze the tiny Channel Islands, still held by the enemy, sticking up very rocky against the blue of the sea.

The water stretched all around us now, broken only here and there by the wakes of a dozen little ships zig-zagging in convoy, like minute and distant water-beetles drilling upon an enormous pond.

Now far ahead, but rapidly looming larger, came the cliffs of England. I was beginning to feel hungry and discovering some American K rations abandoned by the crew, to Nobby's evident distress, I started to eat them.

The cliffs rose higher now and the green fields, the tiny cows and midget houses, began to stand out beyond them.

'You are flying against England, Hans,' I told him in French, with a grin. 'You didn't think it would be like this, did you?'

'No, I did not think it would be like this,' he replied, 'but anyway my war is over.' The plane bucked a bit as it hit the air currents over the cliffs.

Below me I could see England. How beautiful it looked in the sun and how peaceful. Somewhere we passed over a stately mansion, its lawns well kept, its ornamental pools and flower beds making a lovely pattern from the air. It was good to be back in English skies.

We circled an airfield and ran in to land. We thanked our pilots, assembled on the tarmac and waited for transport which took ages to come. This was Nether Wallop and we must get back to Fairford. A staff car arrived, with Major Poat and John Tonkin, the latter wearing an MC that looked very new. Johnny Wiseman, who for the past two days had infuriated me by being thoroughly and unnecessarily rude every time anyone offered to help him, suddenly left Alex in charge and drove off in the staff-car to get on with his leave as quickly as possible. I guess we were all a little strange, our nerves suddenly relaxing after the tension of three months playing cat-and-mouse and never sure whether one was the cat or the mouse.

It was truly wonderful to hear everyone speaking English again. The WAAF suddenly seemed all to be very beautiful and Dickie and Alex and I went into the RAF mess and had our first decent pint of beer for a very long time.

Then the trucks came, we all piled on board and back we went to the concentration area that we had left seemingly an age ago. We dumped our kit, gave people the particulars that they wanted and had a meal. Tony knew some people who lived in Fairford village and we stayed with them, for I could not bear the thought of another night with the fleas in my sleeping-bag. They talked sanely and sensibly and the war was miles away. I rang up Margot, whom I had hoped to go to meet at her station in Cornwall. She dissuaded me and we agreed to meet at home in a day or two, as soon as she could get away. I rang my mother who was at a bridge party and she was surprised and pleased to hear my voice. I said I'd be home as soon as I could. I had a hot bath and I slept snug and sound between clean cool sheets. So this was England.

The next day Tony left very early and I collected my warrants from the camp, packed up my kit again and got a lift into the nearest town, where I cashed a cheque and caught my train. As I crossed London by tube I met two of the boys. What extraordinary sights we were. Our clothes were old, torn and battle-stained. My pips were still those makeshifts of parachute silk. We carried our Bergen rucksacks in which we had piled all that was left of our belongings, and I still carried my trusty Schmeisser slung across my chest. We were fat of face and not very tanned considering the time of year; and, in my case, an enormous, blonde, bedraggled moustache crawled aimlessly across my upper lip. This sedentary life in the woods had not improved our looks.

I had said that I would have a drink with the boys when we got out at Kings Cross, but my train was due and I had to run to catch it.

I got to Hull very late. It was after the last train had departed for Hornsea and the Station Hotel was full. I could get no one to put me up, but managed at last to find a YMCA rest house not far from the station. There I had a bed, a couple of blankets and a good sleep.

The first train next morning saw me home. I was rapturous with joy. I ate an enormous breakfast. I spent the day washing and cleaning and becoming again respectable. I remember I went to tea with my Aunt Ivy, whose only son, David, had been killed in the Battle of Britain. I was in a curiously emotional state.

That night, I went to bed tired but strangely lonely and miserable. More than anything in the world, I wanted to see Margot again. I counted the hours till I would be seeing her. Then as I laid my sleepless head upon the pillow, I got to thinking back — to living back — all those varied experiences of a most memorable summer.

I thought of those wet cold trees and the drip of the rain on the parachute tent; the dull drone of the wireless as we tuned in to those everlasting broadcasts, and our silent misery as the rain trickled down the tent walls. And I remembered that broadcast which had come very near the end of our time in the woods and which is a fitting ending to this tale. It was a personal message to the SAS by Lieutenant-General F.A.M. Browning, DSO, at that time Director of Airborne Forces at the War Office. He said:

Now that the story of your operations and exploits since D-day is becoming known and confirmed, I am speaking to you this evening in order to tell you what Field-Marshal Montgomery and the Commanders in the Field feel about your activities.

I saw the Commander-in-Chief yesterday and told him I would be speaking to you today. He proposes to send you a personal message and in the meantime I am going to tell you what views are held about your efforts.

It is considered that the operations you have carried out have had more effect in hastening the disintegration of the German 7th and 15th Armies than any other single effort in the Army. Considering the numbers involved you have done a job of work which has had a most telling effect on the enemy and which, I fully believe, no other troops in the world could have done.

I know that the strain has been great, because operating as you do entails the most constant vigilance and cunning which no other troops are called upon to display.

I personally have kept in the closest touch with all your activities and have attempted to direct them as a result of the information the armies, and you, have supplied. So that, firstly, you were given fair, reasonable, but vital tasks, and at the same time those tasks were designed to have the most effect against the German armies as a whole.

To say that you have done your job well is to put it mildly. You have done magnificently. There is still a lot of clearing up to be done and in this you are pulling more than your full weight.

You will get Field Marshal Montgomery's message shortly, but in the meantime I want you to know how we and the rest of the Army feel about you. In this short talk I hope that I have made that abundantly clear to you all.

Good luck and Good Hunting!

*   *   *

Next day when Margot did arrive it was to tell me that she was in love with someone else and wanted a divorce. I ought to have remained in the Morvan after all.

Index

223